Politics in Taiwan

Politics in Taiwan is an accessible and highly readable survey of the Taiwanese political situation covering the period from 1949 to the present. With a focus on the issue of democratization, Shelley Rigger covers Taiwan's complicated and unique political history, and tells the story of how the Taiwanese, demanding a stronger voice in politics, drove their government to reinvent itself on a democratic blueprint.

Taiwan's experience of democratization is unusual. Taiwan began confounding theorists of political development more than thirty years ago; in the two decades after Taiwan weaned itself off US foreign assistance in 1965, it stood as a counter-example to modernization theories which saw a link between industrialization and democratization. When political reform took hold in the mid-1980s, it was driven by ethnic and political injustice rather than by the predicted class-based demands born of economic success.

This book shows that Taiwan, unlike other countries, avoided serious economic disruption and social conflict, and arrived at its goal of multi-party competition with little bloodshed. Nonetheless, this survey reveals that for those who imagine democracy to be the panacea for every social, economic and political ill, Taiwan's continuing struggles against corruption, isolation and division offer a cautionary lesson.

This book is an ideal one-stop resource for undergraduate and postgraduate students of political science, particularly those interested in the international politics of China and the Asia Pacific.

Shelley Rigger is Brown Associate Professor at Davidson College, North Carolina. She has published articles on recent political developments in Taiwan, local factionalism, electoral behaviour, national identity and political opposition.

Politics in Taiwan
Voting for democracy

Shelley Rigger

London and New York

In memory of Reverend Robert Donnell McCall
and Virginia Montgomery McCall, dear friends of
Taiwan

First published 1999
by Routledge
11 New Fetter Lane, London EC4P 4EE

Simultaneously published in the USA and Canada
by Routledge
29 West 35th Street, New York, NY 10001

Routledge is an imprint of the Taylor & Francis Group

©1999 Shelley Rigger

Typeset in Goudy by Routledge
Printed and bound in Great Britain by MPG Books Ltd, Bodmin

British Library Cataloguing in Publication Data
A catalogue record for this book is available from the British Library

Library of Congress Cataloging-in-Publication Data
Rigger, Shelley
    Politics in Taiwan : voting for democracy / Shelley Rigger.
        p. cm.
    Includes bibliographical references and index.
    alk. paper
        1. Taiwan—Politics and government—1945– 2. Democracy—Taiwan.
    I. Title.
DS799.816.R54   1999   99-22354
320.95124'9'09045—dc21   CIP

ISBN 0–415–17209–8 (pb)
ISBN 0–415–17208–X (hb)

Contents

Figures

Tables

Acknowledgments

I would like to express my gratitude to Davidson College, which provided consistent research funding throughout this project and granted me a sabbatical to complete the book. Thanks also are due to the Chiang Ching-kuo Foundation for International Scholarly Exchange, which assisted me twice, once with a grant for dissertation research and again with a post-doctoral fellowship grant. Some of the data cited in this paper were collected by the research project "The Social Image Survey in Taiwan" funded by the National Science Council, Republic of China. The research project was conducted by the Sun Yat-sen Institute for Social Science and Philosophy, Academia Sinica. The data are released at the Office of Survey Research, Academia Sinica. I appreciate the assistance of these institutes. Thanks also to the Central Election Commission for providing ready access to recent election results.

This book includes information from more than a hundred formal interviews with candidates, public officials, campaign workers, journalists and scholars. I am deeply grateful those who agreed to be interviewed, and to the many other Taiwanese who have shared their thoughts and experiences with me over my years of research and travel there. I owe a special thank you to Chen Chu, who introduced me to her colleagues in the Democratic Progressive Party. I also have received help and support from many generous and patient colleagues in Taiwan's scholarly community, especially at National Chengchi University's Election Studies Center, the Institute for International Relations, National Taiwan University's Department of Political Science and the Academia Sinica. In particular, I wish to acknowledge my good friends Professor Hwang Jau-yuan of the NTU Faculty of Law, Ms Deborah Shen at the *Free China Journal*, Ms Fan Mei-yuan and Mr Wang Sheng-hong and his family.

In the United States, I have benefited greatly from the wisdom and support of Ambassador Richard Walker and Professor James Myers at the

University of South Carolina, Professor William C. Kirby of Harvard University, Professor Alan Wachman of Tufts University, Ms Nancy Hearst of the East Asian Research Center at Harvard University, Professor Jean C. Oi, Professor Roderick MacFarquhar, and my colleagues in the Department of Political Science at Davidson College. Above all, I wish to thank Professor James A. Robinson, Regents Professor and Professor Emeritus of the University of West Florida, for all his help and encouragement over the years, and especially for reading this manuscript. His comments improved it greatly.

Without my husband, David Boraks, I could not have written this book. His encouragement, good cheer, sense of adventure and intellectual companionship make all my work possible. Perhaps it is a sign of changing times that one of my deepest debts of gratitude is owed to Mrs Libby McAmish, who provided reliable and loving care to my daughter Emma during the crucial months of this project.

Above all, I wish to thank the people of Taiwan. Their bottomless hospitality made researching this book a delight, and their fearless embrace of social and political change is an inspiration.

The views expressed and errors herein are my own.

Note on romanization

Recognizing that most readers who have studied Chinese are comfortable with Pinyin romanization, I have used that system to transliterate Mandarin words, both in the text and in the footnotes. Most people in Taiwan use the Wade–Giles romanization system to transliterate their names, so I have followed this convention for proper names (some commonly recognized proper names are idiosyncratic; I have used those spellings to facilitate recognition). In the notes I have used Chinese name order for authors of Chinese-language sources and English name order for the authors of sources in English.

1 Voting for democracy

Friday 22 March 1996 was a night of celebration in Taipei, Taiwan. Thousands jammed parks and public squares for huge rallies, then spilled into the streets for impromptu midnight marches. The warm, humid night had a carnival feeling. Vendors sold souvenirs of every description – from commemorative plates to videotapes of other political rallies. The scents of Taiwan's favorite street foods – sausages, oyster omelets and tofu – mixed with the odors of traffic and sewage and incense that permeate Taipei's crowded neighborhoods. What seemingly had drawn all of Taipei's citizens out of their homes was not a holiday, but the final night of campaigning before the island's first-ever direct, popular presidential election. The giant block party was a celebration of democracy, a celebration barely dimmed by Beijing's missile tests just off the Taiwan coast.

Four candidates and their running mates took part in the historic competition, and each stood before his supporters that night. On the grounds of the Sun Yat-sen Memorial Hall, an enormous mosaic of video screens towered over a stage draped in the white and blue of the Nationalist Party, or Kuomintang (KMT). The screens displayed a succession of celebrities and politicians praising the party's nominees, Lee Teng-hui, the incumbent president of the Republic of China on Taiwan, and his running mate, Lien Chan. As the rally ended, the crowd swayed in unison and sang Lee's campaign theme song, "Hand in Hand," while fireworks exploded overhead.

Within earshot of the Kuomintang gathering, in the plaza adjoining Taipei City Hall, stood another stage, this one draped in the green and purple whale motif of the Democratic Progressive Party's presidential campaign. The throngs gathered before this platform waved their party flags and glow-in-the-dark wands in support of Peng Ming-min and Hsieh Chang-ting, the DPP's presidential and vice-presidential candidates. The location held a special savor for the DPP, which two years earlier had captured city hall in the first direct mayoral election in almost thirty years. Across town, supporters of the Lin Yang-kang and his running mate Hau Pei-tsun gathered under the yellow flag of the Chinese New Party, while independents pledged their loyalty to presidential hopefuls Chen Li-an and Wang Ching-feng.

The next day, 76 percent of Taiwan's eligible voters exercised their right to select their country's head of state. Fifty-four percent cast their votes for President Lee, defying Beijing's warnings against supporting the incumbent. The government of the People's Republic of China found Lee too sympathetic with the notion of Taiwan independence; it reinforced its stern rhetoric with missile tests in the waters near Taiwan. The presidential election truly was historic: For the first time ever, citizens of a Chinese state were entrusted with the ultimate political choice. For many observers, the presidential election completed Taiwan's democratization, and even those who believed more remained to be done before Taiwan could claim to be fully democratic agreed that the presidential election was a critical milestone in the island's political development.

Another milestone came less than two years later, in November 1997, when the opposition DPP outpolled the KMT in elections for Taiwan's twenty-one county and city executives. That election was the first in which votes for opposition candidates exceeded KMT votes on an island-wide scale. But if electing their president and giving the opposition a majority were new to the people of Taiwan, elections themselves were familiar. Taiwanese had been casting ballots for local officials for fifty years, while seats in national legislative bodies were opened to popular election as early as 1969.

Formosa Today, a collection of essays published in 1963, paints a bleak portrait of Taiwan in the 1950s. The book has no use for Cold War-inspired pro-Nationalist propaganda. John Israel's essay on politics is especially unsparing. He writes,

> The difficulties of moving from party tutelage to democracy are evident in Formosa's local elections. Sometimes, non-Nationalists are given a fighting chance of victory, but the ruling party never allows a real challenge to its supremacy.... Democracy has been debased to a contest for the spoils of office.[1]

There is much truth in his description. But what Israel could not have foreseen was that, although profoundly flawed, Taiwan's elections would play a key role in propelling Taiwan toward that jubilant election eve in March 1996.

The creation of a democratic political system in Taiwan followed a long process of pressure and counter-pressure, struggle, negotiation and compromise between the Kuomintang-led authoritarian regime and its opponents. Although people on both sides shed blood for their views over the years, political change has been smoother and more peaceful in Taiwan than in many other countries. The 1996 presidential election can trace its lineage directly to the mid-1970s, when isolated politicians outside the Kuomintang joined forces in an organized movement that would become Taiwan's first true opposition party. But the reform process also had roots in short-lived democratic movements of the 1940s, 1950s and 1960s.

Many factors have shaped Taiwan's political development since 1945. Some are common to many countries – economic development, exposure to mass media, rising levels of education – while others are unique to Taiwan – the leadership of its late president, Chiang Ching-kuo, and the island's precarious international position. This book will look at all of these factors, and trace their role in Taiwan's evolution toward a more democratic political system. Indeed, it is impossible to provide a complete explanation of political change in Taiwan without looking at many different causes, domestic and international, social, political and economic.

But while this book will discuss each of these causes, it will pay special attention to a factor that is often overlooked in studies of democratization: the electoral process itself. This is not because elections were the only factor, although I will argue that they were an important one. The reason we will emphasize elections is that most studies – whether of Taiwan or of democratization in general – pay attention to them as a result of political change, not as one of its causes. This book seeks to add a dimension to our understanding of democratization by showing how elections can help to transform an authoritarian system.

Ordinarily, political scientists think of elections in authoritarian nations as charades aimed at giving a veneer of democracy to undemocratic systems. Indeed, this is often the case. In Taiwan, a major function of elections was to facilitate mobilization; that is, participation that was controlled and channeled by the ruling party. This is why we characterize the ROC's pre-reform political system as "mobilizational authoritarianism." However, as Taiwan's experience demonstrates, the very limited and imperfect elections that are permitted in some authoritarian countries can set down roots that grow in unexpected directions. Our guide for this study is Bolivar Lamounier, a Brazilian political scientist who analyzed the role of elections under authoritarianism in Brazil's political reform process.

But first, what is Taiwan?

When it comes to Taiwan, even the simplest questions are hard to answer. Is Taiwan a nation? If so, what should we call it? If not, what is it? Taiwan is an island on the Tropic of Cancer, off the coast of southern China's Fujian Province. Shaped like a slender leaf, the main island is 394 kilometers long and 144 kilometers wide at its widest point, and about the same size as the Netherlands. The political authorities who govern Taiwan also control a number of small islands and island groups surrounding it, including Orchid Island to the south, Green Island to the east, the Pescadores (or Penghu) Islands to the west, two small islands very close to the coast of mainland China, Kinmen (Quemoy) and Mazu (Matsu), and a number of smaller islands. Taiwan itself is mountainous. About two-thirds of the island is covered by rugged peaks up to 3,952 meters; most of the population lives in the broad coastal plain to the west of the central mountains.[2] The rest live in the narrower, more isolated eastern plain. With 600 persons per square kilometer, Taiwan is second only to Bangladesh in population density; given its many mountainous areas, the population density in the inhabited parts is extremely high.

Taiwan's tropical climate sustains a huge variety of plants which grow year round, sprouting out of cracks in asphalt, blossoming atop concrete skyscrapers and flourishing alongside severely polluted highways and rivers. City-dwelling farmers cultivate vegetables on balconies and postage-stamp-sized lots and sell them in rambling street markets. On Roosevelt Road in downtown Taipei, an ancient tree grows up from the sidewalk, passes through the first and second stories of a building and sprouts out of the roof. Junk left along roadsides is quickly engulfed in vines and weeds. This abundance also applies to agriculture; for decades, Taiwan has exported many agricultural products, including rice, pork, fruit and sugar.

Taiwan (or Formosa, as it is sometimes called) has been a disputed territory for centuries. The island's earliest inhabitants were South Pacific Islanders who migrated northward from the Philippine Islands and settled on Taiwan. This population included many different groups, most of whom lived on the island's fertile western plain. Beginning in the seventeenth century, people began arriving from the Chinese mainland, driven by overcrowding out of Fujian Province across the Taiwan Strait. Their superior technology quickly overwhelmed the existing peoples, some of whom assimilated into the Fujianese migrant population, others of whom moved to higher elevations. Nine major groups of the so-called Aboriginal people survived into the twentieth century, mostly on the thinly settled east coast or in the high mountains of central Taiwan. At the end of the twentieth century, the Aboriginal population is about 350,000 out of Taiwan's total population of 21.6 million.

Since the 1600s, the largest ethnic group in Taiwan has been the

Fujianese, or Hoklo. And because Fujian is part of China, most Hoklo people, who constitute about 70 percent of Taiwan's population today, also identify themselves as Chinese. Another 10 to 15 percent belong to the Hakka minority; they, too, are of Chinese provenance. But their ancestors are not the only connection between Taiwanese and China. For centuries, successive Chinese governments claimed Taiwan as Chinese territory. In the seventeenth century, Spanish and Portuguese explorers made short-lived attempts to colonize the island. In a strange foreshadowing of a later era, when Manchu conquerors defeated the Ming empire in 1664 the Taiwanese adventurer Cheng Ch'eng-kung (known as Koxinga in the West) used Taiwan as a base from which to oppose the newly formed Qing Dynasty. Eventually, the Qing military suppressed Cheng's rearguard action and established its jurisdiction on the island. But Taiwan proved difficult to manage, earning the description "a small rebellion every year, a big rebellion every five years." Thus, the Qing government was never able to assert its authority over Taiwan very strongly, and the islanders grew accustomed to running their own affairs.

In the late 1800s, the Qing Dynasty was in difficult straits. Weakened by rapid population growth, a deteriorating dynastic leadership and internal strife, the regime was vulnerable to the predations of imperial powers and subversive movements. In the 1840s, China was forced to open treaty ports and give other concessions to Europeans as a result of the Opium War. The following two decades saw China eviscerated by the homegrown Taiping Rebellion, which took more than 20 million lives in its central provinces. In 1895, China suffered a disastrous defeat at the hands of the Japanese. As part of the war settlement, China was forced to hand over Taiwan to Japan. For the next fifty years, Japan strove to make Taiwan a model colony. It invested in Taiwan's infrastructure and education, achieving a remarkably high level of economic and social development. At the same time, however, the Japanese promoted a policy of cultural superiority that denigrated Taiwan's Chinese identity and traditions.

At the end of World War II, Japan was forced to surrender its colonies, including Taiwan. Although there was no treaty to settle Taiwan's sovereignty, the Allied powers allowed the Republic of China (ROC) to accept the surrender of Japanese forces on the island, effectively handing control to the ROC leader, Chiang Kai-shek. The ROC called this event "retrocession." But the situation on the Chinese mainland was about to change radically. A civil war between Chiang's Nationalist government and the Chinese Communist Party ended in the Nationalists' defeat. In 1949, Mao Zedong declared a new state on the mainland: the People's Republic of China. Just ahead of the communist advance, Chiang and his government retreated to Taiwan, where they established a regime in exile. At first, most observers believed the communists would advance quickly to Taiwan to take the island, but the outbreak of the Korean War in 1950 brought the ROC on Taiwan under the protective umbrella of the United States. Chiang Kai-shek's holdout regime suddenly became a bulwark against communist expansion in Asia.

According to its ruling party, the Republic of China was not defeated, but only biding its time on Taiwan while it waited for an opportunity to recover the mainland and re-establish its rightful rule over all of China. Thus, the institutions of state that the Kuomintang-led government set up on Taiwan were transferred directly from the mainland, including an administrative apparatus designed to rule the entire country. For example, the national legislators chosen in China-wide elections in 1947 and 1948 held their seats without facing re-election for more than forty years, for after 1949 they could not be replaced by new representatives from the provinces that had elected them. Likewise, Taiwan had two layers of government to administer almost the same territory: the central government (which also claimed, but of course did not actually rule, the provinces of mainland China) and a provincial government for Taiwan itself.

In addition to these new institutions, the KMT regime introduced a new population into Taiwan's mix. These were the soldiers, government officials and their dependents who followed the ROC government to the island. Although they shared the Taiwan residents' Chinese ancestry and contained within their numbers men and women from every corner of China, these newcomers came to constitute a coherent group distinct from the island-born Taiwanese. Families whose ancestors arrived on Taiwan before Japanese colonization were "originated in this province" (*benshengji*, normally translated "Taiwanese"), while those who came after World War II were said to have "originated in other provinces" (*waishengji*, or "Mainlanders").[3] Within the Taiwanese group, distinctions among Hoklo, Hakka and Aboriginal people remained, but the split between Taiwanese and Mainlanders became the island's primary social cleavage. The two groups spoke different languages (most Mainlanders were comfortable with Mandarin, even if it was not their mother tongue, while few Taiwanese had learned the ROC's official dialect before 1945), but the most divisive distinction between them was their unequal access to political influence and power.[4]

In 1991, the KMT changed its policy toward the mainland. It adopted the position that the ROC and PRC were two halves of a divided nation, two entities of equal status in search of a formula for uniting them. The PRC government takes a very different view. To it, the ROC is a defeated remnant that survives only under the protection of an imperialist power, the US. It is still Beijing's position today that China's national destiny will be realized only when Taiwan is restored as a province under the control of the one true, legitimate government of China: the People's Republic. Even though Beijing has offered Taiwan substantial autonomy in a reunified China, it still understands "China" to mean the PRC.

Where does this leave Taiwan? Is it a country? According to both governments – the ROC and the PRC – Taiwan is not a country, but a province of China. Where they disagree is about the nature of the "China" of which Taiwan is a part. In practice, however, Taiwan (or the ROC on Taiwan) functions very much like any other country. It has a clearly defined territory, which it defends with military force. It has a government that decides how to manage the affairs of the 21.6 million people who hold citizenship documents issued by the ROC. It has an economy that is one of the largest and most internationalized in the world. And it even has a limited diplomatic identity: it enjoys official diplomatic relations with about two dozen countries (most of them small and developing), and unofficial relations with many more, and it takes part in a number of international organizations. Ordinarily, these conditions would qualify it as a country under international law, but Taiwan's complicated history twists normal logic. For many years, the government on Taiwan itself insisted that Taiwan was not a country. Later, when most other nations switched their recognition to the PRC, Beijing required them to abandon recognition of Taiwan altogether.

The Republic of China on Taiwan is a political entity with all of the characteristics of a country – except formal recognition from other nations. And that may be the closest we will come to defining what it is. As for what it is called, its official name is the Republic of China, but nearly all government statements nowadays append "on Taiwan" to the end of that appellation. In ordinary conversation in Taiwan and abroad, it is most often called, simply, "Taiwan." There are those in Taiwan who would see it declare formal independence and abandon any reference to China, but they are a minority, both because the PRC has promised to take Taiwan by force if it does so, and because most Taiwanese believe themselves to be part of the Chinese nation.[5] In sum, then, the island's status is peculiarly undefined in formal terms, and its future is cloudy. But at the same time, it is capable of acting forcefully and decisively in both its internal and its external affairs.

If the existence of the ROC as a country is debated, the existence of the ROC state – the institutions of government through which the ROC exercises jurisdiction over its territory and people – cannot be denied. The purpose of this study is to describe the nature of that state and its evolution over time. When the KMT-led government first moved to Taiwan in 1945, it brought with it a set of highly centralized and authoritarian values and institutions. Sun Yat-sen, the father of the Republic of China, took his inspiration from democratic philosophies and practices. But China's political reality in the first half of the twentieth century made it impossible to realize the ideals Sun cherished. To hold together a nation in the throes of dynastic overthrow, warlordism, occupation by Japan and civil war, Sun's successors put their democratic aspirations on hold, creating instead a highly authoritarian regime. On Taiwan, the ROC crafted a variant of authoritarian government that I shall call mobilizational authoritarianism.

In this form of authoritarianism, the institutions of government encouraged political participation by ordinary citizens. But they channeled that participation in ways that favored the regime. For example, the ROC government encouraged workers to join labor unions. But the unions they joined were not independent advocates of workers' interests, but organizations established, funded and guided by the ruling party and the state. Independent unions were not allowed. Thus, there was participation, but within strict limits. The ROC state that established itself on Taiwan in 1949 was far from the democracy Sun envisioned. Nonetheless, over the next five decades, that state evolved, slowly at times, quickly at other times, until it came to resemble very closely the democracies on which it was modeled.

The problem of explaining democracy's emergence has bedeviled political science since the 1960s. Scholars have offered numerous theories naming different factors as causes of democratization (political culture, socioeconomic development, world trends, economic crisis, external forces, the declining legitimacy of authoritarian regimes, national leadership), but none of these theories provides a comprehensive explanation for the many different cases of democratization (and failure to democratize) that puzzle social scientists. While it may be true that certain preconditions, such as a large middle class, make democratization easier, history shows that none of these preconditions is necessary or sufficient for the introduction of democracy.

Studies of Taiwan have focused on three categories of independent variables: socioeconomic development (including industrialization, urbanization, rising educational and living standards, the spread of communications technologies, the growth of a middle class and the proliferation of unofficial associations); elite decision-making (which emphasizes changes in the strategies and behavior of the leaders of Taiwan's ruling party, especially President Chiang Ching-kuo); and interactions between elites within the KMT regime and the opposition.[6] Each of these variables is useful in helping to understand Taiwan's democratization process. Certainly, Taiwan's much-touted economic miracle provided resources, both material and psychological, for ROC citizens to question the authoritarian practices that characterized the island's politics before the mid-1980s. And the actions of President Chiang and other important leaders, both in the regime and in the opposition, must not be discounted. However, these factors cannot explain why Taiwan's democratic transition occurred when it did.

While many forces and conditions contribute to democratic development, one step is indispensable: a decision by political elites to accept democratic institutions. As Huntington points out in *The Third Wave*, whatever preconditions may or may not exist in a country, purposeful action by the leadership is a necessary condition for democratization.[7] In many cases, successful democratization grew out of a compromise between existing (non-democratic) elites and pro-democracy opposition forces. Thus, the most broadly explanatory theories of democratization are those which emphasize the negotiated, or "pacted," nature of democratic transitions.

If democratization is the product of a pact between a non-democratic leadership and advocates of reform within a society, this opens the question of why the leadership would choose to move in a democratic direction. As Adam Przeworski has pointed out, democracy entails uncertainty for all groups; elites in a non-democratic regime are able to act more freely in accordance with their own interests under authoritarianism than they are under democracy.[8] Why, then, would they accept reform? First, elites may make an ideological decision that democracy is preferable for their country. Second, the authoritarian elite may decide that because of domestic or international opposition, the regime cannot survive without compromise. In other words, the elite undertakes reform to avoid an even less desirable outcome: popular rebellion, military coup or international sanctions.

In Taiwan's case, both of these factors played a role. As we shall see, the Republic of China was established according to democratic principles articulated by Sun Yat-sen. Its constitution guarantees popular participation and civil liberties. Even as a state of emergency suspended many of its provisions, the constitution stood as an unfulfilled democratic promise. Taiwan's leaders were socialized to believe that their mission to was to realize Sun's doctrine in the ROC. At the same time, however, ROC elites were willing to set that mission aside in the favor of another goal: maintaining political, economic and military stability in preparation for unifying Taiwan and the rest of China. Thus, for decades, Taiwan's leaders justified authoritarianism even as they paid lip service to democratic aspirations.

This state of affairs might have continued indefinitely. As the PRC's military and diplomatic strength increased, Taiwan became less, not more, secure. The conditions justifying the authoritarian elite's deviation from its ideological ideal had not abated when it decided to implement democratizing reform. To explain the timing of this decision we must look to the second motivation, avoiding a situation even less favorable to the elite than the uncertainties of democracy. In Taiwan's case, the regime faced severe internal and external threats – the loss of support from the United States and the United Nations, financial scandals, popular dissatisfaction – that brought its long-term survival into question. Above all, the regime found itself facing a growing opposition movement determined to bring about reform of the ROC political system. Ultimately, the elite recognized that authoritarianism was unsustainable, a realization consistent both with the elite's ideological predisposition in favor of democracy and with the preferences of Taiwan's friends in Washington.

After 1972, Taiwan's diplomatic isolation was accelerating rapidly. Chiang Ching-kuo, the ROC president and ruling party chair, along with the members of his inner circle, decided to improve the regime's domestic and international image by broadening the range of political opportunities open to ROC citizens. Twenty years later, Chiang's successor, President Lee Teng-hui, sat down with the opposition at the National Affairs Conference to negotiate constitutional changes that would cement democratic reforms; in short, he made a pact with the opposition. But why? What did the opposition bring to the negotiating table that could persuade the regime to accept its demands? This book will argue that the opposition's decisive resource was popular support, expressed through elections. Even though the KMT won large majorities in most elections, the fact that candidates who openly criticized the regime steadily increased their vote share revealed that the KMT's mobilizational authoritarianism was breaking down. At the same time, interest groups and opposition-oriented publications gave voice to popular demands for reform. But elections proved most important, because elections gave the opposition regular opportunities to demonstrate its popularity and to publicize its ideas. The regime was experienced in suppressing civic organizations and opposition publications. But elections were a fundamental, institutionalized component of the ROC political system. They also were its Achilles' heel.

Most of the literature on Taiwan's political reform focuses on widely accepted theories of democratization. These studies generally define democratization in procedural terms, as the introduction of free and open elections. Thus, they treat democratic institutions, especially elections, as the result of the process – the dependent variable – and they offer a variety of causes – independent variables – to explain why elections emerged. But like this book, some recent studies take a different approach. Two political scientists at National Taiwan University, Hu Fu and Chu Yun-han, have suggested that elections should be treated not as the dependent variable in the study of Taiwan's political reform, but as an independent variable that can help to explain how and why the ROC has moved in a more democratic direction.[9] They write, "elections for national lawmakers not only have increasingly acquired the normal function of popular accountability and system legitimation in a representative democracy, but in the transition they actually functioned as a catalyst of democratization in Taiwan."[10]

If we want to treat elections as an *explanation* for democratization, we cannot also use elections to *define* democratization. In a study like this one, the existence of regular elections does not in itself qualify a state as democratic. Because this study treats elections as an independent variable, we must define democracy more precisely. Of course, no definition will satisfy everyone. Some political scientists would even argue that no country is fully democratic, because all political systems include undemocratic elements: campaign finance systems that give the wealthy disproportionate access to politicians; economic inequalities that make political participation more difficult for some citizens than others; and mass media that fail to provide complete, unbiased information to every voter.

In this book, we will use a procedural definition of democracy developed by Samuel Huntington. He wrote that

> a 20th century political system [is] democratic to the extent that its most powerful collective decision makers are selected through fair, honest and periodic elections in which candidates freely compete for votes and in which virtually all the adult population is eligible to vote.[11]

This means that in a democracy, the chief executive and the legislature are chosen through an electoral process. For that process to qualify as fair, honest and competitive, the political opposition must have the opportunity to participate in elections as an organized entity, and to formulate, articulate and disseminate its policy positions and ideological viewpoint. Also, voters must not be constrained by fear of punishment or a government-imposed lack of information from choosing opposition candidates. Once elected, these decision-makers must be capable of creating and enforcing policy at the national level, without interference from non-elected executive officials, the military or foreign powers.[12] By this definition, we can say that the ROC on Taiwan achieved democratization with the 1996 presidential election.[13]

Hu Fu's suggestion that elections are not only the result of democratization but also are one of its causes opens an extraordinarily fruitful avenue for research. However, no Taiwan specialist has yet produced a fully developed analysis of the dynamics of the relationship between elections and democratization in the ROC. In particular, we need a way of addressing two fundamental questions: Why would an authoritarian state institute elections? And how, specifically, do elections help bring about democratization? Fortunately, Bolivar Lamounier's work on political reform in Brazil provides a framework for exploring these questions. Like Hu and Chu, Lamounier finds the electoral process to be, "not the symbol and culmination of a transition ... [but] almost the point of departure of the process."[14]

At the core of Lamounier's argument is the notion of reform as a "mobile horizon."[15] The motion of this horizon in an increasingly democratic direction constituted the reform process in both Brazil and Taiwan. And elections were one of the most important engines driving that process. Elections, Lamounier argues, were acceptable to both regime and opposition in Brazil because they appeared to provide a process through which the range of what was possible (the "horizon") could move forward at a controlled pace. In Taiwan, too, elections were a sufficiently moderate mechanism to pacify all but the most hard-line authoritarians within the regime, while at the same time they held enough promise of change to win the cooperation of all but the most radical oppositionists. In other words, mobilizational authoritarianism offered the best of both worlds: elections provided the appearance, both domestically and internationally, of a political system consistent with Sun's ideology, and at the same time facilitated cooptation and helped channel popular political energies into support for the regime. Meanwhile, authoritarian institutions – the insulation of the central government from popular pressure, one-party politics, corporatism, and so on – ensured that policy-making would remain under the control of KMT leaders in the party and state – or so it seemed.

"Opening through elections"

Lamounier's theory of opening through elections begins with a question: Why did political scientists fail to anticipate the democratic breakthrough that occurred in Brazil in 1974? First, he found that social scientists were too busy listing reasons why the military regime would not fall to notice growing evidence that change was imminent. Even before the watershed

1974 elections, Brazil was in a period of liberalization: authoritarian pressures were easing, and the state was allowing a wider range of political activity. Lamounier suggests that scholars might have anticipated that liberalization would lead to a democratic opening had they paid more attention to what he calls the "calculus of decompression,"

> an interactive model in which the various actors, whatever their ideologies, calculate the costs of the status quo and of alternative solutions. From this point of view, electoral and competitive mechanisms may seem even to frankly illiberal political actors, and even to hard-line military officers, to be a rational form of accommodation to highly uncertain situations.[16]

Once begun, he argues, decompression has its own momentum, driven, to a great extent, by elections: "the process of decompression produces its own effects. Competitive elections can have liberalizing effects within non-competitive political systems. The existence of an electoral calendar with a minimum of credibility is in itself a source of pressure in this direction."[17]

Second, no regime can institutionalize itself unless it has a legitimacy formula that fits its nation's ideology and history. Even before 1974, Brazil had a tradition of elections and a strong democratic strain in its national ideology. Thus, a regime that did not adhere to democratic norms needed to justify itself on other grounds. As Lamounier points out, legitimacy is at least as important to state employees (such as police, soldiers and public servants) as it is to ordinary citizens, because they are the people who must enforce the rules and carry out policy decisions. The search for a legitimacy formula also is influenced by international forces, including international models, international opinion and a state's particular international role and entanglements. All of these considerations, we shall see, are relevant to Taiwan as well as to Brazil.

The second question Lamounier addressed is: Why would an authoritarian regime institute elections? Brazil's military regime perceived elections as a safe, moderate way to offer a legitimacy formula that was consistent with Brazilian history and ideology, but would not commit the state to any particular substantive policy outcomes. The regime could control the trajectory of the "mobile horizon" because it "could monopolize the initiative regarding the politico-institutional changes to be made."[18] Meanwhile, setting up an electoral calendar helped persuade the opposition to work within the system, reducing the threat of subversion and insurgency. Even if elections are flawed procedurally, and even if elected officials have little influence over policy-making, if the opposition perceives that it has some chance of gaining a foothold in the power structure through the electoral process, it may well choose to "play the game." Lamounier's data show that as Brazil's opposition began to achieve victories at the polls, its commitment to the electoral process increased. What the regime was not expecting, of course, was that the opposition eventually would use these victories to press for a more meaningful policy-making role for elected officials.

This brings us to Lamounier's most fundamental question: How do elections bring about the decomposition of an authoritarian regime? Lamounier identified six processes through which Brazilian elections helped bring down the military government. First, despite institutional manipulations that kept the regime in power – including "legal or institutional changes which directly or indirectly affected the electoral chances of the opposition," "direct intervention in the legislative branch" and providing the executive with special powers to override legislative decisions – members of the opposition (and some ruling party members) began to use elected offices as platforms for criticizing the regime. Even though the regime maintained its legislative majority, voters knew who the anti-authoritarian politicians were, and they used their ballots to support them. The message coming from the electorate was clear, and even ruling party politicians had to shift their positions in the direction favored by the voters if they wanted to be re-elected.

Sending messages about issues was the second way Brazilian voters used elections to undermine authoritarianism. Lamounier calls these elections plebiscitary. Voters in plebiscitary elections are not driven by ordinary concerns such as the performance of the regime or the promises of the opposition, but by the desire to make "a pronouncement about the regime and the situation of the country as a whole."[19] Paradoxically, this effect is strongest when the power of elected officials is weakest: voters are not afraid to send a strong symbolic message if they know the people they elect have little power, since their choices will have few practical consequences. In other words, knowing that built-in obstacles will prevent the opposition from overturning the political order or implementing radical new policies frees citizens to cast protest votes.

Third, elections are a potent tool for political socialization and education. Among other things, they create party identification among voters, making it difficult to halt or roll back electoral reform. Through elections, parties develop clearly defined images among voters. In Brazil, the electoral process highlighted the ruling party's connections to the government and to the upper class; the opposition came to be viewed as the party of the poor and of pro-reform forces. Fourth, opposition victories inspire the opposition to get its own house in order, because suddenly it has something to lose. Fifth, the messages voters send in elections strengthen reform factions within the authoritarian regime. Finally, the momentum of elections eventually carries the opposition into power, and the authoritarian regime, reduced to minority status in elected bodies, is forced to yield control.[20]

Taiwan's "opening through elections"

Why does this study focus on elections? As we have said, international forces, political leadership and socioeconomic development played important roles in Taiwan's reform process, and many scholars have explored these dynamics. But these explanations leave important questions unanswered. Why did Taiwan's leaders choose reform instead of continuing the repressive practices that had kept them in power in the past? And once they chose reform, why did they lose control of the process? Also, as Chen Ming-tong has pointed out, leadership and socioeconomic development cannot explain the timing of the reforms, because "In the twenty years after Taiwan's economic take-off began in 1970, there was no relationship between the opposition party's vote share and economic development."[21]

For decades, critics of the theory that socioeconomic development would lead to democratization used wealthy, authoritarian Taiwan as a counter-example. Why did Taiwan, which for so long seemed immune to the democratizing forces of economic development, finally respond to those pressures in the 1970s? Chen, like Lamounier, looks to the internal dynamics of politics, especially electoral politics, for a more satisfying explanation. Indeed, each of Lamounier's major insights – the need for a legitimacy formula, the calculus of decompression and the momentum of elections in authoritarian decomposition – resonates in significant ways with Taiwan's experience.

The legitimacy formula

The search for a workable legitimacy formula has been an abiding concern of Taiwan's ruling party. At the end of World War II, the KMT expelled the Japanese colonial authorities and imposed its government on Taiwan with little thought of consulting the local population. It immediately set to work creating a one-party state that placed a mainland-born political elite above the native-born Taiwanese. In 1947, frustration over the regime's heavy-handed treatment of the local population erupted in a violent uprising, which the KMT quashed with military force. This event, dubbed the February 28 (or 2–28) Incident, created a wedge of distrust between the Taiwanese, who constituted about 85 percent of Taiwan's population, and the Mainlander minority that dominated the ROC state. Under these circumstances, the KMT was challenged to find a legitimacy formula capable of securing the loyalty of the Taiwanese people and ensuring unity within the regime. It settled on a formula combining two strains: democratic ideology and a commitment to recovering mainland China. Over the course of Taiwan's political reform process, the emphasis of the legitimacy formula shifted from mainland recovery to democracy.

The KMT's ideological foundation is the political thought of Dr Sun Yat-sen, summarized in his Three Principles of the People: nationalism (*minzu*), popular sovereignty or democracy (*minzhu*) and economic justice (*minsheng*). Sun asserted that democratic governance – complete with constitutional supremacy, separation of powers and other institutional arrangements associated with Euro-American liberal democracies – was the appropriate model for China's long-term political development. He also recognized that achieving this objective would take time, so he designed a series of incremental steps to lead China toward democracy. First, he said, China needed military government to secure its independence from foreign powers and warlords. Once its borders were secure, the nation would enter a period of "political tutelage" during which the executive branch and the Kuomintang would rule with special powers while raising the citizens' civic and educational level. Once the citizens were ready to take on the responsibility of their own governance, the period of constitutional government would begin, and the ROC constitution would be implemented fully.

The retreat to Taiwan left the KMT-led ROC government facing unanticipated challenges. Under the new circumstances, the ROC's democratic framework and ideological tradition took on a new dimension. The KMT's attachment to democracy, although imperfect and abstract, became its primary claim on international sympathy and support. It was "Free China;" throughout the Cold War, the Western world compared Taiwan favorably with "Red China."[22] Thus, propagating Sun's democratic ideology was an important element of the KMT regime's domestic and international legitimacy formula.[23] In the long run, however, this democratic ideology was to haunt the KMT's efforts to maintain a one-party political system. As Jauhsieh Joseph Wu put it, "Sun's revolution and the democratic ideas advocated by him formed a legacy that people could utilize to challenge the authoritarian rule of the KMT government and which contributed to the rise of the democracy movements of the 1980s."[24]

Sun's writings do not give a precise time line for realizing constitutional government. Nonetheless, the promise of full democracy is omnipresent in ROC ideology, and deviation from that norm required justification. This brings us to the second component of the KMT regime's legitimacy formula, mainland recovery. From its founding early in this century, the KMT's rallying cry has been national unity and sovereignty. Through decades of warlordism, Japanese occupation and civil war, the ROC government carried this standard. After it lost the civil war and moved to Taiwan, the regime continued to insist that its mission was to restore legitimate government (i.e., ROC rule) to all of the territory claimed by the Qing government in the late nineteenth century, including Taiwan, Tibet and Outer Mongolia. Fulfilling this destiny would require great and noble sacrifices on the part of all patriotic Chinese. Among these sacrifices were the delay of full constitutional government and the implementation of emergency measures that limited the degree to which Sun Yat-sen's democratic dream could be realized. ROC leaders constantly referred to democracy as their goal, but they insisted that this objective must be pursued gradually.[25]

In the 1950s and 1960s, when the threat of PRC attack was strong and civil war rhetoric was at its height, few on Taiwan questioned either the desirability or the plausibility of mainland recovery. The few who expressed such opinions openly risked long prison sentences. After the February 28 Incident, few people doubted the KMT's willingness to use draconian methods to silence dissent. One who did challenge the regime was the Mainlander intellectual Lei Chen. Lei's efforts in the early 1960s to found a political party earned him ten years in prison. Another indication of the degree to which mainland recovery dominated the KMT's agenda during these years is the heavy representation of the military on the party's all-important Central Standing Committee. From 1957 to 1969, nearly a third of the CSC members were military men.[26]

Despite the regime's best efforts to keep the dream alive, the plausibility of the ROC recovering mainland China by force grew increasingly remote over the years. At the same time, confidence in Taiwan itself increased. The economic miracle that unfolded in the 1960s and 1970s convinced a growing number of Taiwan's residents that emphasizing the island's own development was more likely to yield a good life for its people than continuing the preoccupation with mainland recovery. At the same time, Taiwan's international position was deteriorating, and international support for the mainland recovery project was dwindling. In 1971, Taiwan lost its seat in the United Nations, and with it, its status as the internationally recognized government of China. The following year, President Nixon visited the PRC, setting in motion the process of de-recognition of the ROC by its most important ally. Meanwhile, the influence of international models was growing. Human rights advocates questioned the ROC's characterization as "Free China" and called attention to the regime's authoritarianism and unmet democratic promises. Taiwanese dissidents living overseas voiced increasing criticism of the regime. These international set-backs increased the pressure on the KMT to reinvent itself.

As the likelihood that the ROC would recover the mainland diminished, the KMT leadership shifted its rhetoric from mainland recovery to the "reunification" of China under Sun Yat-sen's three principles. To this day, the ruling party's stated goal is the convergence of Taiwan and the PRC on a common democratic and capitalist model that will permit their peaceful and voluntary reintegration. However, the likelihood of such a convergence strikes most Taiwanese as exceedingly remote, and many are convinced that even if the PRC and Taiwan were to converge, Taiwan would stand to lose a great deal more than it would gain by wedding itself to such a vast political, economic and demographic entity.[27] In sum, the shift from mainland recovery to reunification failed to persuade most Taiwanese that democratization should be delayed further, and by the mid-1970s cries for lifting the restrictions on civil liberties promised in the ROC constitution had grown very loud indeed. The mainland recovery component of the ROC's legitimacy formula could no longer justify short-changing its democratic promise.

Of course, the fact that many Taiwanese no longer accepted the KMT's reasons for maintaining an authoritarian state need not have brought that system down; the KMT could have resorted to repression. But according to Lamounier, a regime without a workable legitimacy formula is unstable; it feels pressure from its supporters as well as its subjects. The fact that the first major challenge to the ROC regime on Taiwan came from Lei Chen, a trusted and respected insider, illustrates this point, as does the constant jockeying for position by high-level KMT factions. To hold party, state and society together, the search for legitimacy continued, and pressure for democratization increased.

Along with the search for legitimacy, wrote Lamounier, authoritarian regimes need to appear consistent with their own past practices. Both Brazil and the ROC had electoral traditions that complemented their democratic ideologies. These traditions forced the two regimes to at least maintain, if not increase, the role of elections. Even under Japanese colonialism, some Taiwanese were exposed to elections, although in a very limited way. But in 1946, the ROC introduced grassroots elections with universal suffrage in the form of township representative contests. In 1950, the electoral calendar expanded to include elections for township heads and municipal executives and council members in Taiwan's nearly two dozen counties and cities. In 1951, Taiwanese elected the first Taiwan Provincial Assembly. These elections continued on a regular schedule without significant interruption, along with elections for village executives and councils. In 1969, a few seats in the central government became open to election. Direct elections in the 1970s and 1980s filled a handful of supplementary seats in the Legislative Yuan (the ROC legislature) and the National Assembly (which elected the ROC president before 1996, and still is responsible for amending its constitution). In fact, as Table 1.1 illustrates, few years have passed without an election since the ROC assumed control.

Taiwan's early elections had many limitations; in fact, there still is much to criticize in the late 1990s. Studies of ROC elections emphasize both the institutional weakness of elected officials and the degree to which elections reflect patron–client relationships and calculations of self-interest, as opposed to a desire for representative government.[28] However, as Lamounier observes in his discussion of Brazil, the fact that voters are not motivated by party identification or issue preferences does not necessarily undermine the usefulness of elections as a tool of political reform. Whatever their motivations for choosing a particular candidate may be, citizens who are accustomed to casting ballots on a regular schedule and having those ballots determine the identity of office-holders will learn to value this process and expect it to continue. Even if the powers of elected officials are limited, winning office brings significant rewards for both office-holders and their supporters. Thus, both groups have a stake in continuing the electoral process. In Taiwan, as in Brazil, scholars dismiss elections as a mere formality at their peril, for ROC citizens clearly have invested much in elections, both emotionally and materially. And, as Wu reminds us, the KMT itself inflated the importance of elections, claiming legitimacy based, in part, on its "outstanding electoral performance."[29]

The calculus of decompression

Lamounier observed that decompression, or liberalization, rests on the authoritarian regime's calculation that it can control the pace and direction of political reform. This confidence allows the regime to undertake a reform process that (as it learns too late) has a momentum and direction of its own. There is no question KMT leaders believed that the institutional framework they put in place in Taiwan would give them a firm grip on the liberalization process. These institutions are explained in detail in Chapter 3, but some of the most important are worthy of mention here.

First, until 1991, the KMT regime maintained a firewall between the central government and the electoral system, ensuring that the top decision-makers would be selected by the KMT's core leaders.

Table 1.1 Elections in the Republic of China on Taiwan, 1946–1998

Year	President	National Assembly	Legislative Yuan	Provincial Assembly	Municipal executive	Municipal council	Township executive	Township representative
1946	X	X	X	X	X	X	X	X
1947								
1948	indirect							X
1949								
1950					X	X	X	X
1951				X				
1952						X	X	X
1953								
1954	indirect			X	X	X		
1955							X	X
1956								
1957					X	X		
1958						X		X
1959							X	
1960	indirect			X	X			
1961						X		X
1962								
1963				X				
1964					X	X	X	X
1965								
1966	indirect							
1967								
1968		appointed	appointed	X	X	X	X	X
1969								
1970								
1971								
1972	indirect	supplem.	supplem.	X	X			
1973						X	X	X
1974								
1975			supplem.					
1976								
1977				X	X	X		
1978	indirect							X
1979								
1980		supplem.	supplem.					
1981				X	X			
1982						X	X	X
1983			supplem.					

(cont. over)

Table 1.1   Elections in the Republic of China on Taiwan, 1946–1998 *(cont.)*

Year	President	National Assembly	Legislative Yuan	Provincial Assembly	Municipal executive	Municipal council	Township executive	Township representative
1984	indirect							
1985				X	X			
1986		supplem.	supplem.			X	X	X
1987								
1988								
1989			supplem.	X	X			
1990	indirect					X	X	X
1991		X						
1992			X					
1993					X			
1994				X		X	X	X
1995			X					
1996	X	X						
1997					X			
1998						X	X	

Source: Ch'i Kuang-yu, *The Political Development of the Republic of China*, (*Zhonghua Minguo de zhengzhi fazhan, Minguo sanshiba nian yilai de bianqian*), Yangchih Publishing Company, 1996, pp. 1090–1093.

A second powerful constraint on the emergence of a truly democratic system in Taiwan was the imposition of emergency provisions. Claiming the civil war as its justification, the regime imposed martial law on Taiwan from 1949 until 1987. Martial law not only gave the government broad powers to arrest and imprison dissenters, but also imposed a complete ban on the formation of new political parties, effectively enshrining the KMT regime as a one-party state. Martial law also allowed the state to control the mass media.

A third set of institutional controls operated within the electoral system itself. The regime set aside seats in the major representative bodies for members of functional constituencies, which the KMT easily controlled. In addition, the peculiar electoral formula used in Taiwan – single, nontransferable voting in multi-member districts, or the SVMM system – permitted competition and broad participation in local elections under the ruling party banner. The KMT used local elections to recruit authentic grassroots leaders, whom it then coopted into the party. Local factions and individuals competed fiercely among themselves for votes in grassroots contests, but nearly all of them were affiliated with the KMT, and they rarely questioned its policies or ideology. However, it would be unwise to dismiss this clientelistic electoral behavior as unimportant; even though elections in pre-reform Taiwan had little or no effect on national policy, at the local level these elections were fiercely fought and highly valued. One indication of this phenomenon is Taiwan's consistently high voter turn-out. In fact, as Figure 1.1 shows, voter turn-out is generally very high in Taiwan, but paradoxically, it is highest in grassroots

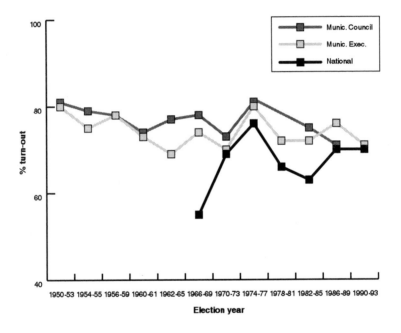

Figure 1.1 Voter turn-out in elections

Sources: Chi Kuang-yu, *Political Development of ROC* (*Zhonghua Minguo de Zhengzhi Fazhan*), Taipei, Yangzhi Cultural Publishing Company Ltd, 1996, pp. 1088–1093; Lin Chia-lung, "Local Elections and the Marketization of the KMT," in Chen Ming-tong and Zheng Yungnian, eds, *Basic-level Elections and Socio-Political Change on Both Sides of the Taiwan Strait*, Taipei, Yuetan Publishing Company Ltd, 1998, pp. 180–181.

Note:
National elections include Legislative Yuan and National Assembly elections; municipal elections are municipal executive elections; sub-munic. elections are municipal council elections. Turn-out given for periods in which both Legislative Yuan and National Assembly occurred is an average of the two turn-outs.

elections (municipal council), slightly lower in mid-level elections (municipal executive) and lower still in national elections.

Another consequence of the SVMM electoral formula is its tendency to provide well-organized parties with large "seat bonuses." If a party can estimate its potential vote share accurately, it will be able to calculate precisely the number of seats it can win in a given district. If it is further able to allocate its votes among its candidates evenly, it can turn a relatively modest vote share into a much larger percentage of seats won. Small parties and independent candidates find it difficult or impossible to maximize their performance under this system, leading to their disproportionately low representation in elected bodies, as Table 1.2 shows.

This recalls Lamounier's observation that the Brazilian military regime's electoral manipulations "have much more effect on the conversion of votes into seats than on the distribution of votes itself."[30] As Hu Fu and Chu Yun-han put it in a discussion of the KMT's persistent seat bonuses,

> These simple statistics explain why the [opposition] DPP has placed so much emphasis on democratic reform, without which much of their hard-won electoral support has been sidetracked. This also explains why the ruling party has been willing to initiate the transition. With these archaic arrangements, there is little chance that the opposition ... posed a real challenge to the KMT regime.[31]

In light of the KMT's well-constructed arrangements for maintaining power, it is not so difficult to understand why this authoritarian regime was willing to give ground on demands for limited political reform. But why was the opposition willing to accept these unfavorable terms? Despite the repression Taiwan's political dissidents faced in the 1970s, opposition activists continued to participate in elections. While some opposition activists complained that elections were a useless formality, the opposition

Table 1.2 Seat bonuses in Legislative Yuan elections (percentage of seats won minus percentage of votes won)

Year	1980	1983	1986	1989	1992a	1995a
KMTb	+8	+16	+11	+11	+2	+4
TW/DPP	-6	-12	-8	-10	0	0
Independent	-2	-4	-3	-1	-2	-3

Source: Chu 1992:183–184, World Journal 20 December 1992, election returns.
Notes:
a Excludes Aboriginal, overseas and at-large representatives.
b Includes KMT members running without nomination or endorsement.

constantly intensified its electoral effort. The reason for this was, as Lamounier suggests, opposition politicians' recognition that elections provided a consistent and relatively safe mechanism for expanding their influence.

Even when the offices opposition candidates were elected to fill carried with them little policy-making authority, they did confer significant status (not to mention immunity from prosecution for statements made in the legislature). Meanwhile, electoral campaigns were an opportunity to transmit the opposition's message to huge numbers of citizens. Although the KMT held an overwhelming majority in every elected body in the land, the possibility of incremental victories – especially in such high-profile contests as municipal executive and supplementary legislative elections – encouraged opposition politicians to work within the system.

Authoritarian decomposition

The notion of authoritarian decomposition implies that the direction of political change is antithetical to the interests of the regime. Thus, some scholars might argue that the concept does not apply to Taiwan, since the regime itself led the democratization process. For example, Chao and Myers make a strong case that President Chiang Ching-kuo's personal leadership was the single most important factor driving Taiwan's democratization.[32] But as they explain, Chiang believed in a "Chinese-style democracy in which only the virtuous elite could represent the people and govern them"; he was no advocate of messy, unfettered pluralism.[33] Yet by the end of the century, Taiwan's political marketplace had become extremely messy. Non-stop revelations of political corruption had long since put to rest any illusions that a virtuous elite was governing the island. So even if Chiang Ching-kuo and the KMT regime were devoted to a particular kind of democratization, they eventually lost control of the process. To understand why, Lamounier points us toward elections.

According to Lamounier, elections have momentum and consequences apart from their role in selecting office-holders, and these forces push the liberalizing regime in the direction of more and more meaningful elections. One of the first signs of liberalization in Taiwan was the KMT party reform of 1972. The early 1970s marked a shift in party leadership from President Chiang Kai-shek to his son, Chiang Ching-kuo. Although the elder Chiang remained in office until his death in 1975, the succession began several years earlier. According to Bruce Dickson, an expert on KMT party history,

> The new generation of leaders believed that more rapid political reform was necessary for the survival of the party. The main goals and

tasks of the KMT changed: Rather than concentrating on plans to retake the mainland, the party devoted more of its energy to issues of immediate concern to Taiwan and its own reputation. It underwent both functional change (such as a greater concentration on elections) and generational change, as new leaders with new skills were introduced to important posts at all levels of the party bureaucracy.[34]

Two important aspects of this reform targeted the electoral system. First, the KMT decided to recruit more native Taiwanese in order to shed its image as a Mainlander-dominated exile party. Party leaders hoped that a more indigenous party would have greater electoral appeal and legitimacy. Second, President Chiang Ching-kuo sought to improve the quality of elected local officials by taking a more active role in cultivating and nominating "good government" candidates to replace local bosses. This increased emphasis on elections also meant that the KMT began to use elections as "an institutionalized feedback mechanism on the party's performance."[35]

This is not to say that the party suddenly decided to give the voters everything they wanted. As the sacking of a string of KMT organization heads attests, the blame for electoral losses fell not on policy-makers, but on the party strategists responsible for mobilizing the KMT's electoral machine. So while Dickson makes a good case that the KMT was more willing to listen to messages from the electorate than it had been in the past, its primary concern continued to be winning elections.

Accompanying these changes in party organization and strategy in the 1970s was a limited, but noticeable, relaxation in the repression of dissidents. While critics of the regime continued to risk arrest even into the early 1990s, the so-called "White Terror" that reigned from the February 28 Incident through the 1960s was easing by the early 1970s. The clearest evidence of this change was the proliferation of opposition magazines in the 1970s.

These publications shared two central themes: the desire for democratization and the demand for fair and equal treatment for the Taiwanese majority (which I will call "ethnic justice"). The regime did not fully tolerate these publications; they were routinely and regularly harassed, censored, confiscated and closed. However, unlike in the earlier period, when long prison terms silenced dissident editors, the opposition journalists of the 1970s faced relatively mild penalties, most often economic sanctions aimed at the publications themselves. They played a cat-and-mouse game with the government, reopening sanctioned publications under slightly different names, registering as book series to evade censorship, and generally defying the regime's efforts to put a stop to their activities. Rather than acting decisively against them, the government attacked the publications piecemeal.

Activists demanding democratization and ethnic justice grew bolder in other ways, too. In 1977, supporters of opposition candidate Hsu Hsin-liang rioted when they thought he was about to be defrauded out of a county executiveship. Two years later, activists from the dissident magazine *Formosa* (*Meilidao*) sponsored a rally in the southern city of Kaohsiung. When the rally turned violent, police arrested the magazine's leaders, including some who were not even present at the rally. In the short run, the regime's swift and punitive reaction stifled opposition activity. But public opinion quickly turned against the government, as many Taiwanese found its reaction disproportionate and brutal. The tide of sympathy and outrage found expression in the 1980 supplementary elections, when the wives and attorneys of several defendants sought National Assembly seats. These candidates did extraordinarily well, in one case winning a district's highest vote total. Their performance was interpreted widely as a statement of sympathy and support for the Formosa group, and a gesture of protest against the regime's heavy-handed treatment of dissidents.

In sum, by 1980, the KMT government was finding it increasingly difficult to suppress dissent and ignore calls for further liberalization. When it did take strong action, as in the Kaohsiung Incident, it incurred a heavy cost, as revealed in the 1980 election results. Repression also cost the ROC dearly in increasingly precious international support. Elections drove up the cost of repression further because once an opposition activist had been elected to office, he or she not only enjoyed elevated public stature and legitimacy, but also had access to the bully pulpit of public office. Suppressing isolated dissident intellectuals was one thing; suppressing elected officials whose popularity had been demonstrated at the polls – and most of whom possessed extraordinary charisma – was another matter. As Hu Fu puts it, "it became increasingly costly for the ruling elite to use repressive measures against popularly elected opposition leaders. To do this the KMT regime had to pay a considerable price, at the cost of its own legitimacy."[36]

Another sense in which elections complicated the regime's efforts to control the reform process was the expectation created by the electoral calendar. Canceling elections when the outcome looked unfavorable to the ruling party was simply too risky. Even KMT politicians would have protested, since they, too, had a great deal at stake in elections. Indeed, the only significant interruption in the ROC electoral calendar came in 1978, in response to US President Jimmy Carter's decision to normalize relations with the PRC. Even some opposition leaders believed the postponement was justified, given the ROC's sudden and severe reversal of fortune.[37]

Lamounier's analysis emphasizes the importance of elections for creating sites for criticism of the regime – and not only by the regime's opponents. He noted that Brazilian law-makers of the pro-regime ARENA and opposition MDB parties alike used their positions to speak out against the military government. Likewise, gaining elected office offered ROC politicians the opportunity to criticize the regime – and created pressure for them to do so. In the early years of the reform, most criticism came from opposition politicians, some of whom took advantage of legislative immunity to speak freely. Over the years, KMT politicians added their voices to the chorus of criticism, especially on such popular issues as controlling corruption and seeking UN membership for Taiwan. As Joseph Wu writes,

> KMT leaders face challenges from their own elected representatives who are increasingly demanding a role in party policy-making. They argue that as popularly elected representatives of the people, they have more right to decide KMT policy than the top decision-makers, including the president, the premier or the members of the Central Standing Committee, none of whom are popularly elected.[38]

After 1990, the legislature was more than a bully pulpit for critics of the regime; even with a KMT majority in the legislature, the party leadership lost some important legislative battles, including a 1993 contest over a financial disclosure law.

Another dimension of Lamounier's analysis is his characterization of some elections as plebiscitary; again, Taiwan's experience supports the theory. In particular, the 1980 legislative election fits Lamounier's definition of a plebiscitary contest. In 1980, the opposition was small and weak; some of its leading figures were in prison or exile. Still, opposition candidates made their strongest showing yet in 1980. Many of these candidates themselves were the relatively unknown spouses and attorneys of the Kaohsiung defendants. Their startling electoral success can only be understood as a plebiscite on the regime's treatment of the opposition, what Lamounier calls "a pronouncement about the regime and the situation of the country as a whole."[39] The supplementary legislative elections held in the 1980s were, as Lamounier expects, especially conducive to plebiscitary voting because their function was symbolic. Given the overwhelming majority of seats occupied by senior legislators, virtually all of whom voted the KMT line, no one expected that the results of these elections would alter national policies directly. The sole logical reason for choosing opposition candidates was to send a message to the ruling party. Yet, the Dangwai's vote share increased (see Figure 1.2).

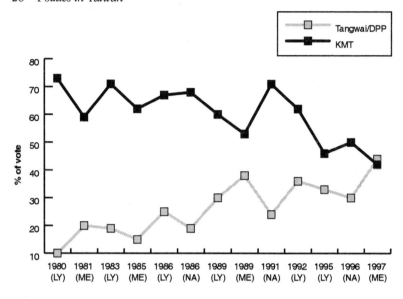

Figure 1.2   Dangwai/KMT vote shares

Sources: Hung-mao Tien, *The Great Transition: Political and Social Change in the Republic of China*, Stanford, CA: Hoover Institution Press, 1989, pp. 176, 186, 187; Yun-han Chu, *Crafting Democracy in Taiwan*, Taipei: Institute for National Policy Research, 1992, p. 55; John Copper, *The Taiwan Political Miracle*, Lanham, MD: University Press of America, Inc., 1997, pp. 238, 239, 283, 306, 307.

Symbolic or protest voting may not carry much expectation of influencing national policy in the short term. However, the long-term consequences of such voting can be profound. This was the case in Taiwan. First, as Lamounier predicts, the feedback provided by plebiscitary elections reinforced the reform faction within the KMT leadership. This dynamic operated on two levels. First, the reformers were able to demonstrate that the cost of retreating from, or even slowing the pace of, reform would be a substantial loss of popular support and legitimacy. By casting their ballots for the opposition, voters demonstrated their support for continued reform. KMT hard-liners' arguments in favor of slower reform flew in the face of tangible evidence that a significant and growing segment of the population opposed their position. Surveys of Taiwan residents' political attitudes echoed these election results. For example, in 1984, 41 percent agreed that "Government affairs should be decided by top government leaders." By 1990, the proportion had fallen to 33 percent, and in 1996, it was down to 30 percent. Likewise, in 1984, more than half of those surveyed agreed that multiple political parties would lead to chaos; by 1990, only 18 percent believed this, while 65 percent believed an opposition party was necessary to supervise the government.[40]

Second, the reformers used their electoral successes against their hard-line opponents within the regime. Especially after Lee Teng-hui succeeded Chiang Ching-kuo as president in 1988, elections became a weapon in the struggle for power between factions in the KMT leadership.[41] For example, conservatives fought to maintain the privileges of the senior legislators (those elected on the mainland in the 1940s), but a Council of Grand Justices sympathetic to reform forced the seniors to retire in 1991, a move that enjoyed overwhelming popular support. Opening the national law-making bodies to complete re-election further eroded the KMT's dominance. The rationale for keeping the seniors in office was the civil war. Once new parliamentarians were elected, it became much more difficult to justify other abridgments of the constitution on the same basis. For example, if Taiwan could safely elect new law-makers, why not the provincial governor? Indeed, by 1991, more than three-quarters of Taiwan's residents believed the governor and big-city mayors should be popularly elected.[42] And if the provincial governor could be elected, why not the president?

Lamounier's analysis predicts that electoral success will increase the opposition's organizational strength and popularity. This, too, is evident in the Taiwan case. As Huang Teh-fu writes, "Local elections and the limited opening of representative bodies to electoral competition expanded the opposition's political leverage and ability to mobilize."[43] Throughout the 1970s, the opposition steadily intensified its efforts to form a unified movement. They called their movement the *Dangwai*, which means "outside the party" (i.e., outside the KMT). Activists organized a variety of groups to house their proto-party activities. In the late 1970s, Dangwai politicians established a chain of service centers to coordinate campaign efforts across district lines and to assist with grassroots recruitment. Opposition politicians defied election laws forbidding coordinated campaigning, sponsoring joint rallies and publicizing their cooperative relationships. And as the Dangwai's organizational framework solidified, popular support for the movement, as measured by election results, also grew. Dangwai candidates' vote share in supplementary legislative elections doubled from 8.3 percent in 1980 to 16.7 percent in 1983. In the 1986 legislative race, held just three months after Dangwai activists founded the Democratic Progressive Party, DPP candidates captured 22 percent of the vote.[44] In other words, elections provided a venue for the opposition to improve its organization, while its improved organization helped the opposition attract more votes.

Elections also helped to strengthen party identification and enthusiasm for democratic institutions in general.[45] This is a function Hu Fu labels "political socialization." For decades, surveys of voting behavior in Taiwan found little evidence of party identification. However, recent research finds a new trend. According to Liu I-chou's study of the 1992 legislative election, partisanship was the strongest variable for predicting voting behavior.[46] The roots of this partisanship, he argues, lie in the experience of elections: "After the partisan contests between the KMT and the DPP in 1989 and 1990 ... the success of applying the concept of party identification to voting behavior seemed more certain."[47] Hu Fu and Chu Yun-han reported similar results in a 1992 study. They found that, "intensified electoral competition, the growing national significance that elections have acquired, and the increased symbolic meaning accorded to party label have accelerated the growth of partisanship among the electorate."[48] Concluded Hu,

> the DPP is a formal party organisation rather than just a statistical sum of non-KMT candidates. With its leadership and organisation, the DPP can integrate its popular support from various constituent bases into a coherent national political programme. The DPP, as a party, has already won its identity among a substantial portion of the electorate. Its rise has actually bolstered the growth of partisanship among the electorate. More importantly, the DPP has built its electoral support largely on the demand for a comprehensive political reform to realise majority rule. To a degree, the rise of the DPP has elevated elections increasingly to a test of the legitimacy of the KMT regime.[49]

Lamounier concludes his analysis of authoritarian decline with a discussion of the ARENA party's loss of its absolute majority in the Brazilian legislature. Taiwan has not yet experienced a change of party leadership at the national level. However, the 1997 elections, in which DPP candidates won a larger vote share than the KMT's nominees, brought DPP executives to power in 12 of Taiwan province's 21 towns and cities. Combined with the 1994 election of a DPP mayor in Taipei City, the 1997 results left more than 70 percent of Taiwan's population under local executives from the opposition party. Moreover, the transformation of the KMT itself has been so profound that one can plausibly argue it constitutes the replacement of the old regime. Under President Chiang Kai-shek, the ROC government's top priority and raison d'être was re-establishing KMT government in mainland China. Democracy was an instrument of KMT control over Taiwan; full implementation of the ROC's democratic promise awaited the victory over communism. Taiwan served an important function as the base from which the ROC would retake the mainland, but had little value or importance in its own right.

As President Chiang Ching-kuo gradually assumed his father's roles in the KMT party and ROC state in the 1970s he guided a subtle shift in priorities. Although the leadership continued to cling to the goals of mainland recovery and unification, it gave greater emphasis to policies aimed at improving the status and security of Taiwan itself.[50] Of course, Chiang Ching-kuo did not intend his reforms to bring about the end of KMT rule on Taiwan; on the contrary, he sought to ensure the party's long-term survival by modernizing and "Taiwanizing" it. To do so, he encouraged recruitment of native Taiwanese into the party leadership (especially at the local level), nomination of Taiwanese for elected office and a more active role in the nominating process for the party center. As a result, "the KMT grew more responsive to society and to the aspirations of its own members"; in effect, a new government based on democratic accountability replaced the authoritarian regime.[51] The new government was, like the old, led by the KMT, but it was a very different KMT than had existed forty years earlier.

One of the most profound changes the KMT underwent during the reform process was its split in 1993. This, too, can be traced to electoral pressure. In 1991, the KMT faced a rebellion within the party. The conservative faction, which called itself the New KMT Alliance (NKA), demanded that the party take a stronger stand in favor of unification, and that it punish the DPP for including a pro-independence plank in its party platform. The KMT leadership, however, recognized that most Taiwanese – including many KMT politicians – did not approve of strong unificationist language, and would oppose efforts to crack down on the opposition. Accommodating the NKA's demands "would run the risk of alienating the majority of native Taiwanese."[52] Choosing voter preferences over party unity cost the KMT its unity: two years later, the NKA broke away from the KMT and formed the Chinese New Party. The loss of the New Party reduced the KMT's legislative majority to the barest of margins in the 1995 election and forced the ruling party to negotiate with the opposition on a range of legislative proposals.

Within an authoritarian regime, elections redistribute power from hard-liners to reformers. Taiwan's experience further suggests that they redistribute power from the regime center to the grassroots by increasing the regime's reliance on the individuals directly responsible for delivering votes – party activists, candidates and local networks, or factions. These are the people who can provide tangible evidence of ruling party legitimacy. As Lamounier points out, even if an election's significance is symbolic, the plebiscitary messages it generates are important. In the final analysis, the ruling party needs to win. And once it faces significant opposition, winning requires the active cooperation of grassroots election workers. Taiwan's experience offers many examples of this phenomenon. Above all, most observers agree that – despite Chiang Ching-kuo's original goal of replacing local bosses with good government candidates – the democratization process has increased the clout of local politicians.

As the regime loosened its restrictions on opposition activity, elections became more competitive. In order to win, local politicians had to redouble their efforts. In exchange for this extra effort, local factions demanded more control over nominations, and ratcheted up their expectations of material rewards. When the party center denied local politicians the benefits or nominations they expected, some rebelled. In many cases, they simply refused to give a particular campaign their best effort. In other cases they covertly supported opposition or independent candidates. In a few cases, factions defected from the party entirely, and affiliated with the opposition.[53] In short, reform gave local factions political leverage over the party center. The result was that party policies had to cleave more closely to the desires of local politicians, whose primary concern was re-election. Politicians and voters alike favored the continuation and expansion of reform, creating upward pressure on the party-state.

According to Chen Ming-tong, the KMT's disappointing performance in the 1977 municipal executive elections, when it nominated good government candidates "made the KMT slow its pace of fighting local factions. In the 1981 and 1983 mayoral elections, the factional nominees for mayor exceeded the nonfactional ones."[54] In 1989, the party attempted to reimpose the good government strategy. The effort backfired, and the party lost 7 municipal executiveships as well as 21 Legislative Yuan and 15 Provincial Assembly seats. Huang Teh-fu has calculated the percentage of KMT nominees linked to local factions and their likelihood of victory in legislative and Provincial Assembly elections. Both figures declined steadily from the 1970s until 1986, at which point they rebounded sharply. In 1992, 82 percent of the KMT's successful legislative candidates had factional affiliations – compared to an average of 53 percent in the six previous legislative contests.[55] In sum, writes Chen:

> As Taiwan's political system becomes more democratic, elections are increasingly becoming the only institution that can allocate political power legitimately. To solidify its power base at the grassroots level and to face the opposition challenges in elections, the KMT has

increased its political involvement in local society. Local factions have once again become most crucial allies.[56]

The expansion of electoral competition was possible in Taiwan because both the regime and the opposition recognized the benefits of a "mobile horizon." The ruling party believed it could use elections to enhance its legitimacy in an unstable era. At the same time, it expected to control the pace and direction of reform, because it was confident of its electoral ability. The opposition saw elections as an opportunity to gain influence and to reach a larger audience. Although dissidents recognized the limitations of the electoral system, the majority of them were convinced that working to change the system from within was the most fruitful course open to them. And so the horizon began to move. No one anticipated, however, how fast or how far it would go. Each election created pressure for further reform, as elected officials found themselves forced to compete for votes in a society that valued participation. Elections inculcated Taiwanese citizens with partisanship and democratic values; they created opportunities to send pro-reform messages to the regime; they altered the balance of power between hard-liners and reformers and between state and society. By 1996, the horizon of the possible in Taiwan's political system had moved far beyond what anyone had anticipated or predicted even five years earlier. Four presidential candidates stood before their supporters and the world, staking a claim to Taiwan's newborn democracy.

2 Learning to vote
The origins of Taiwan's electoral system

The Japanese era

Throughout the nineteenth century, Japan's leaders worried that their nation would attract the attention of European and North American empires looking to expand into the Pacific. Thus, the Meiji period, which began in 1868, was marked by vigorous campaigns to convince the West that Japan was neither *terra nullis* nor isle of savages, but a modern nation on the road to economic and political self-development. When China signed the Treaty of Shimonoseki ceding Taiwan to Japan in 1895, the Japanese government seized the opportunity to establish a model colony on the island. Taiwan would prove that the Japanese could out-colonize those who might dream of colonizing Japan. As it turned out, the project was a success. Within two decades, Taiwan no longer required subsidies from Tokyo. And by the time the Japanese withdrew from the island in 1945, Taiwan outpaced mainland China in nearly every measure of material development – per capita income, economic infrastructure, health, educational attainment, and so on. Decades later, this gap contributed to serious problems.

Japan's Taiwan policy responded to a variety of competing concerns. First, the Japanese worried about subversion from mainland China. As Japan and China moved toward war in the 1920s and 1930s, colonial authorities intensified their efforts to keep the island free of influences from the mainland. Japanese policy combined assimilation and discrimination. For example, students in the widely available primary schools studied a Japanese curriculum. However, Taiwanese university students were steered toward technical fields (such as medicine) and away from potentially "subversive" disciplines (such as social sciences), while graduates faced employment discrimination.

Meanwhile, the Japanese colonial government strove to maintain Taiwan's social stability and economic prosperity. Their most difficult challenge on this front was on-going resistance from Taiwan's indigenous peoples. The Japanese insistence upon eradicating the Aboriginal peoples' way of life – and exploiting the resources of their mountain homelands – provoked violent confrontations. In 1930, an Aboriginal attack on a police outpost in the central mountains left more than two hundred Japanese dead. The Aboriginal fighters and their families eventually were wiped out, but the incident shook the island's Japanese community.

A third important factor driving Japanese policy in Taiwan was the shifting political climate in Tokyo. While conservatism reigned among Japanese officials at Taipei, Taiwanese found a more sympathetic hearing among liberal forces in the home government. The Diet enacted a number of political reforms for Taiwan over the objections of the Taipei authorities. Taiwanese who advocated local autonomy for the island thus found encouragement in some quarters, but also faced daunting obstacles, especially when they attempted to expand their activity from Japan to Taiwan itself. The authorities on the island had ample resources to keep the activists on edge, threatened and factionalized. Nonetheless, in the 1920s a home rule movement appeared.

Taiwan's movement for greater local autonomy began in 1918. Taiwanese students living in Tokyo found inspiration in President Woodrow Wilson's campaign for national self-determination and human rights; they took further encouragement from Japanese rhetoric (addressed to Western governments) asserting the principle of racial equality. In 1921, a group of Taiwanese in Japan founded the Taiwan Culture Society. Japanese authorities tolerated the group, although they declared some of its activities illegal. The organization advocated for a Taiwanese parliament to check and balance the colonial administration; it submitted petitions to the Diet annually requesting a parliament and a Taiwanese representative in the national legislature. Despite harassment and persecution by colonial authorities, more than 17,000 Taiwanese signed these petitions between 1921 and 1934. Some students even used their vacations to travel from village to village in Taiwan stumping for home rule.

In 1927, the Taiwan Culture Society split. The moderate faction founded the People's Party, which "worked to legalize labor unions and win a larger role for Taiwanese in local governance."[1] This marked a shift in the home rule advocates' approach: instead of fighting for an island-wide parliament, they pushed for locally elected assemblies and councils at the prefectural level and below.[2] When the People's Party split in 1930, one of the offshoots was the League for Local Self-Government.

As it turned out, the new strategy meshed with Tokyo's own plans. In 1919, Tokyo for the first time dispatched a civilian to be Taiwan's governor. The following year, islanders gained a modicum of political participation when the colonial government established assemblies in each of Taiwan's prefectures. These appointed representatives were charged with advising local executives; most were Japanese. Of the Taiwanese members, a handful urged greater autonomy for Taiwan, but the great majority were conservatives. In 1921, the colony's governor-general appointed nine Taiwanese to his consultative council, the highest office Taiwanese would obtain under the Japanese empire.

In the early 1930s, with war on the horizon, Japan needed the support of its Taiwanese subjects – especially the landlords, whose economic contributions and social influence were great. The central government handed the colonial authorities a mandate to institute local elections in 1935, in which voters would choose half the members of local assemblies, with the other half to be appointed. The assemblies' job was to "discuss and act on the local budget, certain local tax matters, and a few unimportant administrative questions."[3] The effect of the reform was to "draw local elites into a political apparatus controlled by the colonial authorities, and also to set them against one another and make them dependent on the higher-ups."[4] The franchise for these early elections was extremely limited: only men over the age of 25 who paid more than five yen in taxes each year could vote, and voter rolls and campaign materials were subject to police approval. In 1935, 187,000 persons were qualified to vote, comprising 14.6 percent of Taiwan's Japanese residents and 3.8 percent of the Taiwanese population.[5]

The decision to permit local elections eliminated all hope of establishing an island-wide parliament, but most home rule advocates accepted their partial victory and made the best of it. In 1935, the League for Local Self-Government voted to support candidates in the local elections, effectively changing its mode of political participation from social movement to electoral competitor. According to Chen Ming-tong and Lin Jih-wen, elites in the home rule movement made the shift to electoral politics because they recognized it was the only mode of participation available to them.[6]

The electoral process the Japanese instituted in Taiwan mimicked the system used in Japan itself. Administrative orders stipulated one vote per elector, with no transfers among candidates. Electoral districts followed administrative boundaries. To equalize representation, the number of members elected from each district varied according to district population. The winners in these multi-member races were those who received the largest number of votes, until all the district's seats were filled. Taken together, these regulations established a system of single, nontransferable voting in multi-member districts (SVMM).

As the League for Local Self-Government soon discovered, the SVMM formula presents political organizations with daunting challenges. The League hoped to maximize its representation in the first local elections by dividing its support among several candidates in each district. This strategy was impossible in most areas, where the League's organizational base was weak. However, in Taichung the League was confident enough to implement a unified electoral strategy.[7] It chose four candidates, who agreed to limit their campaign expenditures and staff size, emphasize issues in their campaigns and refrain from door-to-door campaigning. The goal was to present a united front that would carry all four candidates to victory.

As it turned out, the League's efforts foundered on the same shoals that would frustrate political strategists for generations to come. As Chen and Lin put it, "As soon as electoral combat began, the agreement fell apart,"[8] with the result that the League won only two of the four seats it contested. In Pingtung, where the League also felt strong, too many home rule candidates were nominated; only one out of the five managed to win a seat. In other prefectures, the League left its nominees alone, with better results. In Chiayi and Tainan, the League's candidates won three out of three and four out of four seats, respectively. In Taipei, the single League candidate won more votes than any other candidate. The lesson of this first election was this: high-minded campaigns based on issues and collective restraint are a less effective way to win SVMM elections than individually managed campaigns in which socially prominent candidates mobilize supporters on their home turf. As Chen and Lin write,

> The situation in Taichung reflects the difficulty facing a rational party under the SVMM system. If it chooses to follow the path of publicizing and promoting its ideas, it immediately will face the problem of dividing votes. If only one candidate adopts the strategy of localized campaigning, it will be impossible to maintain the agreements negotiated beforehand. Thus, carrying out local elections not only factionalized local elites, but also made it impossible for existing anti-government elites to resist this trend.[9]

After 1935, Taiwan's assemblies had 172 members. Of these, 109 were Japanese (60 appointed and 49 elected), and 63 were Taiwanese (26 appointed and 37 elected). In 1937, another round of elections took place, and the governor-general's advisory council was enlarged to 40 members, including 17 Taiwanese. These early elections had lasting political consequences. They neutralized the home rule movement by redirecting its leaders' energy away from the struggle for a Taiwan parliament, toward electoral competition. They divided local elites, encouraging ambitious Taiwanese to develop individual political bases instead of joining organized movements. They rewarded elites who took a local rather than island-wide perspective, and they diminished incentives to join a united opposition.[10] In a more positive vein, however, the elections introduced Taiwanese to regular, peaceful political participation. As of 1939, almost 300,000 Taiwanese were registered to vote, and more than 3,000 had held elective office.

These reforms were short-lived. By the late 1930s, military adventurers had displaced civilian authorities in Tokyo, a development which spilled over into colonial policy. On Taiwan, policies promoting assimilation and mobilization for war and war production brushed aside the tentative steps toward home rule. Nonetheless, Taiwan's brief experience with elections set the tone for the future. As George Kerr writes, "The Formosans ... were becoming familiar with all the devices of political campaigns and electioneering ... elements of training and experience that ultimately were to form a frame of reference for future (post-Surrender) demands and expectations."[11] Lai, Myers and Wei echo this view, writing: "the Taiwanese started to become accustomed to the idea of basing local government on local elections. This was certainly one of several reasons why the KMT initiated local elections in Taiwan as early as it did, in April 1946."[12]

Retrocession

Taiwan returned to Chinese control upon the Japanese surrender in 1945. ROC president Chiang Kai-shek dispatched a military leader, General Chen Yi, to the island to serve as its first Chinese governor in five decades. One of Chen's first items of business was instituting local elections. In 1946, Taiwanese chose representatives to district, city and township consultative councils. These elections gave the Taiwanese more representation than they had under the Japanese, and more than other Chinese provinces enjoyed at the time.[13] Competition in the elections was keen; almost 37,000 candidates vied for fewer than 8,000 seats. Above the district level, representatives were chosen indirectly; lower-level assemblies elected those above them. The provincial consultative assembly, in which more than 1,000 candidates competed for 30 seats, chose Taiwan's representatives to the ROC government on the mainland. The provincial body, which was charged with advising and interpellating the provincial administration but had no legislative authority, generated great public excitement. Its early meetings turned into raucous forums for criticizing the provincial administration.[14]

The 1946 elections shared a great deal with elections under the

Japanese. Among the 1,180 candidates for the provincial consultative council, for example, 38 percent had held seats in advisory bodies under the Japanese. Another 6 percent were anti-Japanese political activists, while most of the rest belonged to the colonial era political elite.[15] In fact, between 1945 and 1947, years that Chen and Lin call the "honeymoon period," the switch from Japanese to Chinese sovereignty had little effect on Taiwanese elites' political involvement.[16] A second important area of similarity between the 1935 and 1937 elections and the 1946 contests was the electoral system. The ROC adopted Japan's basic rules of competition, and SVMM elections became a permanent feature of Taiwanese politics.

Single, nontransferable voting in multi-member districts

It still is possible today to see the influence of Taiwan's Japanese colonizers on the island. Japan left behind a solid infrastructure for economic development, including schools and universities, rural electrification projects, roads and railroads. It also contributed to Taiwan's culture: Taiwanese take off their shoes indoors, eat sashimi, use words borrowed from Japanese and install Japanese-style rooms with platforms, sunken tables and sliding screens in their homes. Perhaps the colonial era's most significant political legacy is the system of single, nontransferable voting in multi-member districts (the SVMM system). What follows is a description of that system and its effects on political behavior and outcomes generally.

Taiwan's electoral districts follow administrative boundaries. Most legislative districts consist of a municipality (a county or city),[17] while Provincial Assembly and National Assembly elections follow township and city lines. As a result, electoral districts are not remotely consistent in population. In order to provide for equal representation, the number of representatives elected from each district – the district magnitude – varies according to population. For example, in 1995, Taipei County residents elected seventeen national legislators, while voters in the five smallest municipalities chose only one representative each. The average district magnitude in that year was 4.5. Under SVMM, candidates are ranked according to the number of votes each receives, and those with the largest number of votes, up to the district magnitude, are elected. For example, in Taipei County, the seventeen top vote-getters were the winners.[18] This electoral formula is called single, nontransferable voting because each voter chooses one candidate (unlike the Italian two-vote preference voting system), and votes are not redistributed (as they are in the Irish system). Any votes a candidate receives beyond the number he or she needs to win are, in effect, wasted.

To win an SVMM election, a candidate does not need a majority or even a plurality of the votes cast; it is necessary only to finish near the top. The larger the district magnitude, the smaller the percentage of votes required to win. A handful of Taiwanese districts have only one representative; these effectively are plurality elections, not SVMM elections. But where the district magnitude is large, the percentage of votes needed to capture a seat can be quite small. For example, in a district with five candidates (a modest-sized field by Taiwanese standards), one might well be elected with less than 20 percent of the votes cast. In the 1992 legislative election, one district in Taipei County had 48 candidates competing for 16 seats. The sixteenth finisher was elected with less than 3 percent of the total vote.

The SVMM formula has far-reaching consequences for parties and voters. As the League for Local Self-Government discovered in 1935, it poses formidable strategic challenges for parties and other political groups. Assuming that a party's goal in legislative elections is to maximize the number of seats it wins, an electoral system that requires candidates from the same party to compete for votes is certain to create intra-party conflict. Indeed, this is precisely the effect of SVMM elections. In Taiwan's 1995 legislative elections, on average, 11.6 candidates fought for the 4.5 seats available in each district. Of these, 3.5, on average, were KMT nominees. Thus, in most districts, maximizing the KMT's share of seats required the party to coordinate campaign strategy among three or more candidates, in an environment made highly competitive by non-KMT challengers. To make matters worse, members of the same party are likely to compete for the same votes, since their party label and issue positions are similar. To overcome the logical inclination of party comrades to compete for votes, parties try to allocate the votes available to them to their various nominees.

As long as the KMT suppressed alternative parties, the SVMM formula actually reduced intra-party conflict and encouraged cooperation among KMT candidates, thereby enhancing the KMT's control over electoral outcomes. An SVMM race is not a zero-sum game; one candidate's victory need not spell another candidate's defeat. Instead, SVMM elections have many winners, allowing the KMT to reward several factions in each district – factions among whom single-member districts would inspire cut-throat competition. In the absence of challengers from outside the party, SVMM elections rewarded cooperation, not competition, among KMT factions. But to maximize its share of winning candidates, a party also must ensure that none of its members receives such a large share of the vote that its other nominees fall short. One strategy for combating this tendency would be simply to assign people to vote for particular candidates. But this would require perfect information about who the party's supporters are and perfect compliance with the party strategy. Such conditions are unlikely, although not inconceivable.[19]

To maximize its share of seats in SVMM elections, the KMT uses a strategy of "dividing the vote" (*pei piao*) and assigning candidates to "responsibility zones" (*zirenqu*).[20] Before elections, potential candidates meet with party leaders and faction bosses to estimate the number of votes the party can capture in the district. In general, the party nominates only as many candidates as it can elect, given the number of votes reported. Before 1986, that often meant nominating a candidate for every open seat, a strategy known as "full nomination." However, the party left room for outside candidates when local cadres believed they might defeat KMT nominees or provoke factional conflict. This "partial nomination" strategy ensures that the party's votes are not spread so thinly that it cannot maximize its seat share.[21]

Once the KMT's slate of nominations is set, party cadres meet with the nominees to negotiate the division of the district into responsibility zones. It is the candidates' responsibility to mobilize the votes in their zones. The allocation of responsibility zones balances several factors. First, zones are assigned to give all the candidates equal access to KMT voters. Second, candidates are assigned to zones in which they have good personal connections, and in which their demographic profile (especially ethnic origin) matches that of the neighborhood. Third, incumbents are normally assigned to the same zones in each race they contest. Fourth, while most zones are geographical in nature, some are functional; that is, the members of a particular occupational group (veterans, postal workers, etc.) are assigned to the same candidate, regardless of where in the district they live. A few such groups are held aside and deployed in the last days before an election to prop up lagging KMT candidates. These are called "spare zones."[22] The KMT's most reliable voters are known as "iron ballots" (*tie piao*).

ROC political campaigns have two faces. A campaign's public face includes speeches, rallies, posters, newspaper advertisements – beginning in 1991, even television commercials appeared. The private face of a campaign – the mobilization of the responsibility zone – emphasizes clientelistic methods. Clientelism is a political style in which politicians (the patrons) form lasting relationships with people below them (their clients). These relationships are based on mutually beneficial exchanges. The patron gives the client access to the spoils of power, and, in turn, the client supports the patron's political ambitions and activities. The benefits a patron provides to his or her clients are known as "particularistic" bene-fits, to distinguish them from benefits that the public sector provides to all citizens equally. In Taiwan, votes are the currency that finances the patronage system. The grassroots political activists who collect those votes on behalf of their patrons are known in Taiwanese as *tiau-a-ka* (pillars).[23]

Clientelistic relationships in a society tend to form chains; for example, a city council member might act as a patron for several neigh-borhood leaders, while simultaneously acting as a client to the mayor. In this case, the neighborhood leaders would rely on the council member to ensure that community complaints were resolved quickly. In exchange, they would mobilize the neighborhood to vote for that council member. The council member, in turn, would encourage those neighborhood leaders to turn out their supporters to vote for the mayor, while the mayor pressured the city bureaucracy to take special care of the council member's neighborhoods. The mayor also might serve as a client to an official in the provincial or national government. Clientelism is a common form of political interaction, familiar to people in nearly every country in the world.

For a clientelistic system to work, there must be a point at which inter-actions between citizens and the state acquire their particularistic character. Whether this takes the form of a precinct boss handing out Christmas turkeys in Chicago, a bureaucrat in Palermo moving a supporter to the top of a public housing waiting list, or a village head informing a group of Taiwanese farmers that their road is to be paved, somehow the system must put a human face on public services. Every state action, no matter how obligatory or automatic, is portrayed as a favor by an individual public official to some small group of citizens, and their grat-itude is manifested as political support. This is the essence of a clientele system. And the clientele system is the essence of Taiwan's electoral mobilization.

Before the DPP came on the scene, mobilizing the votes in one's responsibility zone normally was sufficient to win a seat. But as elections became more competitive in the late 1980s and the 1990s, KMT candi-dates found it necessary to supplement their mobilization efforts in their responsibility zones with appeals to "floating voters." They also found it increasingly difficult to resist the temptation to steal votes out of others' responsibility zones. In theory, KMT nominees are not supposed to campaign outside the responsibility zone, except to mobilize existing rela-tionships with relatives and friends. But as Liu I-chou puts it,

This rule ... is very difficult to enforce. This is an internal rule of the party, thus no legal sanctions can be taken against a violation. Also, it is hard to make distinctions between old and new connections. All Kuomintang candidates in fact pursue old and new support in their colleagues' zones.[24]

The SVMM system's effects on party strategy are obvious. Its consequences for voting behavior are less visible, but no less profound. Many studies have found that SVMM elections are associated with candidate-oriented voting. For example, according to a detailed voting behavior survey, 80.5 percent of Taiwan's voters were "candidate oriented" when making their voting decisions in the 1989 legislative election.[25] Rochon offers strong evidence that the SVMM system causes candidate-oriented voting. He found that Japanese voters (until 1994, Japan's Diet elections used the SVMM system) were no more likely than their counterparts in other countries to base their votes on candidate evaluation when their preferred party nominated only one candidate. But when a voter's party nominated two or more candidates in a voter's district, the incidence of candidate-centered voting shot up.[26] According to his analysis, Japanese vote *in* parties, but they do not vote *for* parties, because under SVMM rules, party preference alone is not enough to select a candidate. With several nominees of the same party competing against one another, voters must resort to candidate evaluation in order to choose one.[27]

Yang Tai-shuenn's essay "The Peculiarities of our Electoral System" takes this argument a step further. In an SVMM election, each voter chooses one candidate from a list. As Yang observes, even candidates in large districts need relatively few votes to be elected, compared to candidates in single-member districts, who must win a majority or plurality. As a result, it is possible to win many Taiwanese elections merely by capturing the votes of people to whom one is personally connected, or to whom one's close followers are connected. So not only is candidate-oriented voting more likely, but also, candidates' views and opinions take a back seat to personal relationships and group mobilization.[28] A 1983 National Taiwan University elections workshop poll found that 71.7 percent of respondents were candidate oriented, but only 30.4 percent rated "candidates' political views" most important.[29]

The candidate-oriented voting that characterizes SVMM elections comes at the expense of issue-based voting and party identification. In a survey of Taipei City voters taken after the 1989 elections, 68 percent of the respondents who preferred the DPP's position on direct presidential elections and 69 percent of those who agreed with the DPP on the independence issue nonetheless reported voting for KMT candidates.[30]

Issue-based voting is more common among DPP voters than KMT voters; still, other orientations are twice as common as issue-voting even among DPP supporters.[31] There is evidence to suggest, however, that issues are becoming more important. A survey by the Workshop on Political Systems and Political Change at National Taiwan University found the percentage of Legislative Yuan voters rating issues in their top three reasons for selecting a candidate dipped from 30.4 percent in 1983 to 23.4 percent in 1986, then rose to 54.2 percent in 1989. At the same time, the percentage who mentioned personal connections or social relations fell from 32.4 percent in 1983 to 21.3 percent in 1989.[32]

Lin Jih-wen has elaborated a detailed theory to explain the interaction between mobilization and issue voting.[33] He points out that SVMM elections force candidates to stake out distinctive identities to attract voters.[34] In most districts, KMT candidates accomplish this by using the responsibility zone system.[35] However, there is a subset of Taiwanese voters for whom issues, especially national identity, do matter. Candidates who wish to appeal to that subset use issues to distinguish themselves from other candidates. They tend to take extreme positions, because that is where the issue voters are most likely to be. To prove his point, he shows that candidates in Taiwan's executive elections, which do not use the SVMM formula, take more centrist positions than candidates in SVMM races. For example, Lin points to Taipei City mayor Chen Shui-bian, who took a strongly pro-independence position when he ran for a legislative seat in 1992, but was far more moderate in his 1994 mayoral campaign.[36]

Mobilizational politics is especially effective in small districts, in which the limited number of candidates makes it easier to negotiate and enforce the division of turf and other agreements. District size is one reason why the opposition's vote share in National Assembly elections lags behind its share in legislative elections, in which the districts are more than twice as large. When the Central Election Commission decided to divide the island into 58 electoral districts for the 1991 National Assembly race the DPP protested vigorously, at one point organizing a demonstration at which its supporters pelted the Ministry of the Interior with eggs. In an SVMM election, the larger the district magnitude, the closer a party's seat share will be to its vote share. Districts with five or more representatives will be nearly proportional; the smaller the district, the greater the disproportionality. Because the KMT traditionally has won the largest seat bonuses, small districts have benefited the ruling party most.[37]

If small districts magnify the influence of clientelism, large districts can contribute to clientelistic voting in another way. When district magnitudes are large, ballots contain long lists of candidates, many of whom the KMT has either nominated or recommended. (See Table 2.1.) This can

Table 2.1   Candidates per district

Year	Office	Max.	Min.	Average	KMT (average)
1995	Legislative Yuan	50	3	12	4
1992	Legislative Yuan	48	2	12	6
1991	National Assembly	29	4	8	4
1989	Legislative Yuan	29	2	9	4
1989	Provincial Assembly	19	2	7	3
1983	Legislative Yuan	25	5	16	
1980	National Assembly	16	1	5	
1980	Legislative Yuan	33	6	19	

Source: *Capital Morning Post*, 3 December 1989; *Independence Morning Post*, 22 December 1991; *World Journal*, 20 December 1992; election results.

make selecting a candidate very arduous. Reading the election bulletin in which candidates list their positions on major issues is of little benefit, since most candidates reiterate the party line. In most districts, voters do have the option of voting against the KMT, since there is at least one non-KMT candidate. But for voters whose preference is for the ruling party, the large number of candidates and their similarity to one another make it difficult to choose one. Lacking any clear basis on which to make an independent selection, voters are more likely to respond to vote buying, personal appeals and other clientelistic tactics.[38]

The problem of choosing intelligently from among a long list of candidates is one with which many Taiwanese are sympathetic. A newspaper cartoon lampooning this predicament appeared shortly before the 1989 election. It illustrated the exertions of a man who decided to make an informed voting decision. He spent all his working hours reading newspapers, so he lost his job. He spent every evening attending candidate forums, so his wife left him. And so on. By election day, he had lost everything – but his voting decision was well informed.

SVMM elections also discourage political parties from emphasizing issues. It is easier to distribute and mobilize votes if a party's candidates all appear very similar. Otherwise, voters may be too "distracted" by the candidates' individual positions to carry out the planned distribution of votes. Thus, until 1992 the KMT always insisted that its members adhere to the party platform. They were permitted to develop independent positions on issues of local concern only. Voters therefore had little to base their votes on, other than the candidates' individual qualities and mobilizing efforts. For the DPP, whose candidates do emphasize issues, allocating votes evenly is a perennial headache.

While there is little doubt that the SVMM formula promotes candidate-oriented voting and clientelistic campaigning in Taiwan, the electoral system is not the only factor that contributes to Taiwan's mobilizational style of electoral politics. A number of other influences, both environmental and institutional, deserve attention. First, Taiwan's social and cultural environment is compatible with clientelistic politics. Taiwanese society provides fertile ground for clientelistic practices from pork barreling to vote buying. Kinship, friendship and other ties have been features of the island's social and political milieu for generations, and gift-giving is a basic principle of Taiwanese etiquette. Some observers link Taiwan's culture not only to personalistic voting, but even to nepotism in government service. According to Lui Fei-lung,

> A customary saying, "to be an official is temporary, to be a man is permanent," sums up the belief that one cannot perform government duties without taking care of personal duties to friends and relatives at the same time.... This is why primary social relations usually come first in measuring the relative importance of factors determining one's voting behavior.[39]

There is good reason to believe that Taiwan's culture tolerates clientelistic politics; still, it is important not to make too much of the cultural explanation. Where on earth is the society in which public officials never try to use their influence to take care of friends and relatives? If anything, Chinese culture is less forgiving of nepotism than most, thanks to its Confucian tradition. Indeed, if we are looking for an explanation for political clientelism in Taiwan, we are likely to find better answers in Taiwan's institutions, which are both more unique and less ambiguous than its culture. In particular, clues to the strength of clientelistic politics can be found in Taiwan's party system, government structure and campaign rules.

The SVMM system, with its long ballots and issue-less campaigns, promotes candidate-oriented voting and strengthens clientelistic electioneering. So, too, does a single-party system. Prior to 1977, the only alternatives to KMT candidates were a few independents. Voters relied on KMT cadres and *tiau-a-ka* to guide them through the complexities of an electoral system without party competition or issue conflict. Between 1977 and 1986, some independent politicians joined together in a loose network, but Taiwan still lacked a true opposition party. And even after more than a decade of multi-party elections, many Taiwanese still are in the habit of turning to vote brokers for advice.

Thanks to its dominant position, the Kuomintang promoted clientelistic political structures directly as well as indirectly. A number of Taiwanese scholars believe the ruling party deliberately channels public resources to clientelistic networks in order to enhance its own power.[40] Others go further, claiming the KMT created the clientelistic networks in the first place. According to Hu Fu, the KMT:

> has built a set of interest exchange-based patron–client networks, taking local political and social forces – through the local factional organizations – and bringing them into the ruling party structure to enhance its manipulation of them. Under such a political operation, local elections could only become a tool of authoritarian politics.[41]

A Tainan County DPP activist put the matter more bluntly: "As long as there are two factions, the KMT is always the big brother (*lao da*), because it has its hands on goodies people want."

The previous sections described how the SVMM formula and the one-party system discourage party- and issue-oriented voting and encourage candidates to use clientelistic strategies to attract supporters. Another factor contributing to the prevalence of clientelistic, candidate-oriented voting in Taiwan is the distribution of power within the ROC state. Assuming issue-based voting is not merely symbolic or expressive, but is intended to influence policy outcomes, when elected officials have no say in policy-making, issue-based voting is irrational. In contrast, candidate-based voting promises immediate pay-offs. The structure of the ROC government exploits this logic by limiting elected officials' authority to precisely those arenas through which patronage and other particularistic rewards are dispensed, while allowing the central government to monopolize policy-making.

The imprint of centralized decision-making is evident in both national and local elections. At the national level, elected officials include the members of the National Assembly, whose powers are limited to amending the constitution, and the Legislative Yuan. Both bodies play limited roles in policy formation. Taiwan's parliamentarians rarely initiate legislation, and the presence until 1992 of a decisive voting bloc of senior legislators in office since 1947 enabled the ruling party to pass any bill it pleased.[42] Also, KMT legislators (whose representation in the Legislative

Yuan has never fallen below 50 percent of the seats) must be careful not to oppose their party too much. Some of the KMT's best-known legislators lost their party's endorsement as a result of their outspokenness. Legislators do, however, enjoy innumerable opportunities to channel economic resources to themselves and their supporters. They have access to information, they have leverage in negotiating with bureaucrats, they can even make laws to benefit their clients.[43] In short, while the legislature still is struggling for its rightful place in the policy-making process, it long ago mastered the arts of patronage and pork barrel politics.

Locally elected officials have even less policy-making authority than their counterparts in the central representative bodies. What power they do have is supervised stringently by higher levels of government and the ruling party. Once again, the source of central control is the ROC constitution, which provides for a unitary state. Power exercised by provincial and municipal governments is delegated by the center. By law, personnel appointments and budgeting at the provincial level and below are subject to central government supervision. Hu Fu summarized the situation facing politicians at the provincial level and below in a 1986 article: "In principle, local governments of each level are responsible to their corresponding representative bodies, but the Executive Yuan is the last power holder, which can overrule any decision made by the local governments at any ... level."[44]

To make matters worse, bureaucratic agencies parallel each elected organ, so elected officials end up sharing power with appointed officials. Often, their terms of office are arranged so that the appointed bureaucrat arrives before his elected counterpart and is therefore more knowledgeable and experienced from the outset.[45] These bureaucrats often serve the party as well as the central government; in 1983, more than 80 percent of ROC civil servants belonged to the KMT.[46] Also, key government agencies may not be under local jurisdiction at all. Police, public health workers, civil defense officials and others report directly to their provincial and national supervisors.

Local governments are further constrained by the lack of a local resource base. Most tax revenues collected in Taiwan go to the central government, leaving municipal budgets in the red. Localities depend on subsidies from the provincial government to pay their expenses. (See Table 2.2.) Nor are subsidies always distributed fairly.[47] According to Tien, "there are no detailed guidelines for the allocation of these subsidies; the amount received by local governments depends as much on politics and favoritism as on merit and need."[48]

This is not to say that elected officials have no power at all. County and city governments are responsible for maintaining local public facili-

Table 2.2   Sources of county and city revenue (as percentage of total revenue)

Year	Local tax income	Subsidies
1965	45	41
1970	47	38
1975	39	45
1980	37	50
1985	45	39

Source: Huang Shih-hsin, "The Problem of Local Financial Administration" (*Difang zizhi caizheng wenti*) *National Policy Quarterly*, 7 (1990), p. 17.

ties, including local roads, schools and markets. They hire construction contractors and some public employees. They also make zoning decisions and buy land for public use, creating lucrative opportunities for those in the know. The Provincial Assembly regulates certain economic activities, including banking. As a result, businesses target assembly members in their lobbying efforts.[49] The prestige of office also can be helpful in persuading police to release a suspect or revenue officials to drop a tax audit. In sum, elected officials in the provincial, municipal and township governments can use their positions to benefit themselves and their supporters, even if they cannot enact far-reaching policy initiatives.

Given that elected officials in the ROC – both local and national – have little power to make policy, we would expect voters to show little interest in candidates' views on the issues. A more pragmatic approach is to vote for candidates who will serve their constituents. Voters receive this message from *tiau-a-ka*, who cite examples of candidate service, and may even reinforce their appeals with gifts. For their part, the *tiau-a-ka* are recruited through the few policy realms in which elected officials do influence outcomes: local contracting and patronage. In short, the distribution of authority in the ROC reduces the effectiveness of non-clientelistic appeals, while encouraging the use of clientelistic political strategies.

The alternative to personalistic, clientelistic politics is a mass-based, media-oriented campaign style in which issue preferences and party identification play leading roles. But as Curtis observed, "By its almost total prohibition of the use of the mass media in campaigning ... [Japan's election] law has inhibited the development of new political techniques similar to those that have developed in the United States and Western Europe."[50] Until 1991, Taiwanese politicians labored under many of the same campaign restrictions as their Japanese counterparts – with similar results. Nor did the mass media make up for the lack of advertising in their news coverage.[51] In part because the island's broadcast outlets cover areas that are larger than most electoral districts, TV and radio news shows report on only the most elite races, leaving voters dependent upon newspapers for information on elections outside metropolitan Taipei. Overall, then, campaign regulations benefited candidates who used the clientele system to mobilize support because the campaign rules curtailed voters' access to the information they needed to choose among the many candidates in SVMM races.

Among the most restrictive provisions of Taiwan's election law were campaign time limits, which ranged from three days for village and neighborhood contests to fifteen days for National Assembly and Legislative Yuan campaigns. Time limits handicapped candidates with low name recognition or weak connections; in practice, this meant opposition and independent candidates. The election law also restricted the activities candidates could use. The law limited campaign activity to direct contact with voters (through canvassing, operating sound trucks, making speeches, and distributing bulletins and handbills). Collective campaign activities, parades, and advertising in the mass media were forbidden. When opposition candidates began attracting large crowds to their speeches, the legislature cracked down on rallies, making it more difficult for the opposition to get its message to the public.[52] Prior to 1989, candidates were not allowed to place advertisements on radio, television, magazines or newspapers.[53] The ban on newspaper and magazine ads was lifted in 1989, and political parties aired their first campaign commercials during the National Assembly campaign of 1991. These reforms reduced but did not eliminate the obstacles facing candidates who lacked access to the KMT's mobilization system.

Measuring success in SVMM elections

So far in this chapter we have traced the origins of Taiwan's unusual electoral system (SVMM) and looked at its implications for candidates, parties and voters. We have seen how SVMM elections promote mobilizational strategies in ROC elections, and we have looked at other factors that reinforced that tendency. The rest of the chapter will be devoted to considering different methods for measuring success in SVMM elections.

Ordinarily, news reports of an election give only the percentage of votes and seats won by each party. These results show the distribution of power within the elected bodies, and how much overall support the parties enjoy. They do not reveal how the distribution of votes and seats was achieved. For example, if party A nominates twice as many candidates as party B, it may not win twice as many votes, but it is very likely to win more, simply because each candidate brings in some supporters. But merely nominating more candidates is not a wise strategy, especially for a small party, which will win more seats if it concentrates its votes on fewer candidates. For a small party to win one seat in every district would require outstanding organization – an accomplishment that would be hard to recognize from the overall election results.

The best way to judge the effectiveness of a party's organization is to compare its performance with its goals. In most situations, a political party's objective is to maximize the number of seats its candidates win.[54] To accomplish this goal in an SVMM election, the party must estimate its potential support accurately, keep unauthorized candidates out of the race and allocate its votes in a way that optimizes its performance. Traditionally, the Kuomintang has used local factions to mobilize support for its candidates. Local factions recruit vote brokers (*tiau-a-ka*), who in turn cultivate groups of voters whose support they deliver to selected candidates, based on the party's overall strategy. If the local factions and *tiau-a-ka* do their job well, the party can allocate just enough votes to each of its nominees to ensure their election, without wasting any votes.

A party cannot allocate its votes efficiently if more than the optimal number of party members join the race. The number of party votes is finite, and if they are spread too thinly among a large number of candidates, fewer will be elected. Thus, one criterion for judging a party's organizational success is whether or not it is able to control its members' entry into the competition. For example, the KMT did a good job of controlling its members in 1991, when only 2.4 percent of the KMT members who registered as candidates did so without the party's authorization. What is more, these unauthorized (or "maverick") candidates took a mere 1 percent of their party's total votes, because the KMT made sure the mavericks did not take votes from its official nominees. In 1992, in contrast, the KMT had a much more difficult time: one-fourth of the KMT candidates in the race were mavericks.

Brown, Moon and Robinson have developed another method for evaluating a party's popularity, controlling for the vagaries of the SVMM system.[55] They compare the ratio of candidates each party nominated to the ratio of votes it received. The DPP cannot nominate as many candidates as the KMT, both because its estimated vote share is lower, so more nominations would be counter-productive, and because it has fewer potential candidates to recruit. However, we would not want to say that the DPP enjoys no popularity in a district in which it had no candidate, even if the lack of a candidate meant that it received no votes. To account for this phenomenon, Brown *et al.* look to see how the DPP's vote share compares to its candidate share. For example, in the municipal council elections held in January 1998, the DPP won only one-third as many votes as the KMT. However, when we consider the fact that the

DPP also nominated only one-third as many candidates as the ruling party, its vote share changes from lackluster to quite respectable.

Another measure of a party's organizational effectiveness is the success rate of its nominees. A party that estimates its strength accurately, nominates the optimal number of candidates and makes the most of the votes available to it will see a higher proportion of its nominees take office. In 1991, 86 percent of KMT nominees were elected, compared to 45 percent of DPP nominees and 2 percent of independents. Looking at a party's seat bonus also is informative, since the seat bonus measures a party's success in translating raw votes into representation in government.[56] The KMT's large seat bonus in 1991 – it captured 78 percent of the contested seats with only 71 percent of the votes cast – indicates that the KMT distributed its votes more effectively than its opponents.

A more subtle way to evaluate a party's effectiveness at mobilizing votes would be to look at whether or not each candidate's votes were concentrated in his or her "responsibility zone." Liu I-chou analyzed the results of the 1989 legislative election in Taipei City's district and found that the KMT candidates who participated in the responsibility zone system won significantly more votes inside their zones than outside. The candidates' vote shares within their responsibility zones were between 1.5 times and 6.2 times as high as their vote shares outside their zones (the average was 2.9).[57] This represented a substantial deterioration in the responsibility zone system's effectiveness since 1980, when Taipei's legislative candidates won, on average, more than eight times as many votes inside their responsibility zones as outside.[58] Liu's method works well for evaluating the effectiveness of mobilization in small areas, but it would be difficult to apply at the national level.

A less detailed – but more manageable – approach would be to compare the parties' overall patterns of vote distribution. If each candidate ran as an individual, we might expect the distribution of votes among candidates to be roughly normal; that is, a few candidates would get very few votes, a few candidates would get many votes, and most candidates would fall somewhere in between. But in the SVMM system, political parties strive to distribute the votes available to them as evenly as possible. Thus, the distribution that maximizes the number of seats a party can win is one in which all candidates receive about the same number of votes. Candidates who score too low will lose; candidates who score too high waste votes that could have gone to less secure members of their party.

The frequency distributions in Figure 2.1 illustrate successful and unsuccessful results. Ideally, all the candidates would finish at or just above the minimum number needed for election (the quota). Graphically,

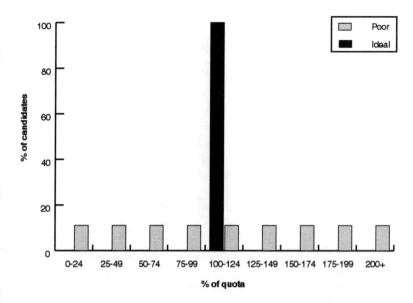

Figure 2.1 Ideal outcome versus poor outcome in SNTV–MMD elections

this distribution would look like the "max" bar in Figure 2.1 (one tall bar in the middle of the graph). On the other hand, if a party were completely incapable of allocating votes among its candidates, instead of concentrating its votes near the percentage needed to win, it would spread them all over – with some candidates losing, some winning, and many votes wasted at both ends. This scenario is illustrated by the "min" bars in Figure 2.1. (Of course, an even worse distribution would be to have all of the party's votes concentrated at the very low end; however, the flat distribution in Figure 2.1 is closer to the distributions parties achieve in reality.) In short, the tighter the curve, the better the distribution approximates the ideal. As Figure 2.2 shows, the KMT's distribution of votes in the 1991 National Assembly election resembles the ideal much more closely than does the DPP's. The KMT's votes are concentrated just above the quota needed for election.[59] The DPP's vote distribution is flatter, so we know that it distributed its votes less efficiently than the KMT.

Japanese colonial rule introduced Taiwan to elections, but the form those elections took was problematic. Single nontransferable voting in multi-member districts brought the colonial authorities' indigenous opponents into the political system and introduced them to electoral competition, but it also splintered them into local factions and

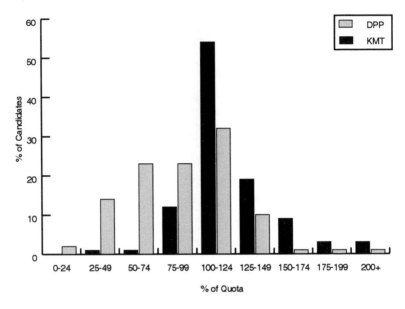

Figure 2.2   National Assembly, 1991

Source: Central Election Commission data

encouraged localism and patronage. The Nationalist regime inherited the SVMM system, along with its advantages and short-comings. The rules of the electoral system profoundly shaped Taiwan's politics, not always in expected ways. As Chen and Lin write,

> After the KMT transferred to Taiwan, it could not avoid compromising with the local factions, but it also used the existing system to monopolize power. However, paradoxically, during the subsequent democratization and Taiwanization of power, this system made it difficult for the KMT to unify the local factions, which gradually reduced its supremacy in elections.[60]

3 Party-state authoritarianism in the pre-reform era (1945–1972)

The Japanese surrender in December 1945 opened a new chapter in Taiwan's history. As Japan's colonial administrators, soldiers and civilians prepared for their departure, the island's residents prepared for the arrival of the Nationalist Chinese government. The Nationalist Party, or Kuomintang (KMT), established the Republic of China in 1912 after the fall of the Qing Dynasty. Throughout the ensuing decades, the KMT fought to unify China's vast territory under its control, struggling first against warlords, then against the Japanese and finally against the Chinese Communist Party. Although technically a multi-party democracy, the ROC government early on fell under the domination of the KMT.

Despite military setbacks, corruption, economic crisis and authoritarian inclinations, the KMT regime gained recognition as China's legitimate government. It joined the Allied forces in World War II, and at the Cairo and Potsdam Conferences Allied leaders agreed that Taiwan would become part of the ROC at the end of the war. According to contemporaneous reports, Taiwanese eagerly awaited retrocession, which they saw as the restoration of their ancestral connection to mainland China. In Taipei, some 300,000 residents turned out to greet the arriving soldiers.[1]

But the Nationalist troops who arrived on the island in 1945 were a bedraggled, rag-tag lot, with far less spit-and-polish than the Japanese whose surrender they accepted. After decades of war, the Nationalist forces were stretched thin and exhausted, their ranks filled with indigent peasant conscripts. George Kerr, a Taiwan specialist posted to Taipei by the US government from 1942 to 1947, describes the early contacts between the Taiwanese and their mainland compatriots:

> Elements of the United States Seventh Fleet escorted troopships into Keelung and Kaohsiung on October 15. Aboard were the 62nd and

70th Divisions of the Chinese Nationalist Army, numbering in excess of 12,000 men. They were acutely conscious of the presence of Japanese troops concentrated inland somewhere near the ports. They flatly refused to go ashore.... Only a rancorous argument forced the Chinese to accept their fate and go ashore. It was an inauspicious beginning, made the more so because these incidents were witnessed by the Formosans. Word soon spread, and lost nothing in the telling. Formosans along the way laughed at the shambling, poorly disciplined, and very dirty Chinese troops. It was evident, they said, that the "victors" ventured into Formosa only because the United States stood between them and the dreaded Japanese. Much evil and many individual tragedies were to spring from these expressions of open scorn, for the mainland Chinese were losing face, dearer than life itself.[2]

Once the ROC administration was installed on the island, relations between the native Taiwanese and the new arrivals deteriorated quickly. To the Nationalists, Taiwan was a sideshow. Their top priority was preventing more territory in mainland China from falling to the Communist Party's Red Army. The ROC leadership handed the job of administering Taiwan to Administrator-General Chen Yi. Chen replaced the foreign, but efficient, Japanese colonial government with a regime preoccupied with mainland affairs and riddled with corruption. To make matters worse, Nationalist officials doubted the loyalty of a population subject to fifty years of colonization by China's enemy, and they favored mainland transplants over Taiwanese at every turn. Among department-level officials of the provincial government, Mainlanders outnumbered Taiwanese nineteen to one.[3] The small number of Taiwanese who had gained positions in the bureaucracy during the pre-war years were replaced by Mainlanders with lesser qualifications – or no qualifications at all. Indeed, approximately 36,000 Taiwanese employees of the colonial government were not retained under the new regime.[4] Taiwanese who expected to be welcome in a Chinese government found themselves even more marginalized than before.

At the same time, the Nationalist regime saw Taiwan's riches as a bonanza for the ROC. They expected the Taiwanese to volunteer their economy and society in the service of the war against communism. They shipped raw materials and foodstuffs to the mainland, seized property owned by Japanese, and imposed monopolies (including one on tobacco) that worsened the lot of a Taiwanese population impoverished by years of war. Taiwan's nascent industrial base, already damaged by US bombing during the war against Japan, was devastated further when Kuomintang officials ordered factories dismantled and transported across the Taiwan Strait. Unemployment and inflation skyrocketed. Compounding the problem, the KMT brought with it to Taiwan the epidemic of corruption that was sapping its strength on the mainland. In a ten-day period in early 1946, the *Min Pao* newspaper reported six incidents of corruption.[5] The Taiwanese, accustomed to a government that was strict but honest, were especially outraged by corruption and abuses of power.

By early 1947, the Taiwanese populace's joy at retrocession had given way to bitter disappointment. On 3 February, a thousand people gathered at Taipei's Longshan Temple to protest rice shortages. Wrote *Min Pao*, "The mentality of the unemployed is deteriorating day by day. They are profoundly dissatisfied with debauched public officials and a landlord and business class that is growing rich off retrocession."[6] A few weeks later, the growing tensions between the Taiwanese population and the Nationalist government erupted into violence.

On 27 February, agents of the Monopoly Bureau beat a woman selling contraband cigarettes in Taipei. When angry onlookers surrounded the group, one of the agents fired his weapon, killing a bystander. A crowd gathered at a local police station to protest, and when the police denied their demand to hand over the officer who had shot the man, the crowd rioted. The following day, the violence spread. Angry Taiwanese beat Mainlanders, destroyed property and attacked government offices. Cities throughout the island were swept up in the tumult. Nationalist officials fled, leaving local governments in the hands of *ad hoc* Taiwanese administrations.

Taiwanese leaders in Taipei formed the Committee to Resolve the February 28 Incident to set the conditions under which they would end their uprising. Among their demands were fundamental political reforms, including equal representation of Taiwanese in the provincial government and in the management of government-owned businesses, immediate municipal executive elections, freedom of speech and protection of private property. Similar committees in other cities demanded sharp restrictions on military and police authority. In a message to Chinese on the mainland, the Taipei committee struck a patriotic tone, apologizing for attacks on Mainlanders in Taiwan, and insisting upon their loyalty to the Nationalist government and their commitment to reasonable political reforms. They ended the message with four slogans: "Improve Taiwan's politics; Long live the Republic of China; Long live the Nationalist government; Long live Chairman Chiang."[7] However, not all Taiwanese agreed with this moderate stance, and on 7 March the Taipei committee submitted a more radical set of demands that included self-government for the island.[8]

In negotiations with the Taipei leaders, administrator-general Chen Yi took a conciliatory line, but when the Nationalist authorities (reinforced by troops from the mainland) returned to island in early March, they exacted a terrible revenge. Troops approaching the island fired indiscriminately into crowds on the waterfronts. After they landed, they rounded up thousands of Taiwanese to be imprisoned or killed. There were mass executions in Taipei, Kaohsiung and Keelung. The troops targeted Taiwanese who had taken leadership positions, especially the members of Taipei's Committee to Resolve the February 28 Incident, as well as students and community leaders. The terror cowed Taiwan's educated class and social elite into a silence that lasted for decades.

In the wake of this event, which came to be called the February 28 Incident, the Kuomintang government took a two-pronged approach to the administration of Taiwan. On the one hand, the Nationalists took swift and brutal action to suppress dissent. Although repression never again approached the level of 1947, political arrests and detentions were common until the 1970s, earning the name "White Terror" (*baisi kongbu*). Legal support for the repression came from a series of emergency decrees enacted in 1947, 1948 and 1949. These gave the government nearly unlimited power to suppress political opposition and punish those who challenged its authority. Thousands of political prisoners, including pro-communist "Red Caps" and pro-independence "White Caps," were incarcerated.[9]

On the other hand, however, the Nationalist government acted to rectify the worst abuses that had helped spark the 28 February rebellion. Governor Chen Yi was dismissed and replaced by the more liberal Wei Tao-ming. (Chen was executed in Taipei in 1950 for allegedly collaborating with the communists.) The ROC government raised Taiwan to the status of a province, and between 1948 and 1951 it held elections for a provincial assembly as well as county and township officials. Taiwan's situation improved even further when the government was forced to move to Taipei in 1949. Suddenly, the KMT regime's hopes of retaking the mainland – indeed, its very survival – rested on defending Taiwan militarily and developing its economy. The facile exploitation of the island ended.

Although Taiwan's status as a peripheral territory of the ROC lasted only four years, it had long-standing consequences. First, the opportunity for a smooth transfer of ROC legitimacy to the island was lost. The Taiwanese who waited enthusiastically for the Nationalists to accept the Japanese surrender were bitterly and irrevocably disappointed by those early experiences. In the wake of the February 28 Incident, winning the hearts and minds of the Taiwanese became one of the KMT's most difficult challenges. Second, the Nationalist government interpreted the rebellion as proof that the Taiwanese could not be trusted. For much of the subsequent forty years the regime strove to balance the need to win popular support against its desire to keep power in Mainlander hands.

Third, the incident planted the seeds of animosity between the two ethnic groups, Taiwanese and Mainlanders. Under Japanese colonialism, few Taiwanese thought of themselves as different from other Han Chinese. But once the ROC government was established on the island, differences between the two groups appeared. Mainlanders were trusted with government jobs, favored in education (where their superior Mandarin put them at an advantage), cared for in military villages. Taiwanese faced discrimination in education and public sector employment; their language and culture were denigrated.[10] Before long, a social and economic gap yawned between the two groups. In later years, this gap would come to be seen in explicitly political terms.

From 1949 to June of 1950, Taiwan prepared for what most observers believed was the inevitable advance of the Red Army into the Taiwan Strait. Nationalist troops dug in on the island's beaches and rail lines; civilians waited. The KMT's strongest ally, the United States, had withdrawn its support in disgust over the Nationalist regime's corruption and incompetence. But the US reversed its position on 27 June 1950, just after the outbreak of the Korean War. With communist expansion in East Asia no longer an abstraction but a bloody reality, President Harry Truman sent the US Seventh Fleet to the Taiwan Strait to deter a PRC attack. At the same time, the US promised to exchange economic and military assistance to Taiwan for a commitment by the KMT government not to attack the mainland. The Kuomintang regime was in Taiwan to stay. The nature of that regime is the subject of this chapter.

The ROC constitution

The constitution of the Republic of China is rooted in Sun Yat-sen's three principles: nationalism, democracy and social welfare. In theory, then, the ROC state is a democracy. In practice, however, both on Taiwan before 1996 and on the mainland before 1949, many of the constitution's democratic provisions were ignored or overridden by emergency decrees. Thus, the discussion of the ROC state which follows is a description of a system democratic in theory but authoritarian in practice.

The ROC constitution was written for a state that encompassed all of the territory controlled by the Chinese government at the height of the Qing Dynasty. It provides for a national government in which the ROC's thirty-eight provinces and municipalities elect representatives to two legislative bodies. The constitution also defines the role and powers of provincial and sub-provincial governments. Given that the ROC state is defined as all of China, its sojourn on Taiwan creates a number of constitutional problems. First, under its constitution, the ROC on Taiwan is incomplete, so recovering the mainland is imperative. Since its constitution defines the nation as all of China, the legitimacy of the ROC state depends upon maintaining the notion that the separation of Taiwan and the mainland is temporary. As its chances of recovering the mainland became increasingly remote, the KMT struggled to find a way out of this predicament.

Following from this dilemma is a second problem: what is the status of Taiwan itself in an ROC whose effective control is limited to Taiwan? In theory, Taiwan is one province of the Republic of China; in fact, Taiwan *is* the Republic of China, at least for the time being. The Nationalist government resolved this conundrum by allowing the territory controlled by the Taiwan provincial government to overlap almost completely with the territory controlled by the central government. Even though the central government controlled only Taiwan, not having a provincial government for Taiwan as well would imply that the island was somehow coterminous with the ROC. So Taiwan was left with two governments governing the same territory.[11]

A third constitutional problem facing the ROC is its international status. When it first came into being after the fall of the Qing Dynasty, the Republic of China established diplomatic relations with the world, which recognized it as the legitimate government of China. Although warlordism, Japanese occupation and civil war prevented the ROC state from exercising its authority in all of the territory it claimed, its sovereignty was recognized internationally. When the communist victory drove the Nationalist army and government off the mainland, many countries continued to recognize the ROC and to support its goal of mainland recovery. With US support, the Nationalists profited from the PRC's international isolation, even holding onto the Chinese seat in the United Nations.

As time passed, the ROC's claim to be the rightful Chinese government became more and more difficult to defend. The PRC government solidified its hold on the mainland, and the likelihood of recovering it diminished. This left the ROC's diplomatic partners in a quandary: because the ROC refused to relinquish its claim to legitimacy on the mainland, recognizing both states was impossible. But continuing to choose Taiwan over the PRC was becoming untenable. After the Sino-Soviet split in the mid-1960s, the US began to question the wisdom of favoring the ROC over the much larger and strategically important People's Republic. In the same period, Taiwan's relations with other nations deteriorated. By the time the ROC government decided to permit dual recognition of the ROC and PRC in the 1990s, the PRC was strong enough to block its efforts, and the ROC was left with barely two dozen diplomatic partners, mostly small, developing countries in Central and South America and the South Pacific.

Sun Yat-sen's constitutional design includes a president (elected by the National Assembly until 1996) and five branches, or Yuan: Executive, Legislative, Control, Examination and Judicial. The head of the Executive Yuan is the premier, appointed by the president and account-able to the legislature. In practice, the ROC has been dominated by its presidents, especially Chiang Kai-shek and Chiang Ching-kuo, but also the current president, Lee Teng-hui. (Each of these men also headed the Kuomintang during his presidency.) ROC premiers gained the upper hand only in brief periods between strong presidents. The National Assembly is responsible for amending the constitution, but from 1949 on it acted mainly as a rubber stamp for decisions of the ruling Kuomintang. Before its renovation in 1991, few constitutional amendments passed the Assembly, and it ratified the KMT's presidential nominees by huge margins.

The Executive Yuan encompasses the cabinet and central government ministries. Its members are appointed by the president and approved by the members of the Legislative Yuan; nearly all of them are Kuomintang members. In addition, all government offices and agencies have within them party cells and committees, which, as Winckler put it, "wind their way like a central nervous system through the entire administrative organism."[12] The Legislative Yuan is an elected body responsible for ques-tioning public officials, approving appointments, and debating budgets and legislation proposed by the Executive Yuan. Legislators initiated bills for the first time only in 1987. Constituencies in the Legislative Yuan are based on municipal boundaries. The Judicial Yuan organizes the court system of the ROC, while the Control Yuan monitors the actions of civil servants. The Examination Yuan administers the civil service examina-tions used to select personnel for state agencies.

The ROC constitution also incorporates Sun's notion of local self-government. It establishes popularly elected executive and legislative authorities at each level of government, which in Taiwan include the province; 2 special municipalities; 21 regular municipalities (counties and cities); 359 cities, towns and townships; and 7,500 wards and villages (see Table 3.1). At first, all of Taiwan fell under the provincial government's jurisdiction, but in 1967 and 1979, Taipei City and Kaohsiung City, respectively, were promoted to the status of "special municipalities," putting them on an equal footing with the provincial government. Until

Table 3.1   Institutions of local government

Administrative level	Representative body	Executive (Zhang[a])
Province	Provincial Assembly	Provincial governor[b]
Special municipality	City council	City executive (mayor)[c]
County	County Assembly	County executive
City	City council	City executive (mayor)
Town (urban)	Town council	Town executive
Township (rural)	Township council	Township executive
County-level city	City council	City executive
Ward (in towns and cities)		Ward head
Village (in townships)		Village head
Neighborhood		Neighborhood head

Notes:
a The word *zhang* is a general term, meaning "person in charge." It is often translated as whichever English term would be used in an analogous situation. For example, *xian zhang* is often translated "County Magistrate," while *shi zhang* is usually rendered "Mayor." To be consistent, I have translated *zhang* as "executive" in those cases where the *zhang* plays an administrative role alongside a legislative body. Otherwise, I have translated *zhang* as "head."
b Until 1992, provincial governors were appointed by the central government. In 1992, the National Assembly restored direct election of the post. A provincial governor was elected in 1994.
c As of 1998 there are two special municipalities: Taipei City (promoted in 1967) and Kaohsiung City (promoted in 1979). Until 1994, their mayors were appointed.

1994, the central government appointed the provincial governor and the special municipalities' executives. Representation in local assemblies is defined according to local municipal boundaries.

In theory, then, the ROC is a decentralized state with democratically elected executives and legislatures at each level of government. In practice, however, the system has rarely followed this constitutional ideal. Until 1991, the ROC government insisted that the on-going civil war made full implementation of the constitution impossible. The emergency provisions that supplanted the constitution undermined both its democratic spirit and its decentralized structure, and they enhanced the power of non-elected elements in the central government at the expense of elected officials and local authorities.

At the national level, the constitution gives the elected members of the Legislative Yuan broad powers. In practice, however, elected officials played very little role in policy formation before the 1990s. (In the 1990s, elected officials in the executive and legislative branches increased their influence in the policy-making process.) As two ROC political scientists put it, "all important and not-so-important policies have to be decided first by the [KMT] Central Standing Committee ... If legislation is required, party members of the Legislative Yuan are asked to fulfill the formalities."[13] The most important limitation on the legislature's power was the presence of "senior legislators" elected in mainland China in 1947 and 1948. When the ROC government moved to Taiwan, these members assumed their seats in a national legislature committed to the goal of recovering the mainland. Since the regime viewed itself as the government of all of China, it needed representatives from all the Chinese provinces in its legislature. When their terms expired, and the mainland had still not been recovered, these legislators remained in office. Instead of proceeding with elections in the territory under its control – which would have allowed one province, Taiwan, to elect representatives for all of China – the sitting members were frozen in office, pending mainland recovery.

By the late 1960s, this arrangement had become problematic, for time was depleting the senior legislators' ranks. At first, those who died or became too infirm to serve were replaced by their long-ago runners-up. Eventually, however, this stop-gap measure could not sustain a quorum in either body. In 1969, the ROC held the first of many supplementary elections, adding 11 members to the Legislative Yuan and 15 to the National Assembly. Nonetheless, as recently as 1988, senior parliamentarians constituted 91 percent of the National Assembly and 76 percent of the Legislative Yuan. Eighty-six percent of Assembly members belonged to the KMT, while opposition-linked representatives held only about 5 percent of the seats in the Legislative Yuan. Thus, the national law-making bodies were compliant captives of the KMT leadership, guaranteeing passage of any bill the Kuomintang leadership proposed.

Political parties

The ROC constitution assumes that multiple political parties will compete for public office in free elections. However, emergency provisions in place from 1949 until 1987 forbade the creation of new political parties. These provisions included martial law and a set of constitutional amendments called the Temporary Provisions Effective During the Period of Mobilization for the Suppression of Communist Rebellion (thankfully, these are usually called simply "the Temporary Provisions"). Under these provisions, Taiwan was in practice a one-party state under Kuomintang leadership.[14] Writes Tien,

> The party completely monopolizes power within the government, the armed forces, and the police force. In theory at least, the government carries out policies made by the party leaders. The vast majority of government officials and bureaucrats are party members. All key

officers in the various branches of the government, the military, and the police force are party members. At times distinctions between the party and the government blur.[15]

The KMT's organization owes a great deal to Leninism. It is a centralized, disciplined party, although it is easier to gain membership in the KMT than in other Leninist parties. It emphasizes democratic centralism, leadership by a professional political vanguard, and mobilization. Its basic unit is the cell, through which each member's political activities are directed and mobilized. The party's elitist orientation has made intraparty democratization difficult and exasperated reform-minded KMT members. As prominent KMT dissenter Kuan Chung explained in the March 1993 issue of the *Free China Review*, "As for the KMT, its policy making body is still the Central Standing Committee. The KMT will lose the confidence of the people if it lags too far behind, so it must address this problem."

The highest party organ is the Central Standing Committee of the Kuomintang. However, even the CSC is probably too large for effective decision-making, and throughout most of its history the party chair has dominated the KMT. Except for a few years, since 1949 the ROC president also has served as KMT party chair. Below the Central Standing Committee is the party's Central Committee, below which are geographically and functionally organized party branches. Full-time party workers, or cadres, run local party headquarters and offices (known as service centers) through which the party interacts with the public. For much of the post-1949 period, Mainlanders outnumbered Taiwanese in the KMT membership and leadership. Prior to Taiwan's reform era, the preponderance of Mainlanders in the party bred resentment among opponents of the regime, who argued the KMT-led government did not represent the people of Taiwan. Even today, while Taiwanese hold a majority of leadership positions, Mainlanders still are disproportionately represented in the party.

Although the ROC lifted the ban on opposition parties in 1987, the legacy of single-party politics still reverberates throughout Taiwan's political system, underlining the tension between the party's democratic ideals and its authoritarian history. A decade after the ban on new parties was lifted, the Kuomintang was able to formulate policies, move them through the legislative and executive branches, and implement them with only minimal interference from opposition parties.

The institutional basis for the KMT's control over policy-making is a tripartite structure, replicated at each administrative level. In the executive and judicial branches, KMT members belong to party cells within their administrative organs. In legislative bodies, all KMT members must join party caucuses. The KMT cells and caucuses implement policies handed down by the KMT Central Committee and Central Standing Committee. To ensure consistency among the different branches of government, the party also operates Policy Coordination Committees at each administrative level (central, provincial, municipal). It also owns a vast business empire and controls many media outlets, either directly (*Central Daily News*, Broadcasting Corporation of China) or indirectly (*United Daily News*, Taiwan Television).

The KMT's ideological polestar, Sun Yat-sen's *Three Principles of the People*, puts electoral competition at the heart of the KMT's mission as a party. But the party's ideological emphasis on democracy conflicts with its Leninist organizational model and its authoritarian history. The contradiction between democracy and authoritarianism is partially resolved in Sun Yat-sen's idea of political tutelage – a temporary party dictatorship during which the nation is prepared for full democracy. However, the Nationalists declared the period of tutelage over before 1949; thus, restrictions on political and civil rights in Taiwan required a different justification. As Chou and Nathan explain, the KMT

> justified itself as a moral and technocratic vanguard capable of guiding national construction and gradually introducing full constitutional democracy ... Upon establishing its rule on Taiwan the party justified its restriction of political and other rights ... not as necessities of the revolutionary state but as temporary measures arising from the condition of civil war between the KMT and CCP [Chinese Communist Party] regimes.[16]

The Nationalist Party's policies in the early years on Taiwan mirror the tension within the party between democracy and dictatorship. The implementation of regular, competitive local elections coincided with plans to strengthen the party's hold on the ROC state and Taiwanese society. In 1949 the Kuomintang launched a campaign to install party cells throughout society to promote loyalty and obedience to the party leadership. At the same time, the KMT – under centralized control – was to seize the reins of power and control decision-making throughout the society. This, even as the ROC regime was promising democracy and self-government. This juxtaposition of party dictatorship against elections offers clues to the origins of Taiwan's mobilizational authoritarianism.

The ROC's ruling party has played an increasingly prominent role in local politics since the 1970s. Earlier, the party was preoccupied with consolidating its power at the national and provincial levels. But in the

1970s, party officials began actively recruiting influential Taiwanese, especially those who had demonstrated electoral potential. According to Jacobs, the KMT's presence at the township level increased markedly between his first field study (1971–1973) and his follow-up studies three and four years later. He wrote, "Party membership had risen, the party's organization had been strengthened, and the party's role in elections had become much greater."[17]

Locally, the KMT supervises administration and coordinates elections. The party makes personnel appointments and vetoes actions that violate its policies. For example, in 1991, the opposition-linked county executive in Kaohsiung, Yu Chen Yueh-ying, made headlines when she protested the KMT-dominated provincial government's decision to appoint a new county police chief without consulting her. In elections, the KMT alternates nominations among local factions, rewards factions and politicians for their cooperation, and coopts promising local politicians into the party. In township representative, county council and Provincial Assembly elections between 1950 and 1955, on average, the KMT boosted its share of seats 8 percentage points by absorbing successful candidates after elections, giving it a two-thirds majority in these bodies.[18] As Chao observes, "The KMT ... absorbs these members of the local elite via a partisan system. Partisanship brings not only political subordination but also loyalty, cooperation, and support."[19] Through local leaders, the KMT penetrates the grassroots of Taiwanese society, taking credit for a broad range of services.

It is not surprising that many Taiwanese want to be associated with so important an institution as the Kuomintang. The number of party members is not published, but current estimates put total enrollment at about 2.2 million, or 10 percent of Taiwan's total population (more than 20 percent of eligible voters). Party membership is especially important at higher levels of government; nonetheless, local politicians, too, seek party membership. In 1958, fewer than one-quarter of all township council members joined the KMT, while twenty years later more than half did so.[20] Many Taiwanese believe it helps one's career to be a party member, especially in the public sector. Not surprisingly, an unknown, but reportedly substantial, proportion of KMT members are members in name only; many neither pay dues nor attend meetings.[21]

Bureaucracy and economic policy

Taiwan's abiding claim to fame is its economic "miracle." From a war-torn former colony in 1945, the island grew into a leading economic power. By the mid-1990s, it was the world's fourteenth largest merchandise trading entity; internationally, only China and Japan had larger foreign exchange reserves. Between 1982 and 1996, its per capita GNP increased from one-fifth of the US level to just under a half, and income was far more equitably distributed in Taiwan than in the US or most other industrialized nations. By 1997 more than half of Taiwan's labor force was in the service sector, and only 10 percent worked in agriculture.[22] The sources of Taiwan's success are numerous: its entrepreneurial and maritime traditions, energetic workforce, strong infrastructure, access to US markets and foreign aid all played a role in the "miracle." But it was Taiwan's powerful and competent economic technocrats who crafted a formula for success from these ingredients.

Before retrocession, Taiwan's economy benefited from Japan's efforts to transform the island into a model colony. The Japanese colonial administration improved and built roads, railways and waterworks to promote economic growth and development on the island. Developing human capital, too, was an important priority. By 1942, 58 percent of the population was literate in Japanese, and three-quarters of the school-aged children were in school.[23] Farmers' associations provided agricultural extension services to introduce modern tools and techniques. Although the Japanese were less interested in industrial development on Taiwan, by the end of the colonial era food processing and other industries had gained a foothold. The number of industrial workers grew from 68,000 in 1935 to 147,000 in 1943.[24]

Thus, when the Nationalists arrived on Taiwan, they found the island ripe for development. In the first two years, rapacious Mainlanders squandered many opportunities to build on the colonial foundation, but after 1949, the KMT made an about-face. Suddenly, developing Taiwan became a national priority, and the regime dedicated vast resources to meeting that challenge. The KMT's economic performance on the mainland did not bode well for Taiwan. For decades, corruption and special interest manipulation had undermined the Nationalists' efforts to promote development. On Taiwan, however, the regime enjoyed two critical advantages: it had learned from its mistakes, and it was an outsider regime. Chiang Kai-shek did not bring all of his party and government officials with him to Taiwan. Those he thought would challenge his power or whose behavior he found especially scurrilous were left behind, or went to live in other countries. The government Chiang led on Taiwan included the most loyal and competent of his mainland supporters.

The benefit of being an outsider regime was that the state did not have to bend to the will of local capitalists and social luminaries. On the mainland, the ROC government found itself unable to implement its most promising economic policies because of resistance from wealthy Chinese.

Because the KMT relied upon landlords and capitalists for financial and political support, policies they perceived as antithetical to their interests were impossible to carry out, no matter how much they might have bene-fited the nation. On Taiwan, the regime had no such entanglements. It owed Taiwan's elite nothing, and Taiwan's elite had no access to ROC decision-makers. Moreover, the February 28 Incident proved that elites were as vulnerable to repression as any group and made them extremely reluctant to challenge the regime. As a result, policies that the KMT considered but abandoned on the mainland became cornerstones of Taiwan's economic development.

The most important of these policies was land reform. Between 1949 and 1951, the government imposed a rent ceiling and redistributed land seized from the Japanese to tenant farmers. In 1953 the Land to the Tiller Act limited land holdings to about 3 hectares. Landlords whose property exceeded this limit were required to exchange their excess land for in-kind bonds and shares in government enterprises. Most landlords passed up the opportunity to become investors, selling their stock at bargain prices. The land, which amounted to about a quarter of the cultivated land on the island, was resold on generous terms to the tenant farmers who worked it. The reform transformed land tenure in Taiwan's country-side, as thousands of tenant farmers gained small, independent land holdings. In 1949, 36 percent of Taiwanese farmers were tenants, and they cultivated 42 percent of the island's farmland. By 1953, tenants made up only 15 percent of the island's farmers, and they farmed only 16 percent of its land.[25] US assistance contributed to the program's success. The US provided Taiwan with economic and military aid well into the 1960s as a strategic measure. During the land reform, it contributed money and advi-sors.

The land reform accomplished three important goals. First, it improved agricultural productivity and increased overall production. This was an important precondition for industrial development, as productivity increases freed agricultural workers for jobs in industry, and agricultural surpluses provided capital for investment. Second, land reform equalized the distribution of wealth, income and social status in rural areas. The structure of traditional Chinese society, with its sharp division between gentry and peasants, was shattered. Taiwan became a land of small, independent farmers, most of whom quickly became integrated into commercial networks. Farmers' Associations provided a locus for agricul-tural extension and marketing. Third, the land reform won the support of many small farmers, and helped to integrate them into the ROC system. While the landlords suffered significant economic losses, the majority of rural dwellers saw both their incomes and their social status improve.

Their rising social position increased their confidence and willingness to participate in political and social activities. As we shall see in the next chapter, the KMT made clever use of local elections to channel this enthusiasm toward regime-supporting political participation.

Although the gulf between the ROC state and Taiwanese society was costly in political and human rights terms, it paradoxically proved to be a boon to the island's economy. In the early years, it smoothed the path of land reform. Later, ROC technocrats used their autonomy to design and implement a highly successful industrial policy based first on import substitution, then on export-oriented industrialization. The technocrats themselves were a small coterie of mostly Western-educated engineers and economists. Both Presidents Chiang gave them wide latitude to chart the course of Taiwan's economic development.

After completing the land reform, the technocrats turned their attention to industrial development. In 1953, Taiwan adopted a strategy of import substitution. The state used direct subsidies, tariffs and price supports to encourage large companies and heavy industries to replace imports with products made in Taiwan. Firms in basic industries, including steel, cement, and petroleum refining, were wholly or partially state-owned. Import substitution created opportunities for entrepreneurs, managers, industrial workers and workers in up-stream sectors, but these economic sectors were the products of state policy, not its producers. As Gold put it, "the state bureaucracy, not tied to the bourgeoisie but increasingly committed to capitalist development, retained its hegemonic position and acted in the bourgeoisie's interest without allowing itself to become its instrument."[26] In other words, the bureaucracy's autonomy allowed it to evaluate and implement policy with an eye to national development, rather than the particular interests of powerful corporations and individuals.

The technocrats' independence proved valuable when, in the early 1960s, they decided to add export-oriented industrialization to their economic strategy. Taiwan's political position as a Cold War ally persuaded the US to open its markets to Taiwanese manufactures; the US government also encouraged American companies to invest there. The ROC, too, took steps to encourage foreign investment, reforming its tariff system, liberalizing its trade rules and creating export processing zones. Gradually, foreign companies were persuaded to set up manufacturing operations in Taiwan and purchase Taiwan-made inputs. One result was an enormous increase in the number of small and medium enterprises (SMEs) established to service the foreign investors. These SMEs were to become the bedrock of Taiwan's economy; by the mid-1960s they out-produced the huge public sector economy. However, the SMEs never received the same benefits as firms in the economic elite, especially when it came to finance. They turned to underground sources for credit, and tax evasion became widespread. The state's favoritism toward large and government-owned firms – at the expense of SMEs – was to become an important source of friction between the state and Taiwanese society. However, in the 1960s and 1970s, what was most visible to observers in Taiwan and internationally was the blossoming of the economy, not the seeds of resentment that some of these economic policies sowed. Between 1960 and 1980, per capita GNP increased from US$130 to US$2,100. Taiwan's GNP growth rate from 1960 to 1982 averaged 8.4 percent per year.[27] At the same time, income distribution remained relatively egalitarian.[28]

Structures of political control

The ROC constitution lays out a democratic structure for the nation, but the KMT used the exigencies of history to justify a long delay in implementing that structure. For the first four decades of KMT rule on Taiwan, emergency measures prevented full constitutional democracy from taking effect on the island. In addition, the KMT regime used its authority over the military, education, propaganda outlets and mass media to suppress opposition activity and ideas. The emergency provisions were enacted in 1948 to give the Nationalist government wartime authority during the struggle against the communists. This rationale remained in place until 1991, when Lee Teng-hui declared the civil war over.

The most important consequence of emergency rule was to exempt the president from constitutional restraints, allowing virtually unlimited powers. They suspended the limitation on presidential terms, and empowered the president to alter the composition of the central government. The temporary provisions froze the mainland-elected legislators in office, and added the supplementary members later on. In sum, the temporary provisions negated the checks and balances built into the ROC constitution and gave the president dictatorial authority.

If the temporary provisions defined the nature of power within the central government, martial law provided the framework for exercising that power at the grassroots. Martial law first went into effect in mainland China in 1934. It was extended to Taiwan in 1949 and enshrined in law in 1950. The job of implementing martial law fell to the Taiwan Garrison Command (TGC), a branch of the military. The TGC maintained oversight of local government and law enforcement, detained political dissidents, disrupted opposition publications, and carried out censorship and surveillance of Taiwanese citizens. Martial law also stipulated military trials for certain crimes, sharply limiting civil liberties and due process. According to Hung-mao Tien, "An estimated ten thousand cases involving civilians were decided in military trials from 1950 to 1986."[29]

The temporary provisions and martial law together all but eliminated opposition political activity. They restricted public gatherings and dissemination of ideas and information and criminalized dissident activity. They outlawed new political parties, cementing the KMT's dominance over public life. They froze the number of newspaper licenses at thirty-one and ensured that the KMT and its allies would control the press. And they restricted other mass media even more fiercely, strictly limiting access to broadcast frequencies for radio and television. In short, the emergency measures gutted the political freedoms guaranteed in the ROC constitution.

In ways small and large, the temporary provisions and martial law created a climate in which political activity outside KMT-approved channels was impossible. Students, intellectuals, military recruits and overseas sojourners were convinced that spies reported their every political utterance. While most of the men and women who faced prosecution under the emergency rules remain anonymous, thousands suffered years of imprisonment for their political ideas, or for associating with others whose politics were suspect. Whispers and rumors about their fates frightened many more Taiwanese into obedience. Throughout the 1960s and 1970s, widely publicized cases reinforced the everyday fear that silenced most Taiwanese. In 1960, a Mainlander intellectual named Lei Chen was sentenced to ten years in prison after attempting to establish a new political party. The official charge was harboring a communist, but his real crime was challenging the established order. The 1964 jailing of National Taiwan University professor Peng Ming-min for pro-independence activities was another high-profile case.

These measures were useful in securing compliance, but the KMT government did not rely on negative measures alone. It also used positive incentives to win the Taiwanese people's support. Economic progress, which brought Taiwanese land, jobs and rising living standards, was an important element of the regime's appeal. So were the local elections discussed in the next chapter. In addition, the KMT mounted a vigorous propaganda effort through the mass media and educational system.[30] Cinemas opened each show with the national anthem, during which movie-goers were required to stand at attention. The 10 October National Day celebration was an annual extravaganza of patriotism, complete with displays of military hardware, parades of uniformed men and women, and enthusiastic crowds.

Taipei and other cities were decked out in billboards and posters promoting mainland recovery; a row of gigantic characters facing the presidential office building in downtown Taipei read, "The Three Principles of the People will unify China." Public service announcements reminding citizens to be vigilant against communist aggression interrupted television and radio programs. The propaganda effort even affected recreation: concrete tank traps lined Taiwan's beaches, where seaward-facing photographs were forbidden, and public parks were scattered with gun emplacements. Taipei residents enjoyed the small parks and playgrounds dotting their neighborhoods; underneath were bomb shelters. Millions of Taiwanese children enjoyed outings and activities sponsored by the China Youth Corps (known in Chinese as the Chinese Anti-Communist Save-the-Nation League), a Young Pioneers-style group devoted to mobilizing and indoctrinating young Taiwanese in support of the KMT.

The educational system, too, was bent to the task of popularizing the regime and its goals. As Chen Ming-tong put it, "schools were the number one tool of political socialization."[31] School curricula at all levels included reverential study of Sun Yat-sen's writings, which played an important part in high school and college entrance examinations. Geography and history lessons focused on the mainland, while Taiwan was relegated to the status of one small province of the ROC. Students were constantly reminded to think of Taiwan as the staging ground for mainland recovery, not a valued homeland in its own right. A peculiarly Taiwanese institution intensified the regime's presence in high schools and colleges. Military instructors (*jiaoguan*) conducted military training, supervised the students and maintained dossiers on each one. They encouraged the better students to join the KMT, even handing out applications in class. Two years of mandatory military service for young men offered a venue for even more intensive indoctrination in the KMT's ideology and mission.

The regime placed great importance on promoting the official language, Mandarin, and discouraging the Taiwanese dialect (the two use the same characters for writing, but the spoken languages are as different as English and German). Teachers punished children who spoke Taiwanese at school by fining them or forcing them to wear humiliating placards. Signs reminding local functionaries to speak Mandarin hung next to the telephones in government offices. The Government Information Office, the agency in charge of regulating mass media, reduced the amount of time allotted to Taiwanese-language programming on TV and radio in favor of Mandarin. The regime promoted the view that Taiwanese was a second-rate dialect, primitive, ugly and low class. The campaign to promote Mandarin succeeded, but the effort to wipe out Taiwanese failed; what the regime created was a bilingual nation in which more than three-quarters of the population speaks both Mandarin and Taiwanese (or Mandarin and Hakka).

The mass media – newspapers, magazines, television and radio – were among the KMT regime's most powerful propaganda tools. In 1945, Taiwan had only one newspaper, but after retrocession dozens more began to circulate. Half of these were shut down after the February 28 Incident, but by 1949 their numbers once again had increased to forty. Economic factors forced some papers to close and others to merge, but press vitality received its worst blow in 1951. In that year, the regime issued strict regulations limiting the length of newspapers and requiring them to register with the state. Most importantly, it froze the number of newspaper licenses at thirty-one. No additional licenses were issued until 1988, although some papers did close and transfer their licenses to new publications.

The central government and KMT owned about a third of the thirty-one licensed papers, and they supervised the rest, making sure that licenses did not fall into the hands of their opponents and keeping close tabs even on their friends. The leading media companies, the United Daily Group and the China Times Group, both cooperated with the regime. According to media expert Lee Chin-chuan, "the party-state … bestow[ed] immense political and economic benefits on the two conglomerates in exchange for their loyalty. Both publishers were recruited into the Standing Committee of the KMT's Central Committee."[32] Editors and publishers at the major news outlets attended KMT "work conferences" at which party cadres instructed them about how their publications could better serve the nation. Nor were officials shy about expressing their preferences for how stories should be reported. In particular, party officials discouraged newspapers from covering the opposition. According to Chen Ching-chien, city editor for the *Taiwan Times*, "Every time I returned to the office after an interview [with dissidents arrested in the 1979 Kaohsiung Incident], I got phone calls from security agents. They would warn me to be careful in writing my story, or worse, they came right out and told me to drop it."[33]

The regime's influence over most newspapers was indirect, but it controlled the broadcast media directly. Taiwan's first television station was Taiwan Television (TTV), opened in 1962 by the Taiwan provincial government. In 1969, the Broadcasting Corporation of China (a public agency) founded China Television (CTV). CTV is KMT-run; as Hung-mao Tien put it, "For all practical purposes, CTV operates as a KMT enterprise; its posts on the board of directors are plums of political patronage dispensed by the KMT."[34] A third station, Chinese Television Services (CTS) was launched in 1970 under the Ministries of Defense and

Education. A fourth broadcast television station, the opposition-linked Formosa Television, finally went on the air in mid-1997. The regime also controlled radio broadcasting until the 1990s. Of the 33 licensed radio networks and 177 local broadcasting stations, most were owned by the government, ruling party or military, or were affiliated with the KMT. No additional radio frequencies were made available to broadcasters from 1959 to 1993. Dissidents objected to broadcasters' biased news coverage, but entertainment programming, too, was of poor quality. And because all three Taipei-based television stations broadcast the same programming to the entire island, news events outside the capital (other than grisly crimes, fires and mudslides) received little coverage.

Cooptation and public ownership gave the regime effective control over the mass media, while martial law allowed it to censor smaller publications. The justification for censorship was national security, but in practice, the censors spent much of their time working to prevent embarrassing information about the regime and its leaders from leaking into the public view. In the 1960s, journalists were sent to prison for writing "treasonous" publications, or "giving comfort to the enemy" (that is, for criticizing the regime). One man was imprisoned for the way he translated a "Popeye" cartoon. In the 1970s, the censors changed their tactics to concentrate on revoking licenses, suspending publications, pressuring printers to turn away dissident publications and seizing magazines before they hit the newsstands.

Party-state corporatism

A more subtle, but nonetheless powerful, form of state power was the KMT regime's control of organizations. Until the late 1970s, nearly all politically relevant groups in Taiwan were organized by the party or the state organs it controlled. Recognizing the necessity for social organization, the regime created groups that the party-state could use to facilitate social and political (especially electoral) mobilization. The overwhelming social, economic and political predominance of party-state sponsored organizations retarded the development of independent interest groups and political pluralism. Still, the KMT regime's control over these organizations was not absolute. Clientelistic networks colonized many local-level groups and appropriated their resources and power for purposes that were not always consistent with the regime's goals.

According to the pluralist theory of interest group formation, groups of citizens organize themselves independently to pursue common interests. The state is merely a referee among these independent groups. A contrasting model of group behavior is corporatism, in which the state itself sponsors and supervises groups. Ruth B. Collier and David Collier define corporatism in terms of three types of state action:

1   state structuring of groups that produces a system of *officially sanctioned*, non-competitive, compulsory interest associations,
2   *state subsidy* of these groups, and
3   *state-imposed constraints* on demand-making, leadership, and internal governance.[35]

Corporatism's defining characteristics – state structuring, state subsidy and state control – describe Taiwan's interest group system well. Most politically active groups originated with the ROC party-state and were sustained by it. The most important group in ROC politics is, of course, the Kuomintang; it is impossible to say where the party ends and the state begins. This is why Taiwan's network of officially sanctioned organizations is best described as party-state corporatism. Since the reform era began, groups have emerged which are independent of the party and state. But their resources and influence still do not approach that of their state-sponsored counterparts.

The notion of party-state corporatism is consistent with Nationalist ideology and organizational theory. ROC leaders since Sun Yat-sen have emphasized mobilization as one of the party-state's central tasks. Sun's theory of political tutelage rested on the notion that citizens needed to be mobilized behind the revolutionary party (the KMT). Sun's successor, Chiang Kai-shek, was committed to the goal of mobilizing the whole population by involving citizens in organized groups.[36] The KMT's 1952 platform called for the establishment of farmers' and workers' organizations to improve living standards, build a foundation for democracy and promote cooperation between labor and capital.[37]

To realize its goal of involving every citizen in one or another organization, the ROC government gave its blessing to a wide range of associations, including Farmers' Associations, Irrigation Associations, labor unions, Chambers of Commerce, Women's Associations, and industrial and professional groups. With the party-state's blessing came the exclusive right to organize a profession or group. Some groups – including farmers, women, labor, industrialists and Aboriginal people – even enjoyed reserved seats in legislative bodies. The regime made no secret of its intention to control these groups. Lerman examined a number of ROC government publications, and found in them "a paternalistic attitude" and ample evidence of "the elite's intention to control the associations closely and to ensure their primary orientation toward approved goals."[38]

In exchange for their privileged position, groups relinquished the possibility of autonomous action. Cadres from the ruling party and government scrutinized their personnel decisions, budgets and policy decisions; in most cases, the leaders of these organizations were themselves KMT members. Among the board chairs of industrial organizations, 51 percent were KMT members; of these, 42 percent had worked as party employees and 33 percent had received specialized training in a KMT institute. Among general managers of these groups, 95 percent were KMT members and more than half had experience as party cadres.[39] As a result, the associations became far more effective at communicating the state's policies to their members than articulating or promoting the members' interests vis-à-vis the state. Group members were not blind to the weaknesses of officially sponsored associations. A 1984 survey found that 66 percent of unionized workers believed the official labor unions to be "useless in promoting their economic interests."[40]

In the ROC, "mobilization" includes electoral mobilization, so corporatist organizations also had a role to play in elections. Their large grassroots memberships made them an important source of votes for KMT candidates. Mobilizing unattached voters was risky, making the corporatist organizations – with their up-to-date membership lists and carefully cultivated esprit de corps – especially valuable to the party. As Table 3.2 illustrates, voters in special constituency elections supported the KMT by extraordinarily wide margins. Only members of the appropriate corporatist organizations and registered Aboriginal persons were eligible to vote in these elections.

Corporatist organizations also played a key role in ordinary elections. Unlike so-called "floating votes," group members' ballots could be targeted to the candidates who needed them most. Ideally, the party could transfer association votes from one candidate to another late in the campaign. In reality, many group members had their own preferences, so

Table 3.2 Performance in special constituency elections (occupational and Aboriginal categories, Legislative Yuan)

	1980		1983		1986		1989	
	vote (%)	seats	vote (%)	seats	vote (%)	seats	vote (%)	seats
KMT	82.4	16	87.5	18	84.7	17	65.5	13
TW/DPP	1.3	0	3.1	0	6.9	1	19.9	3
Indep.	16.3	2	9.4	0	8.4	0	14.6	2

Source: Hu and Chu 1992: 183–184.

telling rank-and-file voters what to do was a touchy business. Still, the party's access to and information about group members was much greater than it was for unaffiliated voters. To illustrate in detail the organizational and political character of party-state sponsored corporatist associations and their role in Taiwan's clientele system, we turn now to a case study of an organization which is not only extremely important politically, but also in many ways is the paradigmatic corporatist group: the Farmers' Association.

The Farmers' Association

Taiwan's Farmers' Associations first formed during the Japanese colonial era, when the Japanese authorities promoted and guided them. At the end of World War II the ROC government took over their administration. Their stated purpose was (and is) to promote farmers' interests through various activities, including agricultural extension, credit and banking services, and cooperative marketing and purchasing. Although the associations technically are autonomous, with the members electing their own boards of directors, officials from the provincial and central levels routinely intervene in local association business. The day-to-day direction of each branch is left to a general manager, who must be chosen from among candidates recommended by government agencies.

In 1974, Benedict Stavis prepared a report for the Committee on Rural Development at Cornell University. He took up the question of whether the Farmers' Associations were run "by and for the farmers" or were, in fact, "controlled by the government and used to organize the farmers and prevent spontaneous independent peasant organization." He concluded: "the latter view is more correct."[41] Farmers' Associations have changed little since Stavis's report; a recent study by political scientists Huang Teh-fu and Liu Hua-tsung asked similar questions and reached the same conclusion.[42]

Farmers' Associations are a key structure for mobilizing rural votes. Given their hierarchical organization and unique service and economic roles, they are well suited for organizing and channeling electoral support. Rural politicians often get their start in the Farmers' Association. "Indeed," wrote Stavis, "the Nationalist leadership considers one of the subsidiary functions of the farmers' associations to be training local leadership."[43] An article that appeared in *The Journalist* magazine in 1991 exposed the extent of the Farmers' Associations' involvement in electoral politics.[44] The article included a transcript of a monthly mobilization meeting held at a town Farmers' Association a few weeks before the 1991 National Assembly election. The purpose of the meeting was to organize support for the association's general manager (identified in the article as "General Manager B") in his bid for a National Assembly seat. The Farmers' Association in the town is dominated by a local faction, identified as Faction X.

"Mr A" led the meeting. A former head of the town's KMT office, Mr A was in charge of Faction X's organization and training for the 1991 election. Before going over the details of the association's strategy he told the activists, "This election will demonstrate whether your town Farmers' Association is united or not," and "The town Farmers' Association's success or failure depends on each one of you." The association's deputy general manager chimed in, "If our *tiau-a-ka* [vote brokers] and the voters handle some things badly our Farmers' Association people are going to be held responsible … If General Manager B succeeds, you will know that it is your victory." Mr A used the stick as well as the carrot: "if we lose this election it won't be General Manager B's loss, it will be your, Faction X's, loss. And everybody will be out. A straightforward dismissal of everybody, and there will be no more Faction X. Every man for himself."

Mr A went on to describe the faction's strategy for mobilizing votes behind General Manager B. "In the town's thirty-two wards, each ward has two workers responsible for it. Each district has a section head in charge of it. Then on top of that we have people like county council members, town representatives, chairs and vice chairs, representatives, ward heads, ward administrators, and the whole Women's Association." He told the association activists, "We have to know whom your friends and relatives are helping. Only by knowing everything about ourselves and everything about the enemy can we win every battle. From pulling votes and encouraging votes to checking up on votes. Who's helping us in every ward? Every neighborhood? Did they get money? Did those who got money vote? This is the work we have to do. Your work won't be finished until after the votes are counted."

He added that having the support of the Farmers' Association carried risks for the candidate, because voters might assume he would win easily and cast their ballots for other candidates. The threat of losing to candidates paying more for votes also loomed. Mr A addressed this possibility, saying, "So we want to use this kind of psychology: If there is somebody paying more, and what General Manager B is paying is more meager, we'll use our skills of persuasion and our smarts to tell them this: General Manager B has been putting out for this society for forty years. That's why we're going to support him. Even though we have less money, the votes we pull are going to be pulled one hundred percent."

Mr A's instructions to the Farmers' Association workers emphasize persuasion, persistence and vote buying, but these are not the only sources of influence the groups enjoy over their members. In fact, Farmers' Association cadres are in a position to provide favored members with a variety of benefits. In the 1960s, the associations collected rice as payment for fertilizer, taxes and land purchased under the Land Reform Program. Cadres could reward supporters by relaxing standards of rice quality and moisture content. In the 1970s, associations selected farmers to participate in pilot programs to develop such profitable export crops as asparagus and mushrooms. Today, associations provide so many services that even township-level offices must hire large staffs, opening the possibility of patronage employment. Potential for abuse also exists in the credit department, where "there undoubtedly are cases in which loans are secured more quickly for friends, relatives, and political allies."[45]

Farmers' Associations are profitable, which gives their officers control over large operating surpluses. Much of the profit is spent on public projects, which may be channeled to construction companies operated by local factions.[46] General Manager B, Faction X's National Assembly candidate, addressed this topic in his remarks to the Farmers' Association monthly mobilization meeting: "I also want to thank the XX Securities Company for bringing us unlimited financial resources. All of XX's money is deposited here. On a total savings account of NT$200,000,000 to 300,000,000 over the past three to five years our profit has been 20 or 30 million." Such heady profits make Farmers' Association work very attractive to ambitious Taiwanese hoping for political careers. A general manager's salary alone rivals that of a national cabinet minister, even without the sideline income available in Farmers' Association work.[47]

In addition to its financial rewards, serving as a Farmers' Association official has political benefits. General Manager B's decision to pursue national office is not unusual; many association officers take part in elections. The cadres working under them serve as vote brokers, making personal appeals to voters on behalf of their patrons. Wrote Stavis, "the farmers association can become, in the context of an election campaign, a very powerful vote-getting machine."[48]

The combination of political and economic benefits available through Farmers' Association work attracted the attention of local factions. It is common for township and county Farmers' Associations to be captured by these local political machines. A 1970 study reported that the Farmers' Association was involved in 84 percent of townships experiencing factional strife.[49] A faction seizes control of a local association by organizing its grassroots supporters to elect sympathetic township representatives, who in turn back the faction's candidates for the Farmers' Association Board of Directors.[50] The Board of Directors appoints a congenial general manager. The faction then uses its domination of the association's organizational networks and resources to reinforce its electoral base. For example, according to a township council chair in rural Kaohsiung County, the county's White faction "owns" the township Farmers' Association. During elections, all the association employees work on the White faction's political campaigns.

Conclusion

The structure the KMT regime created for itself on Taiwan reflected its conflicting core goals: reunifying China under its control and achieving Sun Yat-sen's democratic aspirations. Emergency provisions allowed it to insert authoritarian powers required by its first objective into institutions designed with the second in mind. But in the final analysis, there was a fundamental contradiction between these objectives, a contradiction which sharpened as the hope of mainland recovery faded and Taiwanese society gained in wealth, education and international exposure. As early as the late 1960s, cracks were appearing in the regime's facade of benevolent authoritarianism. The party-state was losing ground to indifference, international opinion was shifting toward the PRC (making repression more costly), senior legislators were dying off, Taiwanese businessmen were feeling their economic muscle more strongly. In short, by the beginning of the 1970s, top ROC leaders, especially Chiang Ching-kuo, had come to realize that the ROC would not survive long without reform.

The reforms President Chiang contemplated were aimed at softening the authoritarian element of Taiwan's mobilizational authoritarianism. But before we turn our attention to those reforms, we need to look at that system's mobilizational component.

4 Electoral mobilization in the pre-reform era (1945–1972)

While the Republic of China in theory is a democracy, the emergency provisions enacted in the 1940s gave Taiwan's government a strong authoritarian cast. But its authoritarianism was not unmitigated. After retrocession, the KMT regime faced an extraordinarily difficult international and domestic environment. It fought to survive in the shadow of the People's Republic, and it struggled mightily to gain a sound footing on Taiwan. Under these circumstances, merely winning the Taiwanese people's passive acquiescence to KMT rule was not enough. To prevail in the face of these difficult odds, the regime needed active popular support. To gain that support, it adopted a strategy of political mobilization; that is, controlled participation that integrated Taiwanese into the state without relinquishing the KMT's policy-making monopoly. A key ingredient in the regime's political strategy, mobilizational authoritarianism, was the electoral system.

Elections have their roots in the ROC constitution, but the KMT government might well have used the state of emergency to avoid elections, just as it negated other constitutional provisions. But elections benefited the regime. Internationally, they helped Taiwan retain the support of its diplomatic partners, especially the US. Throughout the Cold War, Taiwan's friends contrasted the ROC, or "Free China" with the PRC, to which they applied the damning label "Red China." Maintaining the Free China label required the ROC to make at least token gestures in the direction of democracy, and elections were a particularly effective tool for building international favor. Elections also benefited the regime domestically. They gave the KMT ammunition to use against liberal critics and, more importantly, they helped cement the relationship between Mainlanders and the state and draw the Taiwanese into the political system, without actually handing over power to either group.

How is it possible to hold elections without relinquishing power? For political participation to be more than a formality it must involve real competition for meaningful stakes. But unless the ruling group can direct this participation in regime-supporting ways, it inevitably will undermine its ability to make and enforce policy. In Taiwan, the KMT devised institutions to maintain this balance. The constitutional limitations and emergency provisions described in the previous chapter played a central role in protecting the regime. Keeping the senior legislators in office insulated the central government from pressure from below, where Taiwan-elected officials held sway. Martial law ensured that the KMT would not face competition from organized opposition parties, and it gave the ruling party control over political speech and information. In addition, the regime constructed an electoral system that allowed for competition at the local level, but coopted elected officials and channeled their actions in ways that reinforced the regime's authority and legitimacy.

In the 1950s and 1960s, and much of the 1970s, the KMT exercised near-total dominance over Taiwan's elections. Under the emergency provisions, new political parties were banned, and the two legal "opposition" parties operated under the ruling party's thumb. It was obvious to politically ambitious Taiwanese that their best chance of winning public office lay in joining the KMT. Between 1951 and 1985, KMT nominees for municipal executive posts had an average success rate of 88 percent, while the rate of victory for the party's Provincial Assembly nominees averaged 87 percent. In 1980, 1983 and 1986 an average of 93 percent of the KMT's supplementary Legislative Yuan nominees were elected. It is easy to see why ambitious Taiwanese were so willing to attach themselves to the ruling party. Only after an organized opposition party joined the competition did the KMT's success rate begin to decline. In 1989, 65 percent of executive and 79 percent of the KMT's legislative nominees were successful; in 1992, KMT nomination for these offices carried only a 63 percent chance of victory.[1]

The regime did not ban non-KMT members from competing in elections. But electoral conditions were so favorable to the ruling party that these independents (known in Chinese as "personages without party affiliation," or *wudangji renshi*) never threatened the KMT's ruling majority. The small number of independents who managed to win election to public office were either unopposed, tolerated by the KMT or supported by large personal followings. They did not belong to organized political movements seeking to challenge the KMT; on the contrary, they tended to have extremely localized ambitions and agendas.

There were at least two reasons for the independents' weakness. First, the KMT's resources for promoting its candidates overwhelmed those of any other political force. The party not only enjoyed unlimited money and media access for its campaigns, but also controlled the public revenues and agencies that determined whether an elected official succeeded or failed in office. And it operated a security apparatus capable of neutralizing any direct challenge. Second, independents were easily coopted by the regime. In fact, the ruling party used local elections to identify people it wished to recruit for party membership. In the 1950s and 1960s, the KMT routinely added between 5 and 20 percent to its seat share by recruiting successful candidates after local elections.[2]

The fact that the KMT dominated elections does not mean, however, that these elections were non-competitive. Indeed, the genius of Taiwan's electoral system was the way it used competition to encourage political participation and enthusiasm for a regime that imposed itself from the outside and made serious mistakes during its first few years in power. From 1950 on, the ruling party won millions of uncoerced votes from ordinary Taiwanese, many of whom devoted huge amounts of time and other personal resources to making sure KMT candidates won elections. The key to this success lay in transforming the energy of grassroots conflict and interest-seeking into support for the ruling party. The mechanism for performing this alchemy was the electoral system.

Grassroots mobilization

As we saw in Chapter 2, the SVMM formula presents politicians and parties with both challenges and opportunities. Working within the constraints and incentives of the SVMM system, Taiwan's politicians developed informal institutions for mobilizing the votes they needed to win. Officially, electoral mobilization is the responsibility of local KMT offices. Party cadres select the candidates who receive the KMT's endorsement, and they oversee the allocation of responsibility zones to the nominees. They also have resources, including future nominations and access to benefits, with which they reward those who cooperate with party strategy and punish those who do not.

In practice, the fundamental task of mobilizing KMT supporters in their responsibility zones falls to the candidates themselves. To accomplish this feat, many receive assistance from local factions. Local factions, as distinct from national-level party and legislative factions, are a purely local institution devoted to electoral mobilization. They are motivated by their own interests, and they fight fiercely for power and influence. Nonetheless, nearly all local factions are affiliated with the ruling party. That is, the candidates they support run under the KMT's banner and cooperate, for the most part, with its electoral strategy. For example, in 1992, more than 92 percent of the faction-linked Legislative Yuan candidates were KMT members.[3] Thus, local factionalism provides a forum for grassroots political competition within a single-party system. It has allowed the ruling party to maintain its dominance of government while providing outlets for ROC citizens' political ambitions and interest-maximizing behavior.

Local factions

Local factions are characteristic of clientelistic politics around the world. Writes Powell,

> At the level of the village, we find competition among brokers and potential brokers for peasant votes which can be delivered to a particular political patron or potential patron. Such competition, which has been described as "factionalism" in village politics, is an essential ingredient in the process of aggregating clienteles into a widespread network, and linking them to vertical patronage structures in the political system.[4]

In some societies, such as Japan, these "vertical patronage structures" reach all the way to the highest levels of the national government; humble neighborhood vote brokers are linked to cabinet members and prime ministers through chains of clientelistic relationships. In Taiwan, these chains are cut short. Because of the size of ROC electoral districts, Taiwan's factions are confined to individual municipalities (counties and cities).[5]

The primary limitation on the growth of local factions is the nature of Taiwan's electoral districts. The county is the largest unit in which factions have electoral utility, for until the first direct elections for provincial governor (1994) and president (1996), there was no election that could not be won with votes from a single county or city. In the past, the KMT leadership also helped limit the factions' expansion. According to Chen Ming-tong, the top leadership "prepared all kinds of systematic schemes and policies to reduce the local factions' influence, limit the space for their development, ensure that they would develop only at the municipal level and below and avoid their threatening the party center."[6]

Local factions are vital to the KMT's strategy of mobilizational authoritarianism. The ruling party used the spoils of government to coopt local leaders and their factions and draw them into the ruling party. It encouraged a competitive equilibrium between factions in each electoral district by playing factional networks against one another.[7] The key factor facilitating this strategy is the SVMM electoral system. It allows the KMT to nominate at least one representative of each local faction in non-executive races. In executive elections, when rewarding all factions was impossible, the ruling party often split the important posts among factions and alternated the nominations from term to term. Thus, factions became "one of the factors the KMT considers most seriously" when deciding nominations.[8] Indeed, prior to the reforms of the late 1980s, the party center rarely chose candidates from outside the local factional milieu. Writes Chen Ming-tong,

> although on the surface the party center still maintained the upper hand in deciding nominations, in fact, its nominating choices were very limited. Of course, the party center could go after one particular faction-linked personage, but it could not treat all faction members as enemies ... In other words "the supreme leader" could only choose among factions ... under normal circumstances, the KMT dared not nominate non-faction people to compete in elections.[9]

The KMT preferred faction-linked candidates because factional mobilization worked. On average, 83 percent of the local faction candidates in Provincial Assembly elections between 1951 and 1985 won, compared to 32 percent of non-faction candidates.[10]

Maintaining a balance of power among local factions allowed the KMT to enjoy the benefits of competitive local elections at very little cost. The party was able to identify authentic local leaders, enhance its domestic legitimacy and present a democratic appearance internationally. And no matter how viciously the local factions competed, candidates opposed by the party rarely defeated them. When a non-KMT candidate did manage to be elected, the party often drew that individual into the KMT. That is not to say that the KMT had perfect control over the electoral process. Some non-KMT politicians refused to be coopted. If party officials failed to reach a compromise with local factions, the factions occasionally ran independent or maverick candidacies against party discipline, raising the cost of the election and damaging the party's image. As Lerman points out, "The KMT-controlled votes plus the votes controlled by the faction of its nominee must be enough to override the aggrieved faction," or else the disappointed faction "must be given a substitute prize."[11]

Local factions are neither rational nor ideological; instead, they exist to accumulate and distribute material goods and prestige (or "face"). This helps to explain how they manage to exist as separate, competing entities within a single party. Local factions' survival depends on delivering goods to their supporters and taking part in electoral politics. Because they work within the system, they are not inclined to question its legitimacy. The

KMT has tolerated – and even rewarded – factions as long as they do not challenge its basic ideology and policies.

Forced to promote identical political platforms, factions turned to personal and community rivalries to justify their competition. Hating the enemy faction because of real or imagined treachery, local prejudice, and fear of mistreatment substituted for ideological and programmatic appeals. The exchange of benefits between faction leaders and their supporters lends tangible reinforcement to factional loyalty. Even party identification takes a back seat to the faction's particularistic interests. This character-istic was especially galling to KMT cadres in the 1980s and 1990s, who found factions entirely untrustworthy, but nonetheless depended upon them for grassroots electoral support.

Factional competition stirs deep emotions because it involves two of the most fundamental human passions: material interests and personal prestige. Nearly thirty years ago, Gallin observed, "local factions ... are not dedicated to any special principles or objectives, but for the most part are organized around particular personalities."[12] Competition for "face" and for the spoils of office spawned deep animosities among local factions. For example, political activists in Tainan County describe relations between the Ocean and Mountain factions in harsh terms; in interviews, they use the words "enemy" and "hatred" to describe their relationship. A DPP campaign manager admitted that his candidate had received votes from a disgruntled KMT-linked faction in the 1989 county executive race, when Mountain faction supporters preferred to vote for the opposition party rather than see the post go to their KMT "brethren" in the Ocean faction. An Ocean faction activist agreed, observing that it would be inconceivable for Ocean faction members to support a Mountain faction candidate. He added, "I think the Mountain faction thinks the same way."[13]

In order to remain robust, factions must maintain a steady flow of goods to their supporters. Thus, winning local office is not only an end in itself; it also is a means of gaining access to resources that will improve the faction's chances of winning future elections. Taiwanese take it for granted that the factions' fundamental organizing principle is the exchange of benefits (*liyi*) and service (*fuwu*) for political support. As Chao observes, factions must distribute benefits fairly if they hope to improve members' morale and loyalty.[14] Local factions' need for resources further enhances the KMT's influence over them. Chu Yun-han identified four types of economic privileges which the ruling party uses to manage local factions: regional economic activities, such as banking, credit and transport; provincial-level lending activity; provincial and county procurement and contracting; and various local-level interest exchanges, from zoning manipulation to protecting underground businesses.[15] Doling out access to economic rents from these activities helped the KMT forge clientelistic relationships with local factions. After 1951, more than 90 percent of Taiwan's local factions possessed at least one of the following businesses: banks, credit cooperatives, production cooperatives, Farmers' or Fishermen's Association credit bureaus, and transport companies.[16]

In sum, then, factions must elect their candidates to public office to survive. Once in office, the candidates feed benefits back to the faction. The faction then uses those benefits to elect more candidates. Factions live and die by this cycle. But individual faction leaders cannot possibly influence all the voters in a district. For this, they rely on vote brokers, known in Taiwanese as *tiau-a-ka*.

Tiau-a-ka

One person who's very important in local politics is the *tiau-a-ka*. This is a person who helps the county executive with local affairs. The county executive is much too busy to attend to every little thing, so she relies on people in the villages to help out. If someone has a problem and they want to see the county executive about it, first they go to the *tiau-a-ka* in their town, then the *tiau-a-ka* and the voter go to see the county executive together. That way the person is more likely to get what he wants. In recruiting people to be *tiau-a-ka*, politicians look for people who are influential in their communities, respected by local people, loyal to the politician and respectful in dealing with him or her. The local people have to be willing to tell the *tiau-a-ka* their opinions so he can pass them along. *Tiau-a-ka* also need to be able to provide certain services. During elections, the *tiau-a-ka* are the most important people in a candidate's organization. They go around and talk to everybody and drum up support. Not everyone can provide good service. Only if you have power and money can you serve the people. *Tiau-a-ka* have no formal power – their power comes from their ability to get higher levels of government to act.[17]

This is how the head of the China Youth Corps in a rural Kaohsiung County town described a fundamental Taiwanese political institution: the *tiau-a-ka*. Taiwanese often use the phrase "looking up, not looking down" (*kanshang, bu kanxia*) to describe the mentality of public officials, whose primary concern is pleasing their superiors, not their constituents. But *tiau-a-ka* must look in both directions, satisfying those above while at the same time painstakingly cultivating those below. Politicians, factions and party cadres all depend on *tiau-a-ka* to impose a measure of coherence on an unpredictable electorate. The success of Taiwan's electoral mobilization rests on the *tiau-a-ka*'s ability to manage voters.[18]

The earliest scholarly analysis of Taiwan's local politics is Gallin's portrait of Hsin Hsing village, based on field research he conducted in 1961. Gallin found village society in the midst of a far-reaching transformation. The Nationalist Party had not yet penetrated the villages. But traditional village leaders, mainly landlords, had lost the economic basis for their political power as a result of the land reform and were being replaced by informal leaders: "villagers who have more time and money than their fellows and who ... aspire to improve their status."[19] Elected officials were not yet regarded as authoritative; social heavyweights such as clan leaders challenged their power. Gifts reinforced personal relationships between candidates and voters, casting the shadow of corruption over elections: "In general, the villagers consider elections unimportant, and candidates on all levels often buy votes. A few packs of cigarettes or some bath towels and soap may be all that is needed to secure someone's vote."[20]

The phenomena Gallin noted in 1961 continued to grow. Taiwan's electoral mobilization process became enormously complex, evolving into a dense fabric of parallel and overlapping institutions. A farmer living in a rural village might receive voting cues from family members, local factions, Farmers' Association cadres, party workers, temple leaders and the village head – not to mention the candidates themselves. Each voter must decide how to choose among these competing pressures.[21] Because no single institution "controls" all the votes in its domain, mobilization is an inexact science. Candidates and party workers use all the resources they can muster to maximize their position at each step of the electoral process, from nominations to election day. Much of their time and effort is spent recruiting and coordinating three distinct types of *tiau-a-ka*.

Office-holding *tiau-a-ka* hold formal positions in local administration; they include ward heads (*li zhang*), village heads (*cun zhang*) and neighborhood heads (*lin zhang*). The most important of these are the ward and village heads. Their official duties include enforcing decisions made by higher levels of government, managing community finances, evaluating public reaction to various policies, listening to complaints, alerting the town or township authorities to problems in the community (especially problems with public facilities), resolving local conflicts, certifying documents and selecting the neighborhood heads. The great majority are KMT members; for example, as of 1990, there was only one DPP-affiliated ward head in all of Taipei City.[22]

Social *tiau-a-ka* approach voters through social and business networks. The most important of these is the family. The heads of large, traditional families still control many votes. The daughter of a Taipei County clan head told the author that her father plans a vacation abroad before each election to escape the swarm of political candidates who hound him for his endorsement. Another important source of social *tiau-a-ka's* influence is friendship. To Taiwanese, friendship implies reciprocity and obligation as well as companionship. As a Tainan County political activist put it, "I would vote for Mr Huang here no matter what, because he's my good friend."[23]

Taiwanese vote not only for their friends, but also for candidates their friends recommend. Many *tiau-a-ka* are natural leaders who emerge within a group of friends; other people trust their judgment and rely on them for political guidance. As a Taipei County KMT official put it, these *tiau-a-ka* are "persons of principle" whose "broader view of things" gives them influence over others.[24] In addition to friendship and family ties (often referred to as *tong xing*, or same surname) *tiau-a-ka* use business contacts (*tong shi*; same job), alumni networks (*tong xue*; same school) and local ties (*tong xiang*; same home town) to mobilize votes.[25]

Association-based *tiau-a-ka* operate within established organizations such as KMT party branches, Farmers' and Women's Associations, the Huang Fu-hsing Special Party Branch (to which active-duty and retired military personnel and their families belong) and public employees' organizations. These *tiau-a-ka* are mobilized through bureaucratic channels within their organizations. Their superiors introduce the candidates and give instructions on campaign strategy. Employees of corporatist organizations understand that a certain amount of political involvement is part of their jobs.[26]

Incentives for *tiau-a-ka*

It should be obvious by now that acting as a *tiau-a-ka* requires a great deal of work, while the fruits of that labor mostly go to someone else: the successful candidate. Why, then, do *tiau-a-ka* expend so much of their own time, energy and even money to help politicians? What incentives do politicians use to win their support?

Some *tiau-a-ka* are motivated by emotional rewards. Tradition-minded *tiau-a-ka* form long-term – sometimes lifelong – relationships with politicians. A Kaohsiung County *tiau-a-ka* exemplifies this pattern.[27] His relationship with his patrons goes back to Yu Teng-fa, the grandfather of the current county executive, Yu Cheng-hsien. His main accomplishment as a *tiau-a-ka* was persuading the county to cover the sewers in his tiny village, but the villagers know that he can help them gain assistance from the county government on a range of problems. At election time, he visits voters to talk to them about the Yu family and all the good things they have done for the community.

This *tiau-a-ka*, like many others, derives great personal satisfaction from his political involvement. He is proud of his role as a link between his community and the county government. He makes sure the Yu family receives invitations to weddings and funerals in the village; he arranges for a wreath, flowers or a placard to be sent in the county executive's name; and he attends these events as the Yu family's representative. Having a wreath or placard from the county executive, he says, gives a person great face.[28] He believes effort he expends is worth it both because it brings him respect, and because it is a way for him to help his community.

For some *tiau-a-ka*, then, the satisfaction of the job is reward enough. But given the positions most office-holding *tiau-a-ka* occupy – ward, village and neighborhood head – the obligations of office would seem to outweigh its rewards. Although these technically are part-time positions, in fact they are very time-consuming. Village and ward heads need to be available around the clock to respond to emergencies, mediate disputes, comfort angry or distraught residents. Nor can they afford to miss community events; they are obliged to attend (or at least send gifts to) funerals, weddings and other private and public celebrations if they want to stay in office. Yet despite these demands, elections are hotly contested. Why are people so eager to take on these demanding jobs? And how do politicians entice ward and village heads to become their *tiau-a-ka*?

One motive is status, or in Chinese parlance, face. To be elected village or ward head is prestigious, and the closer a village or ward head's relationship with higher officials is, the more opportunities he or she has to accumulate and display face. A local leader who can demonstrate a strong connection with a high-level politician shares the latter's aura. Another reward village and ward heads can expect for their pains is a chance at higher office. Here again, having the support of a more highly placed politician is helpful. For many, service to the village or ward is a stepping stone to more powerful and remunerative offices.

Being a *tiau-a-ka* for a higher official helps an aspiring politician secure the trust of the local KMT headquarters and develop a grassroots support network. The more competent a ward or village head proves to be in local office, the more likely the voters are to trust him or her with higher office. And the better a local official's connections, the better his chances of satisfying his constituents' expectations. The Kaohsiung County *tiau-a-ka* who expressed such pride in his role also admitted its rewards went beyond the satisfaction of a job well done. He said it is easier to be elected village head and to continue up the ladder of local politics if one has a good relationship with the county executive. The Yu family is skilled in helping *tiau-a-ka* advance by making them an indispensable link in the service chain; unlike an ordinary citizen, a *tiau-a-ka* can reach the county executive on the telephone, and will be received in his or her office.[29]

In Taiwan, "service" means using one's political power or access to provide one's constituents with material goods, legal consideration or other assistance that is not universally available. The kinds of service a village or ward head provides include interceding with the bureaucracy, improving public facilities, conferring status and resolving disputes. Of these, the first three require at least the cooperation, if not the active assistance, of higher-level officials. And this is why the ward or village head's connections are so important. If there is a problem with road or sewer repairs, a village whose head has poor connections must wait in line behind other villages for the county bureaucracy to act. A village whose head has connections with a county councilor could get a repair proposal expedited. A village whose head has connections with the county executive could ask the executive to order the repairs to be done immediately.

Electoral mobilization in Taiwan rests on the belief that "service" is the best measure of an official's competence. Service is not understood as corrupt or inappropriate; in fact, for Taiwanese, good service is the hallmark of a skillful, committed public official. A 1984 survey illustrates this point. At a time when most Taiwanese still had relatively authoritarian outlooks on politics (e.g., 41 percent thought national affairs should be decided by the head of government, and barely a quarter believed opposition parties could exist without bringing chaos to the political system), service to the public enjoyed widespread support. Seventy percent of those surveyed disagreed with the view that public officials should concern themselves more with carrying out orders from above than with serving the people, and 82 percent thought the government should pay more attention to the public's demands for public works.[30]

Taiwan's KMT leaders long have emphasized service, especially service to individuals, in party work. Wu Nai-teh labels this the KMT's "patronage mentality."[31] He traces the tendency from the KMT's pre-1949 tenure on the Chinese mainland all the way to the mid-1980s. Initially, the emphasis on service seems to have been strategic, as a 1966 guide to grassroots party work implied:

> Our working procedure should be so arranged that we should directly go into the personal problems of the people and help them to solve those problems. Only when we can benefit them practically and

immediately can we gain their trust and support. This is the function of service works.[32]

Even if the original intent of what Wu calls the party's "obsession" with service work was strategic, it quickly took on a life of its own. In 1962, a report to the KMT Central Committee remarked, "The psychology of the masses is that they are apt to be thankful [for] the personal and individual favors and to forget and overlook the fulfillment of their interests brought about by public policies."[33] Whether or not this generalization was accurate at the time, the party's willingness to accommodate individual service requests helped inculcate precisely this attitude among Taiwanese voters.

Access to politically popular service projects is tremendously valuable to local leaders and other *tiau-a-ka*. But politicians also reward *tiau-a-ka* more directly: they help them make money. It is at this point that *tiau-a-ka* politics can drift into corruption. Some ward and village heads augment their official stipends with illegal payments (including "commissions" on vote-buying transactions) and gifts. During election campaigns, candidates try to secure *tiau-a-ka*'s political support by entertaining them with banquets and trips. Newspaper articles refer to the process of paying *tiau-a-ka* to bring them into one's campaign as "stirring up *tiau-a-ka*" (*bang zhuangjiao*) or "arranging pillars"(*bu zhuang*).[34] Liu I-Chou gives a detailed account of the compensation candidates in one Taipei City election offered their *tiau-a-ka* for their electoral work:

Li leaders received NT$10,000–20,000 (US$400–800) and some gifts such as a cassette recorder, calculator, tea pot set, etc.
Sub-district committee chairs received NT$10,000 (US$400).
Sub-district committee secretariats received NT$5,000 (US$200).
Li administrators received NT$5,000 (US$200).
Lin leaders received NT$2,000 (US$80) from the City Committee.[35]

The benefits described to this point – cash, gifts and service – come out of the politicians' own resources. A far richer source of benefits is to be found in local government coffers; not surprisingly, politicians also use this money to further their electoral goals. Handing out patronage jobs is one way politicians reward "their" *tiau-a-ka*; manipulating construction contracts is another. Although the coziness between politicians and construction firms in Taiwan's municipalities has not yet reached the fabulous heights described in Woodall's work on construction-industry clientelism in Japan, the process by which local governments award public contracts is lax by most standards.[36] Chao Yung-mao's book *Local Factions*

and Local Construction details the corrupting influence of local factionalism on public construction. Of course, incumbents derive the most
political benefit from this practice. In fact, the *tiau-a-ka* system has
contributed to a strong incumbency advantage in local elections, because
out of office, politicians and factions have little to offer potential *tiau-a-ka*.

Incentives for voters

Tiau-a-ka help politicians win elections because they receive material
benefits, social status and a career boost. Politicians help *tiau-a-ka* build
their reputations and bank accounts because they want to win elections.
But what about the voters? Why do they cooperate with the *tiau-a-ka*'s
schemes?

Taiwanese voters cooperate with vote brokers because of a combination of structural factors and incentives. In a nutshell, *tiau-a-ka* use ties of
blood and friendship as well as favors and money to persuade voters to
select particular candidates. But these techniques would be far less effective were it not for Taiwan's political institutions. The SVMM system
generates long ballots with multiple candidates from the major parties.
Until the late 1980s, the ROC's restrictive campaign laws allowed little
useful information about candidates to reach the public, while the ban on
opposition parties ensured that party identification would not be a consideration. These structural factors eliminated many of the cues voters in
other countries use to select candidates, leaving voters in the hands of
tiau-a-ka.[37]

Within this institutional framework, *tiau-a-ka* rely on their relationships with voters. As Wu Nai-teh put it, "As the entrepreneurs collect
money, the politicians collect friends."[38] Affective ties are important
political resources, but *tiau-a-ka* also control a variety of perquisites that
give them influence beyond their networks of friends and relatives.
Village and ward heads are responsible for certifying more than two dozen
different documents, including statements of family income. They also
appoint neighborhood heads (*lin zhang*).[39] Selecting neighborhood heads
helps them build power bases rooted in individual loyalty. *Tiau-a-ka* also
act as go-betweens with bureaucratic agencies, and help to mediate minor
conflicts, such as traffic accidents, contract problems and small damage
claims.

Not all the services ward and village heads provide are directed to individuals. More important are the services they provide to the community
as a whole. Some of these activities do not involve the public sector. For
example, private donations to temples and charities are considered
"service."[40] Although they cannot authorize construction or repair

projects themselves, basic-level officials are responsible for reporting problems to the township or district government. Large construction projects can require the intervention of the municipal executive, which means that unless local officials are well connected, such projects may not go forward. Clearly, voters have a strong incentive to return their *tiau-a-ka*'s patrons to office. Still, while social connections and service are important, they are not enough. For decades, *tiau-a-ka* have supplemented their personal ties and community service with a more tangible incentive: money.

Vote buying

Foreign faces are a rare sight in Chiali, a town of 55,000 in central Tainan County, so I was not surprised when, shortly after I arrived there, two teenaged girls approached me. They asked what I was doing in Taiwan, and in their town in particular. When I explained I had come to study local elections, their responses were revealing. One inquired whether there weren't elections in America I could study. The second observed, "What's to study? They just run around buying votes." In a few words, the young women proved the accuracy of a DPP activist's observation: "Vote buying is an open secret."

It is hard to say which is more difficult: finding someone in Taiwan who denies that vote buying exists, or finding concrete evidence to prove that it does. Naturally, survey research is not very useful for estimating the extent of a practice which is both illegal and widely understood to be morally questionable at best. According to one study, 70 percent of the electorate admitted to having heard of vote buying, while 30 percent said they had been offered a bribe at some time. Perhaps the study's most interesting finding was that, among candidates, 80 percent "believed there was bribery going on."[41] A 1992 *China Times* survey found that a third of the respondents were willing to "accept ... a bribe if approached."[42] One county executive candidate's campaign manager admitted to me in an interview that the campaign bought votes.

Like *tiau-a-ka* politics, vote buying is a complex phenomenon, with subtle meanings and implications. Many explanations have been advanced for why it took root so deeply in Taiwan. Some emphasize cultural factors; others accuse the Kuomintang of deliberately corrupting Taiwan's politics. Neither of these answers is sufficient. Traditional social practices condone behaviors that many would call electoral bribery. But there is no question that most Taiwanese today recognize the illicit nature of the practice, even if they continue to participate. It also is true that the KMT has never acted decisively to bring an end to vote buying. This is no doubt due at least in part to the fact that the main beneficiaries of the practice are KMT politicians. But to accuse the KMT of systematically and intentionally undermining the integrity of Taiwanese elections is unfair. The prevalence of vote buying in Taiwan is rooted in a combination of factors, not the least of which are the ROC's electoral institutions. The electoral system creates strong incentives for candidates and parties to use clientelistic strategies in their electoral campaigns. Even candidates who themselves disapprove of vote buying may be unable to stop their *tiau-a-ka*, who see buying votes as both normal and unavoidable.

Vote buying has been a feature of Taiwanese elections at least since the 1950s. Lawrence Crissman asserted in a 1969 paper that the price of a vote had been rising steadily "for the past ten years at least."[43] Lerman quotes a January 1968 *United Daily* report that in Tainan County, several banks' stock of NT$10 bills were depleted in the days just before an election to pay the NT$40 cost of a vote.[44] Lerman also called attention to the role played by local officials and Farmers' Association cadres in the vote-buying process, and confirmed Crissman's finding that Farmers' Association cadres who refused to buy votes could be fired.[45]

Taiwan's first successful vote-buying prosecution occurred in 1967. According to Ma Ch'i-hua:

> From then on, in every sort of election, bribery has become more and more serious until in 1983 there were rumors of bribery in Control Yuan elections and by 1986 bribery incidents were occurring even in village and neighborhood elections.[46]

Ma blames the increase in vote-buying activity on several factors. Growing support for opposition politicians, first as independents, then as DPP members, made elections more competitive. When KMT nominees lost faith in the party's ability to lead them to victory, they turned to vote buying to improve their chances. At the same time, Taiwan's growing affluence meant many political aspirants could afford to buy large numbers of votes. Ma also cites the prevalence of "electoral oxen and certain village and neighborhood heads" (read *tiau-a-ka*) who were eager to carry out vote buying in order to get benefits for themselves. Neither voters nor candidates disapproved of vote buying, so there was little social pressure to stop. Finally, once a candidate is elected, transgressions during the campaign are quickly forgotten. So, vote buying became commonplace.

When an office-holding *tiau-a-ka* sets out to buy votes, he or she begins by picking up money and campaign literature from a local faction or campaign office, along with a list of potential voters in his or her "responsibility zone." The next step is to canvass the neighborhood, chatting briefly with each family and dropping off campaign literature and a "red envelope" – the Taiwanese euphemism for a bribe. *Tiau-a-ka* who do not hold public office sometimes use their own money to fill the envelopes or to sponsor a dinner or other entertainment for voters they want to mobilize. The amount of money paid for a vote varies widely, according to the office (county executive candidates usually pay more than legislative candidates), the intensity of the competition and how much the candidates can afford. According to newspaper reports, in 1989, the range was about NT$300 to NT$500, enough to buy dinner for two in an inexpensive sit-down restaurant. In the 1992 legislative elections, the average price of a vote seems to have been slightly higher, although the range was similar; conversations with observers of municipal council elections in 1998 revealed little change.

The key to buying votes is personal contact between *tiau-a-ka* and voters. For social *tiau-a-ka*, this is easy, since they specialize in mobilizing their friends, relatives and business associates. It also is one reason why official *tiau-a-ka*'s responsibility areas are kept small, corresponding to the neighborhood or precinct. Political scientist Wei Yung explained the importance of direct contact this way:

> it is still deeply believed that one should only make direct contact with a stranger through an intermediary. That is why the candidates must win over, sometimes at any cost if they expect to win, the local leaders or party cadres in the rural areas. Moreover, since city dwellers live in high-rise apartments, it is an almost impossible task for candidates to campaign house-to-house without receiving prior permission. So, they have to depend on the chief of a *li* [ward] or party cadres to lead the way.[47]

ROC election laws facilitate the office-holding *tiau-a-ka*'s mobilizational work. In order to obtain a ballot, each voter must present a registered voter's identification form at the polls. These forms are distributed by neighborhood heads, who deliver them to each household in person. This affords a convenient opportunity for the neighborhood head to recommend a candidate and drop off a "red envelope." For the sake of subtlety, some *tiau-a-ka* deliver the voter identification form, money and campaign literature on separate visits; an up-to-date motto in 1992 was "first exchange money; bring the handbills later" (*xian jiao qian; hou na chuandan*). (Social *tiau-a-ka* must contrive their own opportunities for reaching their targets, either visiting voters at home or inviting them to special events.) Another of the ward and neighborhood heads' duties is turning out local residents on election day. Voters with little interest in the outcome of the election might prefer to stay home, but under pressure from the neighborhood head at least some will be persuaded to go. Lacking a strong preference of their own, they may be especially likely to cast their ballots for candidates recommended by local officials.

The vote-buying activity of ward, village and neighborhood heads probably constitutes the lion's share of vote-buying transactions in Taiwan. Before the 1992 legislative election, a Hsinchu County *tiau-a-ka* was arrested on suspicion of buying votes for a KMT nominee. The details of the case illustrate vote-buying techniques. At the time of his arrest, the *tiau-a-ka* – himself a township representative – was holding NT$10 million in newly minted NT$500 bills. With the money police found a large amount of campaign literature for the legislative candidate, including sample ballots. Police also found a list of registered voters' names and addresses.[48] In a 1992 local mayoral election DPP "electoral bribery inspectors" confronted a neighborhood head who was visiting voters while carrying NT$5,700 in NT$100 bills in her purse. She admitted that the money came from the ward head, for the purpose of paying voters NT$300 each to vote for the KMT candidate.[49]

Tiau-a-ka buy votes at least in part because they want to prove their effectiveness as vote mobilizers. Those who are able to deliver the promised number of votes – by any means necessary – can expect rewards. Successful *tiau-a-ka* look forward to being courted by candidates in future elections, earning them both prestige and material benefits. Their communities, too, may be rewarded with special projects and funds. In 1991, certain Tainan County village heads complained publicly that the county executive elected two years earlier had failed to deliver promised funds to their villages. They stated forthrightly that the money had been promised as a reward for mobilizing their villages behind Li's candidacy, and they demanded he keep his end of the bargain.

There are two enforcement problems inherent in Taiwan's vote-buying process. First, vote buying as a party strategy is cost-effective only if candidates agree to divide the vote and refrain from poaching (buying votes in other candidates' responsibility zones). Second, the secret ballot system makes it difficult to know whether a voter chose the candidate whose money he or she accepted. On the first point, candidates have an economic incentive to cooperate with the responsibility zone strategy, because it prevents a bidding war for votes, and limits the number of votes each candidate must buy. Poaching raises the cost of campaigning for everyone. In addition, poachers risk being sanctioned by local KMT leaders; they may even lose the nomination in future elections.

But candidates' willingness to compromise has diminished in recent years, because cooperating with party strategy no longer guarantees victory. According to Jacobs, in the 1970s two candidates for the same office would have paid the same price for votes. This generalization no longer holds true. In some districts, the price candidates offered for votes in the 1992 legislative election reportedly differed by as much as NT$200. Candidates from both parties also used the "poisoned well" trick in their opponents' territories: pretending to represent the opponent's campaign, they paid large sums to a few voters, thereby stirring up jealousy and dissension, and raising the rival candidate's costs.[50] According to Taiwan's leading overseas newspaper, *World Journal* (*Shijie Ribao*), in 1992 "election dealers" (*xuanju fanze*) appeared. For a fee, they would handle a candidate's vote buying; some even guaranteed election or your money back.

The second enforcement problem associated with vote buying is ensuring that voters actually cast their ballots as they promise to do, despite the existence of a secret ballot system. One might expect voters with little interest in the outcome of an election simply to abstain. But in Taiwan's highly mobilized political environment, few escape the *tiau-a-ka's* entreaties. *Tiau-a-ka* are active in workplaces, and they canvass neighborhoods, spreading cash. When election day arrives they check to see that those they have paid actually go to the polls. After all, the ballot is secret, but if someone chooses not to vote, any candidate or organization from which he or she has received money can easily find out. *Tiau-a-ka* have a strong incentive to make sure "their" people vote; candidates and faction bosses look at precinct-level results to see which *tiau-a-ka* delivered the promised numbers. The price a *tiau-a-ka* can command for his or her services depends on his or her performance in the previous election. In some cases, candidates use thugs to keep tabs on *tiau-a-ka*; those who fail to deliver the vote may face violent retribution.[51] In short, *tiau-a-ka* see to it that voters do not respond to the absence of party and issue cues by abstaining; rather, they exploit voters' apathy and confusion by mobilizing them behind the candidates they support.

Tiau-a-ka have developed various techniques for ensuring that voters select the candidates from whom they have accepted money. For example, *tiau-a-ka* in rural areas sometimes carry images of deities when they go out to buy votes. They ask the voter to whisper to the god or goddess how they plan to vote. Others try to intimidate voters, implying that they have ways of finding out who voted "wrong"; given the widespread perception that gangsters are deeply involved in local politics, such threats may well be effective. Meanwhile, others point out that if the precinct produces too few votes for a given candidate, the *tiau-a-ka* will receive less money to buy votes in the next election. Still others fret that their community will be punished if they fail to support the assigned candidate by a wide margin. Many Taiwanese view publicly funded community projects as gifts from politicians, rather than as appropriate expenditures of tax money. This gives *tiau-a-ka* a great deal of leverage. Above all, however, *tiau-a-ka* rely on the loyalty of their friends and neighbors. *Tiau-a-ka* cannot successfully buy votes from strangers; among those they know, there inevitably is a certain amount of emotional discomfort with the idea of taking the money without voting as promised.[52]

Vote buying is not an effective campaign tactic, but it is an effective mobilizing technique, because it reinforces the resources *tiau-a-ka* already have at their disposal. Where *tiau-a-ka* are influential, vote buying is a useful weapon in a faction or candidate's arsenal. Where they are less powerful, vote buying gets a candidate's vote broker in the door, establishing the possibility of a vote. As we have seen, the ROC's electoral system builds in incentives for parties and factions to use a strategy of dividing and mobilizing votes rather than allowing candidates to compete head-to-head using an issue-oriented campaign strategy. Until it was dropped in 1987, the ban on new parties prevented inter-party competition and made it easier for the ruling party to carry out its divide-and-mobilize strategy. The SVMM formula also encourages mobilizational politics and vote brokerage in another way: It helps political parties exploit voters' indifference and lack of information to make their mobilizational techniques more effective.

Conclusion

Vote buying and other techniques of mobilizational politics are not uniformly effective. Clientelistic politics works best in rural areas and tightly knit urban neighborhoods, and in local elections. Communities in which friendship and face are important are fertile ground for *tiau-a-ka*. These values are common in rural areas of Taiwan, if only because in the countryside neighbors are stuck with one another for a very long time.[53] Thus, rejecting a *tiau-a-ka*'s overtures is awkward. In cities, many residents do not personally know the *tiau-a-ka* in their neighborhoods, so it is easier to resist their entreaties. In general, this means that the KMT, whose candidates are more likely to be affiliated with local factions and to have access to *tiau-a-ka* networks, out-performs other parties in rural areas. Some scholars are puzzled by the DPP's strong showing in rural areas in certain elections. This usually can be explained by the presence of a DPP-linked local faction (as in Kaohsiung and Taoyuan Counties), or by a temporary alliance between KMT factions and a DPP candidate (as in Tainan and Taipei Counties in 1989).

The mobilization system also works best in basic-level elections (county council, township executive and representative, and village or ward elections) because voters, *tiau-a-ka* and candidates are closely linked. As the number of votes required to win an election grows, the distance between candidates and voters increases, making it harder for *tiau-a-ka* to bridge the gap. This explains an interesting paradox in Taiwan's election turn-out statistics: Historically, turn-out for grassroots elections has been higher than turn-out for national elections, almost as if the level of enthusiasm for an election were inversely related to its importance. The most plausible explanation is that basic-level elections involve voters' and *tiau-a-ka*'s friends and family, so the motivation to vote is greater. The fact that the KMT consistently wins a much larger share of votes and seats in these elections than in county, provincial and national elections is due, in part, to the success of the mobilization system in basic-level races.

The KMT also enjoys a greater advantage over its opponents in representative elections than in executive elections. This becomes apparent when we consider the prevalence of split-ticket voting, in which a voter chooses candidates of different parties for different offices. As Table 4.1 shows, the DPP's executive candidates tend to win a much larger

Table 4.1 Split-ticket voting: DPP vote shares in the 1989 elections

Municipality	DPP exec. vote (%)	DPP legis. vote (%)	Exec.–Legis.
Taipei County	48.8	25.1	23.7
Ilan County	54.5	19.3	35.2
Taoyuan County	41.3	32.2	9.0
Hsinchu County	51.1	34.3	16.7
Taichung County	40.3	20.1	20.2
Changhua County	49.3	13.2	36.1
Nantou County	0.8	29.7	-28.9
Yunlin County	27.1	50.2	-23.1
Chiayi County	22.0	22.9	-00.9
Tainan County	47.3	23.6	23.7
Kaohsiung County	56.3	42.3	14.0
Pingtung County	54.3	42.9	11.4
Taitung County	9.0	19.4	-10.4
Keelung City	42.2	25.7	16.4
Taichung City	38.8	32.2	6.6
Tainan City	7.2	38.1	-30.9
Hsinchu City	31.8	45.0	-13.3

Source: Yang Tai-shuenn, *Elections (Xuanju)*, Taipei, Yung-jan Cultural Publishing Ltd, 1991, p. 274.

Note:
Includes only municipalities in which the DPP nominated candidates in both races.

percentage of the vote than their colleagues running in legislative races. There are two main reasons for this. First, the election of a DPP county executive or mayor is a strong statement in favor of change, whereas the shift of a single legislative seat rarely makes much difference. Second, the mobilization system is more effective in multi-seat races, which candidates can win with relatively small vote shares.

Executive races involve two or three major candidates in head-to-head combat. The ballot is shorter, and voters are unlikely to be forced to choose among several candidates of the same party. Identifying the preferred candidate is therefore less complicated, and voters may be less in need of help from *tiau-a-ka*. In addition, single member district elections tend to exacerbate factional conflict, whereas multi-member elections provide opportunities for several factions to win. Thus, factions are likely to mobilize for the KMT in legislative races, but they may be less helpful in executive elections. As Yang Tai-shuenn writes, "This phenomenon [of split ticket voting] demonstrates our earlier point: in the SVMM Legislative Yuan and Provincial Assembly elections, the KMT is better able to mobilize its long-managed factional relationships and obtain better results for the KMT."[54]

Institutional arrangements at the national level, KMT party strategy, the SVMM electoral system and grassroots political tendencies all combine to support the mobilizational component of the ROC's mobilizational authoritarianism. Local factions, *tiau-a-ka* and vote buying provided a foundation on which the KMT's electoral success in Taiwan was built. They drew ordinary Taiwanese into the electoral system as voters – and sometimes as candidates – both by tugging the strings of family and friendship and by offering concrete benefits in exchange for participation. The ruling party increased the vitality of these informal, grassroots institutions by rewarding their success at the same time as it encouraged competition among them. The result was an electoral system that chugged along with little change from the 1950s into the 1990s.

For many, many voters, taking instruction from a *tiau-a-ka* is standard political practice at the end of the twentieth century. Even so, grassroots electoral behavior was not immune to the changes that swept Taiwan's political system in the 1970s, 1980s and 1990s. Indeed, it was only because voters, candidates and even whole factions were willing to detach themselves from the KMT's political machine that the opposition was able to gain a foothold and force open the system. Nonetheless, conservative grassroots electoral practices reassured the KMT that liberalizing politics would not endanger its position as the ruling party. What KMT leaders did not anticipate was that while the mobilization system might continue to function well at the lowest levels of government, when higher levels of government were at stake, enough voters would be willing to ignore *tiau-a-ka* and local factions to give the political opposition some significant victories.

As we shall see, as Taiwan's political and economic development progressed, the behavior of local factions and *tiau-a-ka* changed. For example, economic liberalization inspired some businesses to cultivate or even "buy out" local factions to ensure their access to political power, while local factions found ways to update their own economic strategies and contacts.[55] Still, the mobilization system continued to occupy an important role in Taiwan politics into the late 1990s. Although politicians complained that the system no longer delivered, they continued to use it, pouring money into the hands of voters and vote brokers. As elections became ever more competitive, candidates dared not leave a single stone unturned.

Even though no one believed that vote buying alone could bring about a victory, only a candidate who possessed a strong base of ideological support (almost certainly a Democratic Progressive Party or New Party candidate) would dare to eschew local factions, *tiau-a-ka* and vote buying. For the vast majority of candidates, working the mobilization system was a major component of a well-rounded campaign strategy. And for the KMT as a party, the mobilization system, for all its faults, was a crucial tool. Anyone who doubted its utility need only look at the results of the 1994 Provincial Assembly races, in which KMT nominees supported by local factions won 93 percent of the seats they contested.[56]

5 Political reform under Chiang Ching-kuo (1972–1988)

During the 1950s and 1960s, Taiwan enjoyed relative stability in its domestic and international politics. Under the strong hand of Chiang Kai-shek, domestic opposition was all but invisible, while the dynamics of local elections turned many Taiwanese into active KMT supporters. Meanwhile, the Cold War encouraged strong international support for the ROC as a defense against communist expansion in East Asia. Thus, in these decades, the ROC leadership was able to ignore or suppress pressure for democratizing reforms.

Taiwan's situation changed markedly in the 1970s. Although its economy was beginning to reveal the vitality that would earn it "miracle" status in the 1980s, the ROC faced serious set-backs – political and economic, domestic and international – throughout the decade. Uncertainty about the succession to Chiang Kai-shek and factionalism within the KMT complicated the regime's handling of these difficulties. In the end, despite occasional attempts at repression, the regime's response to the crises plaguing it was pragmatic. Rather than an authoritarian retrenchment, the leadership undertook political reform. This reform process accelerated after 1977, when the opposition began using elections to demonstrate support for change. In short, the "momentum of decompression" Lamounier describes was building in Taiwan.

The *Free China Fortnightly* episode

The 1960 *Free China Fortnightly* episode was an unsuccessful attempt to set in motion the forces that would come to the forefront two decades later. With support from Hu Shih, the ROC's leading intellectual, a mainland-born scholar named Lei Chen founded a magazine called *Free China Fortnightly*. The magazine reprinted its founding principles in each issue: promoting democracy and democratic values in the ROC, fighting communist expansion, battling for the freedom of Chinese living under communism, and making all of China Free China. Initially, *Free China Fortnightly* enjoyed the patronage of top KMT leaders. It received financial assistance from the Ministry of Education, and public agencies purchased subscriptions. As time passed, however, the magazine's focus shifted from attacks on communism to critiques of ROC policies in Taiwan. This created friction with its erstwhile patrons in the regime.

While the magazine's evolving orientation irritated the KMT leadership, it attracted favorable attention from Taiwanese luminaries who shared Lei's dissatisfaction with Taiwan's political situation. Some contributed articles or joined the magazine's editorial board. At the same time, Lei and his supporters began to envision using local elections as a way to add weight to their demands and advance their democratic goals. To do so, they made common cause with Taiwanese politicians who were organizing their own pro-democracy movement.

In 1957, three local politicians formed a Non-party Candidates' Alliance (by "non-party" they meant non-KMT) to contest municipal and Provincial Assembly elections. They planned citizens' meetings around the island and recommended candidates for various local posts. They also criticized unfair KMT electioneering practices, including using on-duty public employees as campaign aides, allowing incumbents to use publicly owned communications channels for campaign propaganda and permitting KMT cadres to supervise the vote counting process at polling stations.[1] When the election was over, six candidates endorsed by the Alliance had won election to the Provincial Assembly, including Wu San-lien of Tainan County and Ilan County's Kuo Yu-hsin.

After the 1957 and 1960 elections, Lei Chen and his collaborators met with non-KMT politicians, including members of the Alliance, to discuss the elections. They spearheaded a drive to organize independents to challenge the KMT; the magazine openly called for the formation of an opposition party. From the outset, the *Free China* activists recognized that working through existing electoral institutions – not attempting radical change at the national level – offered the best chance for a new party to influence ROC politics. Thus, the work of planning the new party fell to a group called the Local Elections Improvement Association.

KMT leaders profoundly distrusted alliances between central officials and local factions.[2] Thus, they responded angrily to Lei Chen's moves, stepping up the flow of propaganda against the new political party. Organizers complained of harassment by the authorities; Wu San-lien's business received such strong pressure from the authorities that he went abroad for six months.[3] On 4 September 1960, members of the Taiwan Garrison Command arrested Lei Chen and one of the *Free China Fortnightly* editors. Lei was accused of spreading communist propaganda and harboring a communist. Reformers rallied to his defense, but to no effect. Even some in the ruling party believed the TGC had gone too far; legislator Fei Hsi-ping had his KMT membership suspended for a year when he questioned the Lei Chen verdict on the floor of the Legislative Yuan.[4]

Lei's supporters and collaborators tried to carry on after his arrest. On 9 September the organizing group announced its intention to form the China Democratic Party. A few weeks later, the party's spokesmen, Kao Yu-shu and Li Wan-chu, made an illuminating statement to the press. The Lei Chen case, they said, revealed the KMT government's determination to tighten its control and use terror to undermine the efforts of Mainlanders and Taiwanese to work together.[5] In fact, while opposition publications would reappear in the 1970s, and an opposition party would form in the 1980s, never again would liberal Mainlanders work so closely with Taiwanese politicians. One cannot but wonder whether the China Democratic Party might have offered a moderate, non-ethnic alternative to the ideological and ethnic polarization that strained Taiwan's social fabric in the 1980s. In any event, neither the magazine nor the party Lei founded survived his arrest, although the party's organizing committee did support candidates for local office in 1961. As for Lei Chen himself, he spent the next ten years in prison.

The Lei Chen incident is significant for a number of reasons. The *Free China Fortnightly* was the first publication to focus on the problems of KMT administration on Taiwan. As a KMT insider, Lei Chen was one of the White Terror's most highly placed victims; his arrest put to rest any lingering doubts about the regime's willingness to suppress its critics. The abortive China Democratic Party represented the first attempt to form a real opposition party in the ROC, one that would challenge the KMT's power in the name of its founding ideology. In addition, Lei Chen's story is important because it reveals that even in the 1950s, supporters of political reform in Taiwan recognized the value of local elections, and local politicians recognized the value of political reform. The Mainlander intellectuals who founded the *Free China Fortnightly* allied with a would-be indigenous political leadership in the hope of using the electoral opportunities the KMT regime had put into place to pressure the Nationalists for reform. While this particular alliance did not reappear, the strategy of working within the electoral system to challenge the regime's authoritarian tendencies proved to be an important factor in Taiwan's democratization.

The *Free China Fortnightly* incident revealed the dangers and difficulties facing political dissidents; after 1960, few Taiwanese dared challenge the ruling party directly. However, local politicians – including several who had worked with Lei Chen's group – continued to contest elections. In 1964, independents defeated KMT candidates for the mayorships of Tainan and Keelung Cities. Opposition figures such as Wu San-lien and Kuo Yu-hsin criticized the ruling party from their seats in the Provincial Assembly. China Democratic Party spokesman Kao Yu-shu was elected mayor of Taipei City in 1960 and 1964, defeating KMT nominees both times.[6]

The 1970s: a decade of challenges

The 1970s dealt the ROC a series of set-backs, both international and domestic. These events challenged the ruling party to adjust its relationship with Taiwan's citizens. No longer could the regime count on international support and the promise of mainland recovery to maintain its authority. The search for new bases of legitimacy led the regime to open the organs of government and party to a growing number of Taiwanese. At the same time, the fierce repression of the previous decades eased slightly, especially as the day-to-day management of the government shifted from Chiang Kai-shek to his son and eventual successor, Chiang Ching-kuo.

Growing diplomatic isolation

The ROC entered the 1970s in a shaky position internationally; its claim to sovereignty over all China was fast becoming a global joke. After a decade in power, the Chinese Communist Party had consolidated its grip on the mainland and was promoting itself as a leader in the Third World. No longer could Taipei credibly claim to be on the verge of retaking the mainland. Meanwhile, the rest of the world recognized the necessity of coming to terms with the PRC, whose territory and population far exceeded those of its rival. The showdown came in the United Nations.

Since the UN's founding, the ROC had occupied China's seat in the world body. But after 1949, the communist bloc and an increasing number of non-communist countries supported representation for the PRC. Taiwan's friends, led by the US, staved off efforts to seat Beijing, since neither Chinese government would accept dual recognition. But by 1971, the US no longer had the will or the General Assembly votes to keep the PRC out, or to keep Taiwan in. Taipei's delegation withdrew from the UN on the eve of a vote to expel the ROC.

Taipei's bilateral diplomacy deteriorated along with its status in international organizations. In the early 1970s, anti-communism still was strong in the US, Taiwan's most important diplomatic partner. But the

Cold War justification for supporting the Nationalists – walling off communism in Asia – was less persuasive after the Sino-Soviet split. As animosity replaced socialist fraternity in Beijing–Moscow relations, US policy-makers began to consider détente with Beijing. Ideological opposition to communism in all its forms gradually lost ground to a Realpolitik calculation in which "playing the China card" against the Soviets made good strategic sense. Nixon's visit to China in 1972 demonstrated the United States' determination to build a relationship with Beijing; the Shanghai Communique issued before the visit committed the US to a one-China policy.

President Carter announced his intention to normalize relations with Bejing in December 1978. The price of normalization was that the US must sever its ties with Taipei. The normalization process had been underway since 1972; Taiwan's leaders may have been disappointed – or even despairing – at Carter's announcement, but they could not have been surprised. Still, Taiwan had friends in Washington. Before the Senate would approve the transfer of recognition from Taipei to Beijing it demanded assurances for Taiwan. The result was the 1979 Taiwan Relations Act, in which the US promised to provide Taiwan with defensive weapons and to keep an unofficial representative office in Taipei, the American Institute in Taiwan (AIT).

Taiwan's isolation intensified in the 1980s, when Deng Xiaoping's reforms led many in the West to conclude that China's economic and political systems were converging with those of other industrialized nations. At the same time, Beijing took a relatively accommodating stance on foreign policy issues and on the Taiwan question. In 1983 Deng introduced the one-country, two-systems concept, promising to preserve the economic and social systems of Hong Kong and Taiwan if they would rejoin the Chinese motherland. Taiwan responded to the offer with intransigence, announcing the policy of "Three Nos": no contacts, no negotiations, no compromise.

Taipei relaxed its position slightly at the end of the decade. In 1987, President Chiang Ching-kuo lifted the ban on travel to the mainland. This gesture placated Beijing somewhat, but first-hand observation of conditions on the mainland had the paradoxical effect of undermining support for unification among Taiwan residents. In 1989, Taiwan's international reputation received a boost when the Tiananmen Incident revealed the limits of Beijing's reform program. Even so, Taiwan entered the 1990s with fewer than thirty diplomatic partners, and no United Nations seat.

Domestic challenges

These international set-backs compounded Taiwan's domestic problems, which included economic difficulties, declining public morale and confidence, dwindling numbers in the national legislative bodies, a looming succession crisis, a burgeoning overseas movement for Taiwan independence and stirrings of domestic opposition. Taiwan's economy was hit hard by the 1973 OPEC embargo. Taiwan imported nearly all of its oil its from OPEC sources, and oil provided three-fourths of Taiwan's energy needs. Although Taiwan weathered the immediate crisis well, the oil embargo drew attention to the island's vulnerability to changes in the world economy – including a growing protectionist movement in the US, Taiwan's major export market.

Meanwhile, the ROC political system was in need of repair. The national legislative bodies were elected in the 1940s and frozen in office; by 1965 their numbers were in precipitous decline. Many legislators never moved to Taiwan; others left when the prospect of returning to the mainland grew remote. Others died, and many were too aged or infirm to serve effectively. More than 90 percent of the National Assembly's 3,045 members attended its 1948 meeting, but in 1954, barely half were present. In 1984, only 797 senior members remained.

Time affected the executive branch as well as the representative bodies. In 1970, Chiang Kai-shek was 83 years old; the question of who would succeed him could not be put off much longer. Nor could the question be debated openly, however, since Taiwan's leaders were desperate to maintain the appearance of political stability. By 1972, Chiang Kai-shek's son, Chiang Ching-kuo, had taken on many of his father's responsibilities, but there was no consensus among top KMT leaders that the younger Chiang should be the successor. Despite the best efforts of the ROC leadership to conceal the controversy, Chiang Kai-shek's increasing infirmity intensified anxieties about Taiwan's future.

Meanwhile, the Nationalist regime found it increasingly difficult in the 1970s to suppress opposition rumblings at home and abroad. The most serious threat came from overseas, in the form of the Taiwan Independence Movement (TIM). Many TIM supporters fled Taiwan during the White Terror. They believed Taiwan's only hope for freedom lay in replacing the ROC government with a Taiwanese state with no territorial claim to mainland China. Although the regime maintained intense surveillance of Taiwanese living overseas and did its best to infiltrate TIM groups, suppressing dissidents abroad was far more difficult than repressing – or coopting – them at home.[7] Some TIM activists even used violence to achieve their aims. In 1970, TIM supporters attempted to assassinate Chiang Ching-kuo, then deputy ROC premier, in New York City.[8] Six years later, TIM terrorists orchestrated a series of bombings in Taiwan, including one which seriously injured the ROC vice president.

Repression of Taiwan independence activism was intense; according to Ralph Clough, more Taiwanese were arrested for independence activities than for working on behalf of the PRC.[9] As a result, the independence movement made little headway on the island, where the risks of involvement were daunting. One case that did make headlines was the 1965 arrest of National Taiwan University professor P'eng Ming-min. P'eng was sentenced to eight years in prison for preparing a pro-independence manifesto. He escaped abroad, returning thirty years later to compete in the first direct presidential election. He finished second, with 21 percent of the vote.

Another opposition movement aimed not to overthrow the ROC government, but to weaken the KMT's control. While not advocating independence for Taiwan, at least at first, a growing domestic opposition was committed to fundamental reform of the ROC's political system. The first stirrings of a pro-democracy opposition movement came in the late 1950s, when dissidents assembled by Lei Chen attempted to form the Democratic Party. Their efforts ended in failure; Lei Chen went to prison, the group's magazine closed, its editors and writers dispersed. However, many of the participants in these early efforts went on to play important roles in the opposition movements of the 1970s. This first effort to form a genuine opposition party brought together two groups who had not worked together before: liberal Mainlander intellectuals and local Taiwanese politicians. Despite their many differences, the participants shared the dream of realizing the democratic promise of the ROC constitution. Their strategy was to exert pressure both at the elite level, through their magazine, and at the grassroots, through local elections.

In 1971, a new opposition movement appeared. A brouhaha erupted over the ROC government's weak response to Japan's claim on the Tiaoyutai island chain (known in Japanese as the Senkaku Islands). The islands, which are little more than rocks in the sea between Taiwan and Japan, are a major point of nationalistic pride among both Chinese and Japanese.[10] While reports of potential oil reserves partially explain the preoccupation with the islands, for Chinese, the main motivation for demanding recognition of China's sovereignty is a deep sense of outrage over humiliations meted out by Japan since the 1890s.

One of the loudest voices on the Tiaoyutai issue was *The Intellectual* (*Ta Hsueh*) magazine. The magazine's staff included both liberal Mainlanders and Taiwanese intellectuals. Given that their stance was fundamentally patriotic, President Chiang Ching-kuo tried to establish cooperative relations with the group. However, the magazine's twin accusations of selling out China's sovereign territory to a resurgent Japan and behaving supinely in the face of US pressure stung the KMT. Chiang's efforts to woo the activists broke down when protests over the islands intensified and some in the *Intellectual* group used the journal to criticize the KMT's domestic policies.[11] When Tiaoyutai activists overseas were found to be dallying with PRC-based nationalists, the movement took on an even more subversive edge. The authorities switched to a repressive posture. The *Intellectual* group dissolved, and the Tiaoyutai issue subsided.

The reformist response

The KMT-led regime responded ambivalently to these challenges. On the one hand, it jailed dissidents and shut down publications. Some popular Taiwanese figures, such as Kao Yu-shu, were coopted. On the other hand, however, the regime initiated some political reforms. The first of these responded to several different needs at once. The dwindling number of mainland-elected legislators combined with Taiwan's precarious international status and shaky domestic legitimacy to pressure the KMT leadership to expand representation in the national bodies.[12] In 1966, the National Assembly amended the Temporary Provisions to permit supplementary elections for the National Assembly, Legislative Yuan and Control Yuan (Control Yuan members were chosen indirectly, by the Provincial Assembly). A decade later, Chiang Ching-kuo himself argued that the ROC's legitimacy rested on increasing the number of supplementary parliamentarians. He said, "Our people are unanimous in wanting to have a democratic, constitutional political system. This goal is also our unswerving national mission."[13]

The first supplementary elections took place in 1969, adding 15 KMT representatives to the National Assembly, and 8 KMT members and 3 independents to the Legislative Yuan. These representatives, like their mainland-elected counterparts, were elected to indefinite terms. From 1972 on, supplementary legislators were elected for three years, National Assembly members for five. In 1972, supplementary elections added 53 members to the National Assembly and 36 to the legislature. In addition, the executive branch appointed 15 legislators to represent overseas Chinese. The 1975 supplementary Legislative Yuan election brought in 29 new legislators, including 23 KMT and 6 non-KMT members. The ruling party dominated these early national elections, winning 74 percent of the vote in 1972 and 79 percent three years later. Its successes were due in part to its effective electoral machine. In addition, there simply were very few non-KMT politicians with the resources and stature to mount campaigns for national office who were not in prison or overseas.

A second reform initiative increased opportunities for Taiwanese in the KMT and government. Supplementary national elections intensified the pressure on the KMT to make itself attractive to voters, the vast majority of whom were Taiwanese. In response, Chiang Ching-kuo implemented a Taiwanization policy when he became premier in 1972. While positions in the central government continued to go primarily to Mainlanders (many of the Mainlanders promoted in the 1970s were raised on Taiwan), Chiang brought many more Taiwanese into the leadership at the provincial level and below. He chose a Taiwanese, Hsieh Tung-min, to be the provincial governor, and he promoted the first Taiwanese deputy premier. He also pressed for a more prominent role for Taiwanese in the KMT, more than doubling their representation on the party's Central Standing Committee between 1973 and 1979.

Even in the 1960s, Taiwanization was visible at the grassroots level, where the KMT's electoral strategy dictated a strong role for Taiwanese. Still, the number of Taiwanese in leadership positions in provincial and local government and party organs increased more rapidly after 1972. Among the party rank-and-file, the proportion of Taiwanese grew from 39 percent in 1969 to 46 percent in 1972, and 53 percent in 1977.[14] Taiwanese gained leadership roles in local KMT offices, which increased their influence over nominations for local offices. Taiwanization was significant enough to create a backlash: in the late 1970s, Ralph Clough reported, "Mainlanders are now beginning to complain that the government's policy of increasing the appointment of Taiwanese is reducing their job prospects."[15]

Strengthening the party's foundation in Taiwanese society was an important goal, both because of the heightened importance of elections and because waning US support left the regime without outside reinforcement. A new generation of leaders under Chiang Ching-kuo recognized that the greatest challenge facing the KMT party-state was not mainland recovery, which was no longer a realistic near-term goal, but survival. And the only way to ensure the ROC's survival was to set down roots in Taiwanese soil. Thus, in 1972 Chiang orchestrated a major party reform aimed at easing the KMT away from its authoritarian tendencies. Chiang's reform also strengthened his own position by stacking the KMT leadership with his reform-minded supporters.[16]

In addition to Taiwanization, the 1972 party reforms revitalized the KMT leadership and raised its educational qualifications. They set the stage for the political reforms of the 1980s by encouraging party cadres to measure their success by the KMT's electoral performance. The goal was to make elections a more effective tool for building KMT legitimacy. In pursuit of this goal, the party center took a more active role in local party units' electoral work. The party sought to identify and nominate a new generation of local politicians who would be "younger, better educated, and better qualified" than the political bosses promoted by local factions.[17] After nominating an average of only four non-factional candidates in each of the previous five municipal executive elections, the party nominated twelve such candidates in 1972. And the strategy worked: all twenty of the KMT's nominees won.

The party also modified its electoral goals in 1972. Until the 1970s, the KMT valued elections mainly because they offered a smorgasbord of patronage positions, which could be doled out to Taiwanese to secure their cooperation.. But the 1972 party reforms added a new dimension. While the patronage aspect remained important, the party also began to use election results to evaluate its performance. As KMT party historian Bruce Dickson put it, the party began to use elections as an "institutionalized feedback mechanism" to gauge popular reaction to its policies.[18]

President Chiang Kai-shek died in April of 1975. The struggle to succeed him was not as intense as many had feared because Chiang Ching-kuo's post as premier put him in a strong position to move smoothly into his father's role. Chiang became party chair after his father's death; he assumed the presidency in 1978.

The duet of reform

The regime's response to the challenges of the 1960s and 1970s set the stage for subsequent reforms. Instead of digging in its heels and continuing the hard-line policies of the White Terror years, the regime moderated its positions, in what Edwin Winckler called a shift "from hard to soft authoritarianism."[19] The ROC's leaders, especially Chiang Ching-kuo, had no intention of surrendering power, but neither were they willing to risk international opprobrium, domestic subversion and ideological bankruptcy in order to maintain a system predicated on a war-time emergency that had long since grown routine. The resulting reforms opened a crack in the regime's authoritarian façade. Dissidents hoping to win a larger role for Taiwanese in governing the island took advantage of this opening to push for even more reform. Their goals were the democratization of Taiwan's political system and just treatment of Taiwanese.

Taiwanization, supplementary elections and party reform together constituted a tacit admission that change was needed. By conceding the need for reform, the regime gave the opposition legitimacy. Repressing the KMT's opponents became more difficult, since calls for reform now were coming from within the ruling party itself. As long as dissidents did not violate the state's basic tenets – adherence to the constitution and rejection of communism and Taiwan independence – the government would find it difficult to silence them.

That is not to say, however, that the Nationalists agreed with the opposition's views. Although the kernels of the two sides' positions do not appear far apart – both recognized that Taiwanese should have a greater role to play in government, and both accepted the need for political opening – in practice, they were vastly different. Opposition activists demanded that the ROC implement full constitutional democracy. They also wanted Taiwan itself, and the Taiwanese people, to move to the center of the ROC government's attention.[20] The regime, for its part, insisted that the separation of Taiwan from the rest of China justified emergency provisions that overrode key provisions of the constitution. It also clung to the notion of recovering the mainland, which militated against full democratization and Taiwanization, since allowing Taiwanese to replace Mainlanders in the central government would make it a government of and for Taiwan – not China. Thus, while early reform initiatives came from the regime itself, the pressure exerted by the opposition through elections pushed the KMT leadership to make far deeper and more sweeping changes.

Taiwan's opposition activists developed three forums for propagating their ideas: publications, demonstrations and elections. The first two engaged the KMT regime in a cat-and-mouse game, in which the opposition tested the limits of the government's tolerance; in turn, the regime strove to balance its desire for control against its fear of losing domestic and international favor. Opposition magazines and book series relentlessly challenged the regime's efforts to control debate. When publications went too far, state censors closed them down, only to see them reopen under new titles. Demonstrations were a more dangerous tactic, and the opposition used them more sparingly. The public did not oppose the suppression of marches and rallies; most Taiwanese agreed that these activities threatened public order and stability at a time when Taiwan could ill afford internal weakness. Elections, in contrast, offered the opposition a chance to work within the system to publicize its reformist message and to begin to penetrate the organs of the state. To facilitate its electoral strategy, the opposition moved gradually toward forming a political party.

The cat-and-mouse game ended after a little more than a decade. In September of 1986 the main opposition groups took the final step of organizing a political party, christening it the Democratic Progressive Party (DPP). Instead of moving swiftly to crush the new party, as his father had done with Lei Chen's Democratic Party in 1960, President Chiang

Ching-kuo took no action. A few weeks after the DPP was formed, Chiang announced that he intended to lift martial law very soon.

Elections and reform

From the beginning, elections played an important role in the movement for political reform in Taiwan. As we have seen, Lei Chen's efforts to promote democracy included reaching out to local politicians and involving them in his movement. He recognized that local elections could provide a foundation for a political party capable of contesting national races. Although the regime destroyed Lei and his projects, the idea of using local elections as part of a democratization strategy survived. Throughout the 1960s, individual non-KMT politicians challenged the ruling party for posts in city, county and provincial governments. They built personal followings and cultivated local factions, gathering enough support to defeat KMT machines in some districts. But after the *Free China Fortnightly* disaster local politicians made little effort to organize a joint challenge to the regime. Instead, they concentrated on winning their own races and building their individual bases of support.

Nonetheless, as early as 1973 there were signs that local elections might once again become a forum for organized opposition. In that year, several activists from the *Ta Hsueh* magazine group ran a joint campaign for the Taipei City Council.[21] The first widely noticed effort to organize non-KMT candidates for island-wide electoral combat came in 1977, when Provincial Assembly, municipal executive and municipal council elections took place simultaneously. A pair of independent publisher-activists, Kang Ning-hsiang and Huang Hsin-chieh, spearheaded the unified campaign. They called their collaborators the *Dangwai*. Dangwai, or "outside-the-party", was the same name non-KMT politicians used in 1957, but unlike its predecessor, the Dangwai movement that appeared in 1977 was to make a lasting impression on Taiwan's political landscape.

Turning point: the 1977 elections

As political scientist Chen Ming-tong has argued, the 1977 elections marked a turning point in Taiwan's political development.[22] In that year, a split between the ruling party leadership and local factions created just enough of an opening for the opposition to gain a foothold in electoral politics. The KMT lost 4 municipal executiveships and 21 Provincial Assembly seats (27 percent of the total), 14 of which went to Dangwai candidates. For the first time, elections were a forum in which opposition politicians demonstrated the popularity of their cause. After 1977, the

KMT never recovered its electoral monopoly; it never regained its pre-1977 seat share, and each subsequent contest intensified the pressure for change. From December of 1977 on, the KMT found itself squeezed between its grassroots allies – the local factions – and its adversaries in the opposition.

Dangwai candidates took part in elections around the island, but three races had special importance for the developing opposition movement. Lawyers Chang Chun-hong and Lin Yi-hsiung ran for Provincial Assembly in Nantou and Ilan Counties, respectively. A third important race was the Taoyuan County executive contest. The KMT in Taoyuan had long been split into two local factions, one Hokkien, the other Hakka, making the county difficult to manage politically. The party center pinned its hopes on a Provincial Assembly member named Hsu Hsin-liang. Lee Huan, the head of the KMT's Organization Department and a leading advocate of improving the KMT's electoral work, even invited Hsu to take part in a special training program for promising KMT candidates. But Hsu had ideas of his own. In April 1977 he published *The Sound of the Storm (Fengyu zhi Sheng)* in which he criticized his Provincial Assembly colleagues, angering many. When the KMT passed over him in choosing its county executive nominee, Hsu quit the KMT and joined the race as a Dangwai candidate.

The election results revealed a reservoir of popular support for the opposition and a worrisome rift between the KMT and the local factions on which its electoral strategy depended.[23] The KMT's performance was the worst in history; its candidates won only 64 percent of the popular vote in the Provincial Assembly races, although its superior organization allowed it to translate those votes into nearly three-quarters of the Assembly seats. Chang Chun-hong and Lin Yi-hsiung finished first in their Provincial Assembly races, as did six other non-KMT candidates, and Hsu Hsin-liang was elected Taoyuan County executive. Dangwai candidates also captured the executive posts in Taichung City, Tainan City and Kaohsiung County. Overall, Dangwai candidates won 30 percent of the vote in the executive races. Many ruling parties would welcome such results, but for the KMT, accustomed to winning easily nearly any race it chose to contest, the 1977 election results were an ominous sign.

Even more disturbing was a violent outburst in Taoyuan. When the ballots were opened on 19 November, Hsu Hsin-liang's supporters at a polling station in Chungli City suspected fraud. As the crowd swelled to approximately a thousand, rioting erupted. One protester was killed and the Chungli police station was burned. Some Dangwai figures interpreted this event as evidence that the power of the masses was growing. Others saw it as proof that mass demonstrations were dangerous and should be avoided. According to writer and Dangwai activist Li Hsiao-feng, the incident contributed to a split in the Dangwai between the moderate Kang Ning-hsiang and the more radical Huang Hsin-chieh.[24]

Local factions played a key role in the KMT's disappointing performance. Given the success of the anti-faction nominating strategy it employed in 1972, the ruling party was eager to use the same strategy again. Thus, it nominated non-faction linked candidates for 17 of 21 municipal executive posts. This time, however, the local factions fought back. They recognized that the strategy was designed to put them out of business, and they resisted it. In four municipal executive races, including the inflammatory Taoyuan race, local factions' unwillingness to cooperate with the KMT helped Dangwai candidates win. After 1977, the ruling party no longer entertained dreams of easily dislodging local factions. Instead, fearing the opposition more than rebellious local factions, it abandoned the strategy of replacing factions and resumed its cooperation with them. The percentage of KMT nominees with factional connections rebounded.

The Kaohsiung Incident

Supplementary National Assembly and legislative elections were due in December 1978, and once again the Dangwai prepared a joint strategy to contest them. In November, Huang Hsin-chieh and others formed the Dangwai Organization to Promote Elections. But on 16 December, President Jimmy Carter announced the normalization of relations between the United States and the People's Republic of China. While the ROC government must have anticipated the announcement, its finality sent a shockwave through Taiwan. The island's most powerful friend had abandoned it. The timing of the announcement was especially unfortunate, as it came just days before the election was to be held. The government postponed the election, arguing that Taiwan could not afford instability at such a dangerous juncture. Even some oppositionists, including Kang Ning-hsiang, agreed with this view.

Other Dangwai figures were not convinced. The difference of opinion over the postponement aggravated the split between opposition moderates and radicals, a division which grew more evident over the course of 1979. Yu Teng-fa, the Dangwai-linked Kaohsiung County executive, argued the postponement was unconstitutional and reflected the KMT's martial law mentality.[25] Two days before a planned rally to protest the postponement, Yu was arrested. On 22 January, Dangwai activists gathered to protest the arrests. These activists formed the core of a Dangwai group committed to rapid, thorough-going change. They were called the Formosa faction after their magazine, *Formosa* (*Meilidao*).

The events of 1979 revealed an opposition movement that was divided, but determined to present a united electoral front. The Dangwai announced an island-wide effort to coordinate activities by establishing Dangwai People's Representatives Offices, but in the same period, two separate Dangwai publications appeared. Kang Ning-hsiang launched *The Eighties* (*Bashi Niandai*), which reflected the moderates' emphasis on electoral politics and willingness to work within the system for gradual change. The radical faction, including Hsu Hsin-liang, Huang Hsin-chieh and Provincial Assembly members Chang Chun-hong and Lin Yi-hsiung, began publishing *Formosa*, which took a bold editorial line urging street-level protests to demand rapid reform.

The *Formosa* group's ambitions extended beyond publishing; they hoped to use the magazine as the vehicle for an island-wide quasi-party. In September they opened the first *Formosa* service center in Kaohsiung City. The office took its name from the constituent service offices operated by nearly all politicians in Taiwan. They planned to open twelve centers throughout Taiwan. These centers were to serve as headquarters for demonstrations and grassroots organizing. On 10 December, the *Formosa* group sponsored a rally commemorating International Human Rights Day. The demonstration was held in a square in downtown Kaohsiung City. The thousands of marchers found the exits blocked by riot police. There is no consensus about what happened next, but whether out of panic or premeditation or in response to attacks by police or *agents provocateurs*, violence erupted.

No one was killed in the fighting, which came to be called the Kaohsiung Incident, although there were injuries. Nonetheless, government's reaction was swift and severe. The *Formosa* magazine staff all were arrested, along with other Dangwai leaders and activists. Hsu Hsin-liang, who headed the *Formosa* Magazine Company, was traveling when the demonstration occurred. When the Taiwan authorities issued a warrant for his arrest on charges of conspiring to commit sedition, he received political asylum in the US. Eight *Formosa* staffers were court-martialed on sedition charges; thirty-three other activists faced trial in civilian courts.

If the intent of the crackdown was to deter future dissident activity and strengthen the regime, it did not succeed. The trials provoked a strong reaction from the international human rights community. Amnesty International labeled the defendants prisoners of conscience. *Formosa* general manager Shih Ming-teh, fearing that he would be murdered upon arrest, sought refuge with the head of the Presbyterian Church in Taiwan, Reverend Kao Chun-ming. Because he did not hand over Shih to the authorities Reverend Kao was court-martialed, which outraged religious and human rights organizations worldwide.

The low point of this troubling saga came on 28 February 1980. On the 27th, defendant Lin Yi-hsiung's mother visited him in prison. Seeing evidence of torture, Lin's mother contacted Amnesty International. The following day, she and Lin's 9-year-old twin daughters were viciously murdered in Lin's home. A third daughter was stabbed more than two dozen times, but survived. The crime was never solved, despite the fact that Lin's home was under round-the-clock police surveillance when the murders were committed.

All but three of the Kaohsiung defendants – including all of those court-martialed – were convicted. Shih Ming-teh received a life sentence; the rest were given prison terms of 10 months to 14 years. While most Taiwanese disapproved of *Formosa*-style street politics,[26] the regime's response was, to many, unacceptably brutal. The Lin family murders furthered sullied the government's image. The Kaohsiung Incident's chilling effect on the opposition was short-lived; within a few months, the Dangwai once again was pressing its case for political reform. Indeed, the 1980 election results suggest that the Kaohsiung defendants won the sympathy of a significant minority of Taiwan's electorate. Still, with the Formosa faction in jail, Dangwai moderates played a larger role.

Organizing the Dangwai: 1980–1985

With the crisis of US derecognition behind it, the central government rescheduled the postponed supplementary National Assembly and legislative elections for December 1980. These elections broke new ground in several areas. First, the number of open seats was large (97 in the Assembly and 76 in the legislature), increasing the size of the Legislative Yuan by nearly 25 percent. The large number of supplementary members added in 1980 meant that the Taiwan-elected law-makers could exercise more influence over policy-making than before, especially since they tended to be more active than the senior legislators. Second, the 1980 elections were the first to be held under a new election law that expanded the range of permissible campaign activities and created a relatively independent Central Election Commission. Third, the elections were the first in which the ruling party worked with the opposition to negotiate rules for fair competition. The KMT also did little to deter the Dangwai from running a coordinated campaign.[27]

The issues in the 1980 election set the tone for elections well into the future. The KMT ran on its record. Ruling party candidates took credit for Taiwan's economic progress, its high standard of living and its peaceful, egalitarian society. They also called attention to newly created social programs. At the same time, the ruling party used nominations to reward cooperative local factions. The opposition, for its part, emphasized political issues: eliminating martial law; increasing opportunities for Taiwanese; permitting popular election of the national legislative bodies, provincial governor and Taipei and Kaohsiung mayors. Some Dangwai candidates criticized the KMT's record on economic justice and environmental issues, but these issues provoked little public interest. In short, the key issues for the opposition were democratization and ethnic justice.

The results of the 1980 election were mixed. The KMT captured four-fifths of the seats in each law-making body, giving party-sponsored legislation smooth passage, but its vote share in legislative districts – 72 percent – was below previous norms. Nonetheless, by most standards the KMT's vote share was strong, and its superior organization enabled it to translate its votes into an even larger share of seats. Moreover, many Dangwai candidates, especially those identified with radical positions, lost, and the Dangwai as a whole won only 13 percent of the vote in the legislative election.[28] Moderates and Dangwai politicians associated with local factions did better than the radicals, but not nearly as well as they had hoped.

One Dangwai sub-set scored impressive victories, however. Several wives and attorneys of the Kaohsiung defendants not only were elected, but won the largest share of votes in their districts. These candidates' campaigns tapped voters' emotions; some even broke down and wept during speeches as they decried the injustices meted out to their loved ones. The large vote shares handed to the so-called "Wives and Lawyers Faction" demonstrated the public's sympathy with the Kaohsiung defendants. Even though many voters disagreed with the Formosa group's confrontational political style, they used their votes to notify the authorities that they did not condone the harsh crackdown.[29]

Paradoxically, mobilizational authoritarianism encouraged this protest voting. The Nationalist government so thoroughly insulated ROC institutions from popular pressure that the opposition had no hope of implementing its policy agenda. Even if all the Dangwai candidates had been elected in 1980, the KMT still would have enjoyed an overwhelming majority. Since the Dangwai posed little threat to continued KMT control of the government, voters could choose Dangwai candidates secure in the knowledge that they were not undermining Taiwan's economic and political stability. Meanwhile, the Dangwai itself offered a platform centered on protest issues. Few Dangwai candidates bothered to propose solutions to specific policy problems; instead, they concentrated on criticizing the ROC's undemocratic features and the imbalance between Taiwanese and Mainlanders in the government. In short, the authoritarian character of the regime gave voters freedom to treat elections as plebiscites on two fundamental issues defined by the opposition: democratization and ethnic parity.

The effects of mobilizational authoritarianism are visible in the election results. The Dangwai lost three seats in the Provincial Assembly, and its vote share fell to 28 percent from its 1977 high of 34 percent. At the same time, however, the opposition increased its vote share in executive races from 30 percent to 41 percent, but without gaining any seats. These paradoxical results make sense only in light of Taiwan's peculiar mixture of electoral formulas.

In the executive races, the KMT benefited from the disproportionality inherent in winner-take-all elections. Despite its increased vote share, the Dangwai did not win any additional seats because the new Dangwai voters were too evenly distributed to constitute a majority in any additional municipalities. In contrast, the Provincial Assembly races were not winner-take-all races, but SVMM contests. This formula allows for a more proportional result, but only if the participating parties (or in the case of the Dangwai, proto-parties) are sufficiently well organized to achieve an optimal allocation of the votes available to them. As it turned out, the KMT, with its strong central organization and well-oiled local political machines, was more successful than the opposition at estimating, allocating and mobilizing votes. Thus, the KMT achieved a "seat bonus"; its share of seats (77 percent) exceeded its share of the vote (72 percent). This seat bonus translated directly into a deficit for the Dangwai, which won 28 percent of the vote, but only 23 percent of the contested seats.

The 1981 elections also reveal widespread ticket-splitting. The KMT won 72 percent of the Provincial Assembly vote, but only 59 percent in the executive races. Here again, Taiwan's electoral system played an important role. Mobilizing voters for SVMM elections is easier in smaller districts, so the KMT consistently performs better in lower-level elections (see Figure 5.1). Because the mobilization system is based on personal connections and constituent service, it is most effective in mobilizing small constituencies, where direct contact with a candidate or *tiau-a-ka* is easier to arrange, and constituent service is more manageable.

In large constituencies, candidates must rely on *tiau-a-ka* whose connections are more attenuated, and who therefore are less reliable. The difficulty of providing constituent service also increases with district size, as does the cost of vote buying. Moreover, when voters are distant from candidates, it is less awkward for them to accept money from one candidate, then vote for another. With 21 districts electing 77 Provincial Assembly members, winning a seat requires fewer than a third of the vote

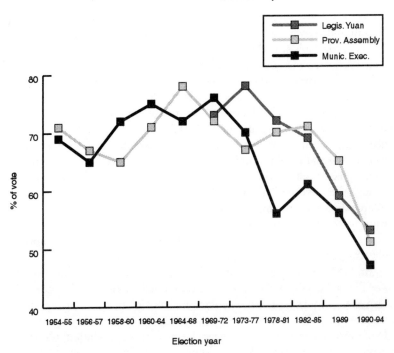

Figure 5.1   KMT performance in local and national elections

Source: Teh-fu Huang, "Elections and the Evolution of the Kuomintang," in Hung-mao Tien, ed., *Taiwan's Electoral Politics and Democratization: Riding the Third Wave*, Armonk, M.E. Sharpe, 1996, p. 109.

in most districts. Where the field of candidates is large, the percentage needed to win is even lower. The chain of *tiau-a-ka* is relatively short. Thus, KMT candidates for Provincial Assembly in 1981 had noticeably better luck mobilizing voters than their comrades seeking executive offices.

On the surface, 1982 was a quiet year on Taiwan. The only elections were at the sub-county level, including township heads and councils, and municipal councils. As usual, the KMT dominated these small-district races. Behind the scenes, however, the conflict among top KMT leaders over who would succeed Chiang Ching-kuo as president was intensifying. To the surprise of most observers, Chiang selected Lee Teng-hui to be his vice president. Lee, a US-educated technocrat, was the appointed Taipei City mayor from 1978 to 1981, when he was tapped as governor of Taiwan

Province. Most noteworthy, under the circumstances, was Lee's ethnic background: Taiwanese.

Lee Teng-hui's selection suggested that reformist leaders in the KMT were beginning to see the party's reputation as a Mainlander redoubt as a liability. The overwhelming success of Taiwanese candidates in elections and the popularity of the Dangwai and KMT Taiwanization strategies appear to have convinced Chiang that Taiwanization even at the highest levels would carry significant political benefits. Nonetheless, many observers initially questioned whether Lee – who was not a KMT heavy-weight – would be able to maintain his position after his patron's death. Thus, anxiety about the succession continued. Some feared a military coup; others worried about a "Chiang Dynasty" with one of Chiang Ching-kuo's sons moving into the top position. President Chiang himself tried to put these fears to rest, promising in late 1985 that no Chiang would succeed him, and that the ROC would never have a military government.

In 1983, facing newly tightened campaign restrictions, Dangwai and KMT candidates prepared for legislative elections. In October, 200 Dangwai candidates agreed on common campaign themes. Their platform attacked the KMT for failing to implement democratic reforms, and for its ineffectiveness in solving such everyday problems as pollution, traffic and economic crimes. According to John Copper, however, "most *tang wai* candidates were unable to offer cogent or realistic solutions other than those already being implemented by the government."[30] The result was that the Dangwai once again centered its campaign on the twin themes of democratization and ethnic justice – although the definition of ethnic justice was beginning to shift from the Taiwanization of the state (in terms of both personnel and priorities) toward self-determination.

Self-determination was, in a sense, a way around the prohibition on Taiwan independence advocacy. Recognizing this, the government banned the word "self-determination" from campaign literature. In another sense, however, self-determination was a genuinely democratic alternative to the hard-line pro-independence approach of the overseas Taiwan Independence Movement. Although self-determination advocates believed that the Taiwanese would choose independence over unification with the PRC (although they could hardly have failed to recognize the preference of most Taiwanese for the status quo), their proposal would not have pre-determined the outcome of the self-determination process.

The KMT, too, adjusted its platform in 1983. Running on its record of economic performance and social stability no longer sufficed. Popular response to the Dangwai's efforts, as demonstrated by its strong perfor-mance in the 1977 elections and the 1980 county executive races, forced the ruling party to justify the slow pace of political reform. The KMT's legislative platform stressed the need for gradualism to forestall economic disruption, social instability (especially disharmony between Mainlanders and Taiwanese) and the PRC threat. But within the leadership, enthusiasm for reform was growing. Even some of Chiang Ching-kuo's closest advisers began to argue that Taiwan needed multi-party politics to check and balance the monopolistic KMT.[31]

As in 1980, the Dangwai's poor organization damaged its electoral performance in 1983. The opposition increased its vote share from 13 percent to 19 percent, but lost three of its nine seats in the Legislative Yuan. The KMT's share of the vote declined from 72 to 69 percent, yet it gained five seats. The ruling party managed this seat bonus largely because its strategy for estimating and allocating votes worked well, while factional disputes plagued its Dangwai opponents. In some districts, the total number of Dangwai votes could have elected two candidates, but a lop-sided distribution left the opposition with only one seat. In other districts, too many Dangwai members contested the elections, and all were defeated. Such was the fate of Dangwai moderate Kang Ning-hsiang.

Once again, the pattern of Dangwai voting suggests that protest voting was widespread. Of the six successful Dangwai candidates, four were either relatives or attorneys of Kaohsiung defendants. Fang Su-min, the wife of Lin Yi-hsiung (and mother of the murdered twins) received the third-largest vote total on the entire island. The second-largest vote total went to the Dangwai's Yu Chen Yueh-ying, daughter-in-law of Yu Teng-fa, the jailed Kaohsiung County executive. On the whole, the Dangwai candidates who won election to the legislature in 1983 were those whose association with major incidents had brought them notoriety. Most moderates, in contrast, did poorly. The Dangwai could not increase its seat share because voters overloaded a handful of Dangwai candidates with protest votes. To gain a foothold in the electoral system the Dangwai needed to make at least three changes. First, it needed to build a loyal grassroots base whose votes could be assigned to less renowned candidates. Second, the opposition needed to master the SVMM system, which meant learning to estimate its support level and allocate its votes effectively. Third, it needed to unify its various strands in order to prevent candidates from undercutting one another in elections – which often meant that *both* Dangwai candidates lost. The Dangwai had three years to learn these lessons before the next national election.

In March 1984 the Dangwai took a major step in this direction: it established a permanent organization, the Dangwai Public Policy Association (later called the Association for Public Policy Research). Previous Dangwai groups had been candidate alliances formed for the purpose of contesting particular elections. They disbanded once each election was over. The new group was designed to provide the Dangwai with a full-time framework for building its grassroots support base and cultivating its leadership.

Toward an opposition party

The KMT's success in 1983 might have allowed it to retreat from reform. The voters were not yet ready to give the Dangwai a significant voice in government, although the strong performance of candidates associated with the Kaohsiung defendants indicated dissatisfaction with the harshest forms of repression. But the ruling party's relief did not last long. Between 1983 and 1986 the KMT suffered a series of embarrassments and setbacks that emboldened the Dangwai movement.[32]

In October 1984, the Taiwanese–American author Henry Liu was gunned down in the driveway of his California home. Under the pen name Chiang Nan, Liu had written an unauthorized biography of Chiang Ching-kuo. Six months later, two agents of the ROC intelligence bureau were charged with hiring a Taiwan-based organized crime gang to carry out the hit. The Henry Liu case hurt the KMT both at home and abroad. Initially, the incident was interpreted as a revenge killing for Liu's unflattering portrayal of President Chiang. Human rights groups in the US decried the murder, adding to the external pressure for reform.[33] As it turns out, Liu was a spy, and the biography probably played little role in his murder. However, this information surfaced too late to spare the Taiwanese government major embarrassment.

In addition to the Henry Liu case, 1985 was a difficult year economically. The island's export-oriented economic strategy seemed to be reaching the limits of its potential; growth was slowing, and investor confidence was weak. Taiwan's GNP grew at less than half the 1984 rate. One reason was growing resentment in the US over Taiwan's trade surplus. The United States was Taiwan's biggest market, so maintaining the existing level of exports was important economically. But Taiwan could not afford to annoy the US. This combination of economic and political dependency made Taiwan especially sensitive to protectionist rumblings in Washington. In addition, Taiwan's strong development and rising standard of living was pricing its workers out of the competition for low-wage manufacturing jobs. If Taiwan was to keep its edge in international markets, it needed to move its economy to a new plane, emphasizing high technology, knowledge-based industry and the service sector.

Taiwan's economic problems were exacerbated by economic scandal.

The government closed a leading financial institution, the Tenth Credit Cooperative, as it teetered on the verge of bankruptcy. The action sparked a financial panic. The scandal spread to the political realm when investors tried to persuade KMT members of the Legislative Yuan to revise Taiwan's banking law to bail out the cooperative. Although the disaster did not bring down other financial institutions, it undermined confidence in Taiwan's economic stability and generated a wave of anger at ruling party officials' complicity in corrupt business dealings.

In November the Dangwai attempted to capitalize on the KMT's difficulties in Provincial Assembly, Taipei and Kaohsiung City council and municipal executive elections. Once again, the SVMM system tripped up the Dangwai in the Provincial Assembly race: although its vote share increased by three percentage points, it did not win any additional seats. As in 1981, the KMT captured more than three-quarters of the total vote in the small Provincial Assembly districts, while the Dangwai won four large-district posts, the municipal executiveships. The opposition's greatest victory came in the Taipei City council election, in which all eleven Dangwai nominees were elected.

After the 1985 elections, preparations for an opposition party accelerated. Founding a party was the natural extension of Dangwai's efforts over the previous decade, but it was a dangerous act. Martial law specifically forbade the creation of new political parties, and there was a real possibility that the regime would disband the party and arrest its leaders. The government already had threatened to arrest activists who set up branch offices of the public policy association. But without a political party, the Dangwai would be forever at a disadvantage, unable to present a permanent, organized façade to activists and voters. And given Taiwan's SVMM electoral system, organization and unity were essential.

At the same time, actions of the ruling party leadership gave the Dangwai cause for hope. At a meeting of the KMT Central Committee in March, President Chiang Ching-kuo raised the possibility of lifting martial law, ending the ban on new political organizations, subjecting the national legislative bodies to re-election and giving local governments greater autonomy. The Central Committee also elected several Taiwanese to the powerful Central Standing Committee, along with leading reform advocate Lee Huan. Lee had been pushed aside after the Chungli Incident of 1977 (Hsu Hsin-liang was his protégé), so his rehabilitation was a good sign for reform. In May, President Chiang facilitated the first direct talks between the Dangwai and the KMT.

Still, Chiang needed to balance his reform efforts with actions aimed at pacifying hard-liners in his government. On the day of the first KMT–Dangwai meeting the Taiwan Garrison Command shut down Kang

Ning-hsiang's magazine, *The Eighties*. In June, a group of leading Dangwai activists went to jail on various political charges. Their sentences were short, but they were timed to prevent the activists from participating in the year-end legislative elections. These defendants organized a series of "farewell rallies" that drew huge crowds; thousands contributed to their legal defense fund. Kang Ning-hsiang, whom several of the jailed leaders had criticized for being too moderate, played a key role in organizing the rallies. Events in the summer of 1986 showed that the momentum was with the opposition and the reformers within the government. A significant fraction of the general public was ready to go into the streets to defend the opposition, and Dangwai leaders of various stripes were willing to work together to push forward their movement.

The birth of the Democratic Progressive Party

Displays of popular support for the Dangwai bolstered the position of reformers within the ruling party. Although they hoped to slow the pace of change and persuade the Dangwai not to form a party, with national elections scheduled for December the KMT could ill afford to appear dictatorial. As Moody put it, "The scandals of 1984 and 1985 meant the KMT had to be on good behavior if it hoped to do well in the elections."[34] Meanwhile, Dangwai demonstrations continued throughout September. Their momentum combined with the regime's conciliatory tone to energize the opposition, and on 28 September Dangwai leaders meeting at the Grand Hotel in Taipei voted to form the Democratic Progressive Party (DPP), with legislator Fei Hsi-ping as its head.

Bolivar Lamounier describes political reform as a "mobile horizon" in which the range of what is possible advances over time. President Chiang's response to the DPP's founding reveals just how much the realm of the possible had altered by the mid-1980s. Instead of rounding up the DPP's organizers and prosecuting them, as the regime did to the Democratic Party in 1960, Chiang's government took no action. And on 7 October, the president made a startling statement to *Washington Post* publisher Katherine Graham. He would, he said, lift martial law as soon as a national security law could be put into place. He also agreed to allow new parties to form, under these conditions: that they respect the ROC constitution and eschew communism and Taiwan independence. DPP organizers, unwilling to make any more concessions than necessary, did not officially accept these requirements, but the new party abided by them in practice.[35]

The DPP continued the Dangwai themes of democratic reform and "Taiwan for the Taiwanese," but these positions were evolving subtly. In particular, the early Dangwai demand for "Taiwanization" of the ROC state and ethnic parity between Taiwanese and Mainlanders lost much of its appeal as the KMT's own Taiwanization efforts matured. While some opposition supporters continued to harbor bitter resentment of Mainlanders well into the 1990s, the selection of a Taiwanese president defused the opposition's claim that Taiwanese could not advance under the KMT. Rather than disappearing altogether, however, the Dangwai's Taiwanization plank gradually gave way to the closely related issue of self-determination. Later, in the early 1990s, self-determination gave way to an outright call for Taiwan independence. In short, while remnants of the raw ethnic politics that motivated the opposition in the early days remained, the focus of the DPP's energy shifted toward resisting pressure for unification with mainland China.

The 1986 National Assembly and Legislative Yuan elections were the first true two-party contests in Taiwan's history. The DPP reiterated the traditional Dangwai demands for political reform, including freedom of expression and fewer campaign restrictions. The KMT emphasized the need for caution to preserve order and national security. On the issues closest to the voters' hearts – traffic, crime and the environment – neither party offered much in the way of concrete solutions.[36] Despite the strict campaign regulations imposed in the Election and Recall law, the campaign was freewheeling. DPP candidates ignored prohibitions on joint campaign appearances and candidates of both parties began their electioneering before the official start date. Accusations of fraud and dirty tricks were commonplace.

The election results show that the opposition benefited from its newly created party structure. The DPP chose a 7-member nominating committee to select its candidates and coordinate its electoral strategy, giving rise to a better performance than any the Dangwai had managed. More than half the DPP's nominees were successful, and the party gained seats in both national bodies. In the Legislative Yuan, the KMT lost 3 seats, while the DPP gained 5; both parties picked up seats from independents in the National Assembly, 7 for the KMT and 8 for the DPP. Still, while the DPP did better than its predecessor, the KMT's campaign coordination still far surpassed the opposition's. If we exclude the functional constituencies, which the ruling party dominated completely, the KMT won a 5 percent seat bonus (it got 72 percent of the contested seats with 67 percent of the vote). The DPP, for its part, captured 33 percent of the popular vote, but only 21 percent of the seats.

The four top vote-getters all were DPP nominees. Their extraordinary success had both positive and negative implications for the new party. On the one hand, it showed that some DPP candidates enjoyed tremendous popular support. On the other hand, it revealed that the new party still could not allocate its votes evenly enough to elect more than one candidate per district. Protest voting certainly played a role in the DPP's success; many voters chose DPP candidates as a way of demonstrating support for multi-party competition. Nonetheless, the election was a victory for pragmatists in both parties; moderates (including the DPP's Kang Ning-hsiang) made a comeback, while ideological candidates generally did poorly.

The DPP and KMT competed ferociously in 1986. But despite some tense moments, the reformist trajectory of Taiwan politics was unmistakable. Since 1977, the opposition had made clear its determination to test the limits of the regime's tolerance. Opposition magazines published intentionally provocative articles, and when the Taiwan Garrison Command closed them, they reopened under new names. Dangwai politicians joined together to contest elections, and even before the ban was lifted, they created a political party. The ruling party, for its part, steadily recalibrated the balance between repression and reform. Persecution and repression gave way to toleration and competition. Instead of cracking down on the newly formed DPP, President Chiang Ching-kuo gave in to its most fundamental demand: ending martial law.

Lifting martial law

Chiang Ching-kuo announced his intention to lift martial law in the fall of 1986, but actually rescinding the emergency provisions required legislative action that carried over into 1987. The rationale for martial law was national security, and the ruling party (and much of the general public) still believed that Taiwan's security situation was tenuous and special protections were necessary. Thus, the spring of 1987 was devoted to passing a national security law. The opposition fought the bill in the legislature and in the streets, and its legislators boycotted the final vote. But the DPP could not block the bill's passage, only delay it. The legislation passed on 23 June 1987. President Chiang Ching-kuo ordered martial law lifted as of 15 July.

Lifting martial had important implications for civil rights. It removed most restrictions on parades and assemblies, so long as they did not advocate communism, Taiwan independence or overthrowing the constitution. It transferred supervision of mass media from a military unit, the Taiwan Garrison Command, to a branch of the Executive Yuan, the Government Information Office. While this was a positive change for civil liberties, it did not entirely resolve the problems of Taiwan's mass media. Shifting censorship to the GIO did not eliminate the practice. Finally, while the limit on newspaper licenses was rescinded along with martial law, the GIO did not expand television broadcasting privileges, leaving the three KMT-linked TV stations with a monopoly.

With martial law lifted, routine censorship was impossible to justify on military grounds.[37] Thus, in January of 1988, the government lifted the ban on new newspaper licenses. Scores of start-ups flooded the market, and although many soon disappeared, they failed for economic, not political, reasons. The opposition jumped into the newspaper business with the *Capital Daily* (*Shoudu Ribao*), published by Kang Ning-hsiang. Taiwan's media market is extraordinarily strong, with about 70 percent of Taiwan residents reading at least one newspaper each day.[38] Nonetheless, the market was not big enough to absorb the huge influx of new publications that appeared between 1988 and 1990. *Capital Daily* folded in the face of tough competition for readers and advertisers. Not all the new outlets failed, however. The thirty-odd papers that were in business before the market opened up remained the most profitable, but in mid-1996, 360 papers had at least a nominal presence in the Taiwan market.[39]

The end of martial law also brought an end to the ban on new political parties. Because the new rules were not retroactive, the DPP technically was still illegal. But no one had a stomach for suppressing the party, and it achieved legal status a few months later. With the end of the ban, a huge number and variety of parties registered, including the Labor Party, the Workers Party, the Social Democratic Party and the Green Party. Despite the enthusiasm of their founders, no third party made significant political inroads until the Chinese New Party was founded in 1993. Only a handful of these parties were able even to run candidates for office; of these, the few who managed to be elected to public office were either in very large districts or were able to tap the candidates' pre-existing personal support networks.

Another consequence of martial law's end was the Executive Yuan's decision in October 1987 to lift the ban on travel to mainland China. At first, permission was limited to people visiting relatives. However, the enormous response to the new policy forced the government to issue permits to more categories of Taiwanese. Neither direct travel nor investment were permitted; Taiwanese traveled to the PRC through third countries (mainly Hong Kong). Nonetheless, many Taiwanese businesspeople ignored the rules and used the opportunity to travel to set up manufacturing plants and export businesses on the mainland. In the decade between 1987 and 1997, Taiwan's trade with the mainland grew to US$22.53 billion.[40]

With an opposition party contesting elections and martial law cast away, politics in Taiwan lost much of its authoritarian quality. The DPP gave the opposition a coherent structure for contesting elections and a unified voice in government. The end of censorship meant the KMT's opponents no longer needed to skirt the law to be heard. Increasingly, non-KMT political forces asserted themselves through institutionalized channels. Nonetheless, significant restrictions on democracy remained. Most importantly, the presence of the senior parliamentarians ensured that the KMT would continue to control policy-making at the national level, no matter how successful the DPP might be in elections. Meanwhile, Taiwan's peculiar electoral system rewarded the KMT's strong organization and grassroots base with large majorities in each election, reassuring its leaders that the ruling party could move forward with electoral reform without risking its dominant position.

After nearly twenty years as the dominant force in ROC politics, President Chiang Ching-kuo died in early 1988. His leadership was decisive in shaping the government's responses to the challenges facing Taiwan in those two decades; his legacy was to play an equally important role in the years to come.

6 The watershed elections of 1989

When Chiang Ching-kuo died in January 1988, Taiwan was a very different place than it had been when he assumed the presidency a decade earlier. Political parties competed for elected offices ranging from village head to national legislator. With martial law lifted, the civilian courts operated freely, without military interference (although political interference was a continuing problem). Newspapers opened at will, and published nearly anything they liked. But if Chiang had imagined that these changes would quiet the voices crying out for reform, he was mistaken. Opposition activists still were dissatisfied. Instead of winning their support, the reforms of the 1980s whetted their appetite for even deeper reform.

At the close of the decade, the DPP was demanding that the senior legislators be retired, and new legislative bodies chosen in comprehensive general elections. These elections, DPP activists said, should be conducted without special privileges for ruling party candidates; government employees should not take part in campaigns, vote buying should be prosecuted and campaign restrictions that put opposition parties at a disadvantage should be removed. The DPP also wanted the state to relinquish its monopoly on television and radio broadcasting. And it proposed profound revisions to the ROC constitution that would refocus the state's mission toward the island of Taiwan itself and de-emphasize the goal of mainland recovery.

There is no question that reformers within the Nationalist government made substantial progress during Chiang's presidency. But liberalization remained controversial. Chiang Ching-kuo's crown-prince status, political savvy and charisma gave him the strength to open some windows in the ROC's authoritarian façade. But his successor, Lee Teng-hui, was not so well endowed. Immediately after Chiang's death, many observers predicted Lee would be unable to consolidate his position as head of the ROC state and the Nationalist Party. Indeed, his opponents were quick to strike. After President Chiang's death in January 1988, conservatives in the KMT leadership moved to prevent Lee from becoming the ruling party head. They attempted to impose a collective interim leadership, which would have weakened his position.

In the end, however, Lee Teng-hui hung onto both the presidency and the party chairmanship. The July 1990 party congress confirmed Lee as KMT chair and elected a new Central Committee. The top ten finishers were all either Taiwanese or reformers; no hard-line Mainlander finished near the top of the Central Committee voting.[1] The proportion of Taiwanese nearly doubled, from 20 percent to 38 percent, and Taiwanese captured a majority of seats on the all-important Central Standing Committee.

Lee used reform initiatives to increase his own popularity with voters, skillfully constructing a platform of public support from which to do battle with hard-liners. Lee's government advanced the reform program with two legislative initiatives in early 1989. In January, the Legislative Yuan passed the Law on the Organization of Civil Groups. The law set the ground rules for multi-party competition. Before the end of the year, more than fifty parties had registered with the government. None of them, however, was able to challenge the KMT and DPP. Taiwan's SVMM elections allow small but dedicated groups to win seats, but even so, only a handful of the new parties (mainly the Labor Party and the Chinese Social Democratic Party) won even a single seat. The second major reform was the Law on the Voluntary Retirement of Senior Parliamentarians. This bill offered mainland-elected legislators and National Assembly members generous compensation to step down. Unfortunately, few senior legislators were interested in taking up the offer, which contained carrots but no sticks.

The effort to dislodge the senior parliamentarians foundered on a basic conundrum of politics: how can a sitting legislature be made to vote itself out of office? The authority to force the senior parliamentarians to retire lay with the National Assembly and the Legislative Yuan, both of which were dominated by the senior parliamentarians themselves. But keeping the seniors in office was unsupportable politically. The DPP's relentless criticism of the "ten-thousand year legislators" and "old bandits" struck a chord with the public. According to a 1987 survey, more than half of Taiwanese favored a comprehensive general election, while fewer than a third opposed it.[2] The aging legislators were an embarrassment, to be sure (some had to be brought on hospital gurneys to cast important votes), but more importantly, they represented an immovable obstacle to democracy. Even if the DPP won every seat in the 1989 supplementary election, the KMT-affiliated senior legislators still would enjoy a large majority in the

Legislative Yuan. The make-up of the legislature was so transparently unfair, irrational and undemocratic that the KMT's top leaders could not defend it. But neither could they persuade the legislators to retire, and forcing them to do so would have torn the KMT apart, for party conservatives insisted that the ROC framework required the presence of mainland representatives in the parliamentary bodies. The DPP exploited the KMT's weakness on this issue, making it a central plank in its platform for the 1989 elections.

Primary elections

It was against this backdrop that three normally staggered electoral cycles fell into synch in 1989. In December, voters went to the polls to select municipal executives, supplementary members of the Legislative Yuan and members of the Provincial Assembly and Taipei and Kaohsiung city councils. The 1989 three-way elections were a milestone in Taiwan's reform process. They were the first in which multiple political parties contended for power, and they occurred in the midst of a transition from the old, martial law era rules to a new set of procedures and regulations. Although individual independents and the Dangwai had challenged the KMT in previous elections, the 1989 elections presented the ruling party with the most competitive situation it had ever faced. To maintain its dominant position in electoral politics, the ruling party would need to appeal to undecided voters and also deploy its mobilizational networks effectively. In the event, attaining these goals proved difficult, and the election results disappointed the KMT leadership. The 1989 elections demonstrated that political patterns established under mobilizational authoritarianism could work against the ruling party as well as for it.

Candidates representing 39 parties and many independents joined the fray, but the KMT and DPP were the only significant organized players.[3] The two parties fielded more than 70 percent of the candidates and together captured more than 86 percent of the vote.[4] The process by which they selected their candidates was new, however. Both major parties introduced primary elections as an important component of their candidate selection processes in 1989. The KMT began experimenting with polling party members as part of its nominating process in the early 1980s.[5] In 1983, the party center used the results of this research, the "Report on Party Members' Opinions," as background information in its Legislative Yuan nominations. In March of 1989, KMT Organization Department head Kuan Chung proposed to the Central Standing Committee that the party move the primary election to the foreground of the nominating process in order to accommodate the effects of "social pluralization."[6] The CSC approved the proposal on 1 April, and the primary election was scheduled for 23 July.

The ruling party's motives for instituting primary elections were complex. At the simplest level, primary elections helped refute accusations that the KMT was undemocratic. This was the rationale offered most energetically to the public, and it reveals the extent to which popular pressure for democratization was driving KMT policy choices. At the same time, party leaders hoped that primary elections would give KMT candidates a jumpstart on the general election campaign, helping them to articulate positions and gain name recognition months before the general election campaign officially began. But most importantly, the primary election was designed to promote party unity. Writes Yang Tai-shuenn,

> Social pluralization, along with the weakening of the authoritarian system, forced the party to search for a non-traditional way of bringing about unity. And the appearance of multi-party competition in the post-martial law era increased the urgency and importance of that unity. The party saw primary elections as a good way to achieve this urgent goal.[7]

Kuan Chung and his supporters believed party primaries would inspire better cooperation between local factions and the party center. Bringing local factions under party supervision (and thereby reducing their influence) was a long-standing KMT objective.[8] Although factions were a fundamental component of the KMT's mobilization system, providing much-needed networks of *tiau-a-ka* and voters, they also were unruly, self-interested and unpredictable, and the candidates they presented often lacked the educational credentials and social graces the ruling party wanted voters to associate with the KMT label. In 1977 the party center used its municipal executive and Provincial Assembly nominations to ease factions aside. But instead of an affirmation of good government candidates, the elections turned into a rebellion of local factions. The party was again forced to abandon the faction-replacement strategy.[9]

Before the appearance of an organized opposition, local KMT officials were in a strong position relative to local factions. KMT nominees were virtually assured of winning, and as long as a local faction cooperated with its party branch, it knew it would soon enjoy the spoils of victory. But the Dangwai's growing strength destabilized this dynamic. Opposition candidates played havoc with the KMT's mobilizational strategy; they made estimating and allocating the party's vote share far more difficult. In response, KMT nominees were tempted to poach votes from one another to ensure their own victories. Local cadres found it ever more difficult to persuade the candidates to cooperate, and success rates for KMT nominees fell further.

Primary elections offered a new approach to the old problem of bringing local factions to heel. As Chen Ming-tong writes,

> Before the institution of the primary system, party members typically took a quarter of the vote, with the other three-quarters allocated among local faction candidates. Because the KMT could not directly control three-quarters of the vote, it had to win indirectly through local factions. But using the party primary system, the KMT could require local factions to bring its members into the party if they wanted to win nominations. Once these candidates were incorporated into the party structure, the KMT could direct them according to its interest.[10]

Moreover, the technical details of the primary system worked to the advantage of party leaders – both national and local. According to rules handed down by the Organization Department, only in districts in which turn-out exceeded 50 percent of party members would the primary election results constitute the "foundation" of the nomination decision; elsewhere, the results would, as before, serve as advisory or background information. As it turned out, only about a third of the districts managed to meet the 50 percent turnout standard. Thus, party leaders enjoyed both the public relations benefits of having organized a primary, and the freedom, in practice, to name the candidates. Also, because the election was so hastily arranged, local cadres enjoyed much more influence than supporters of a fully democratic process would have liked.

Overall, KMT leaders' efforts to use the primary election to promote unity had little success, especially in the zero-sum municipal executive races. While the SVMM contests allowed for all factions to be represented on the party ticket, the executive races pitted local factions against one another in direct competition. Factions made their presence felt in the primaries as well as the general election. Personal and factional networks were many candidates' major resource for attracting primary votes; some even resorted to vote buying.[11] Many would-be KMT nominees accused the party of predetermining the outcome of certain races according to a secret "personnel selection plan" (*guihua renxuan*), either by forcing certain participants to withdraw, or by manipulating the balloting. At least two incumbent municipal executives declined to seek re-election because they believed they would not receive fair treatment.[12]

As a result, KMT candidates cooperated even less effectively in 1989

than they had in previous elections.[13] As political scientist Wu Wen-
ch'eng put it,

> Behind the scenes in the primary election, some local factions
> seemed to become even more divided, and the factions' power
> appeared even more strongly. Thus, some people criticized the
> primary election, saying that it not only failed to unify and harmonize
> party strength, but actually damaged party unity and harmony.[14]

To make matters worse, the primary set candidates in the multi-
member legislative and Provincial Assembly elections at one another's
throats even before the general election campaign began. This, combined
with the destabilizing effect of an organized opposition on the KMT's vote
allocation effort, exacerbated the tendency toward intra-party conflict in
the general election. Also, well-organized groups within the KMT, especially the "iron ballot constituencies" such as retired servicemen and their
families, exerted disproportionate influence in the primary election.[15]
Because these groups were not representative of the general electorate,
the slates they chose often were unelectable. For example, in Taipei's
northern legislative district, all five top-finishing primary candidates were
Mainlanders, forcing the party leadership to choose between losing seats
in the general election and rejecting candidates selected by its most loyal
supporters. In the end, the KMT nominated, on average, 86 percent of
the primary front runners in the legislative, executive, Provincial
Assembly and city council elections held in 1989.[16]

The DPP's primary, which was held on the same day, suffered from
some of the same difficulties as the KMT's. The opposition party
compounded its troubles by declaring the primary results determinative.
This effort to out-democratize the KMT complicated the party's efforts to
nominate strategically. The well-organized New Tide faction, which took
more radical positions on most issues than the party mainstream, placed
several candidates of marginal electability on the party's general election
ticket. The candidate-oriented voting behavior that characterizes
Taiwan's general elections also played a role in the DPP primary.
Candidates with large personal followings but little influence at the party
center enrolled large numbers of their supporters in the DPP just before
the primary (earning them the moniker "paper members"); some even
were accused of buying votes. These abuses weakened the DPP's credibility when it tried to attack the KMT for similar offenses in the
December election.

Platforms and campaigns

As usual, the KMT's campaign emphasized its economic accomplishments and long experience as the governing party. The party reiterated its opposition to independence, while at the same time offering progress on democratization.[17] The platform also promised to enhance the Legislative Yuan's policy-making role, promote the rule of law and improve social welfare.[18] For its part, the DPP continued to emphasize democratization. According to Copper,

> The DPP's main tactic was to make the electorate believe that, in order for Taiwan to become democratic, the public must support the DPP. In short, a DPP victory – or even a better performance in the election – would signify that the elections had been competitive and therefore that political modernization was taking Taiwan in the direction of democracy.[19]

The second item on the opposition's ideological agenda had shifted by 1989, from equity for the Taiwanese to the question of national identity. On this, the DPP was divided. In its policy proposals, the party promised to work within the existing structure of government to "thoroughly revise the constitution in accordance with current realities, and create a new situation in Taiwan."[20] The New Tide faction rejected this approach, however, and in its own statement of principles called for bringing about independence by "using peaceful methods to carry out the ratification of a new constitution by the Taiwanese people, electing a new National Assembly and creating a new state."[21]

Both of these issues enjoyed some popular support. In a post-election survey, among Taipei City voters who were willing to reveal their votes in the legislative race, 44 percent said they agreed with the DPP's position on direct presidential elections and 32 percent said they agreed with the opposition party on the independence issue. This was good news for the DPP, but other survey results were less favorable. For example, fewer than 10 percent of the respondents expressed a preference for the DPP as a party. Even worse, support for the DPP on issues did not necessarily translate into votes for the party's candidates. More than two-thirds of those who said they agreed with the DPP's stance on the issues said they had voted for KMT candidates. The KMT's supporters were much more solid: more than 92 percent of those who agreed with its positions voted for its candidates.[22]

The campaign season was lively and intense, attracting strong interest throughout Taiwanese society. As usual, candidates stretched the campaign rules to their limits and beyond. Candidates of all stripes accused their opponents of unfair play, while dissidents from abroad provided added excitement. In September, the exiled Taoyuan County Executive Hsu Hsin-liang managed to sneak into Taiwan. He arrived on a fishing boat, demanding to be tried for his "crimes" in connection with the Kaohsiung Incident. In November, the head of the illegal World United Formosans for Independence appeared at a DPP campaign rally. When police tried to capture him, he and hundreds of his supporters put on identical black masks, allowing him to escape in the confusion. One particularly entertaining (although ultimately unsuccessful) candidate was the Labor Party's legislative nominee in Kaohsiung City, performance artist Hsu Shao-tan. Hsu used nudity to illustrate her dream of a pure and natural political culture in Taiwan. She drew large crowds, although her political ideas may not have been the main attraction. At one point in the campaign, one of her male opponents responded to her "breast power" boasts by insisting that his "one long thing" (*yitiao*) would defeat her "two points" (*liangdian*).

Election results

In the end, most commentators labeled the election a step forward for democracy and a set-back for the ruling party. Turnout for the election was over 75 percent, the highest in a decade. The KMT continued to hold significant majorities in the legislature and the Provincial Assembly, and maintained control of two-thirds of Taiwan's municipal governments. However, both its seat and vote shares fell below historical standards and the party's own expectations. The KMT's share of elected seats in the Legislative Yuan fell from 77 to 71 percent. In the Provincial Assembly, the KMT's seat share declined from 81 to 70 percent, and it lost 3 more municipal executiveships, leaving it with 14 of the 21 posts. The DPP gained 9 seats in the legislature, nearly doubling its representation to 21 seats. The DPP also captured 6 municipal executiveships; the one independent executive elected had ties to the opposition. In the Taipei and Kaohsiung City Council elections, the DPP won 27 percent and 19 percent of the seats, respectively. In Kaohsiung, another 14 percent of the successful council candidates were independents.

The DPP's successes in the local races were especially important. First, the opposition won the executive seats with a plurality of the vote in direct, party-to-party competition, making it impossible for the KMT to blame its loss on strategic errors. Second, the municipalities the DPP captured in 1989 were among the most important in Taiwan. Taipei County, the largest municipality under a popularly elected executive, chose Kaohsiung Incident defense attorney You Ching. Another very large county, Kaohsiung, gave a clean sweep to the DPP-affiliated Black faction: Yu Teng-fa's daughter-in-law Yu Chen Yueh-ying was elected county executive, her son Yu Cheng-hsien was sent to the Legislative Yuan and her daughter Yu Ling-ya won a seat in the Provincial Assembly. Third, municipal executiveships offered the DPP an opportunity to demonstrate its ability to govern. Success in these posts would help put to rest the argument that the DPP was useful only as a Japanese-style "permanent opposition," good for tweaking the KMT, but unlikely to gain power. Finally, municipal executives are more powerful than legislators or Provincial Assembly members; they offered the DPP its best chance to make an impression on public policy.[23]

The KMT lost votes as well as seats in 1989. In the Legislative Yuan's geographical constituencies, the ruling party captured 60 percent of the popular vote, down from 67 percent in 1986, while the DPP's share increased from the 25 percent won by Dangwai candidates in 1986 to 30 percent. The DPP made a more startling gain in the functional constituencies, a traditional KMT stronghold. From 7 percent in 1986, the DPP's share rose to 20 percent. This was due primarily to a mutiny of voters in the labor constituency, who, for the first time ever, rejected the KMT's nominees, many believing them to be party hacks with no interest in Taiwan's workers. In the municipal executive races, the DPP won 38 percent of the vote (Dangwai candidates captured 14 percent in 1985), to the KMT's 53 percent (61 percent in 1985) – this despite the fact that the DPP did not offer candidates in 4 of the 21 municipalities. As usual, the KMT did better in the Provincial Assembly races, winning 62 percent of the vote and 70 percent of the seats.

The strong performances of several DPP candidates should not obscure the fact that the party itself was in a very weak position in 1989. A province-wide survey of Legislative Yuan voters found very little support for the DPP as an organization. Most voters expressed no preference for either political party, but among those who did have an opinion, the KMT was the clear winner: 35 percent said they liked the KMT and 10 percent disliked it, whereas only 9 percent liked the DPP, and 32 percent said they disliked it.[24] These preferences were rooted in the voters' perceptions of the two parties' stances on issues. The research team gave each respondent a list of issue statements, then asked him or her to choose those that described the positions of the two parties. The state- ments associated most often with the KMT were strongly positive: "stands for unification" (56 percent of respondents chose this statement), "is moderately reformist" (44 percent), "pushes for democracy" (38 percent), "has sole governing power" (28 percent), and "fights for freedom and human rights" (26 percent). The voters' associations with the DPP, in contrast, were more (although not entirely) negative: "tends toward violence" (50 percent), stands for Taiwan independence (33 percent), "emphasizes the representation of Taiwanese" (32 percent), "lacks governing authority" (26 percent), "opposes political privilege" (22 percent).[25] It is interesting to note that of the two issues at the center of the DPP's self-image, democratization and national identity, only the latter was associated with the party in the minds of voters. Indeed, voters were more likely to see the KMT as the party of democratization and reform. Clearly, the DPP's message was reaching voters only intermittently; the successes of 1989 belong more to the party's candidates than to the party itself.

Because so much was at stake and so much was new in 1989, the three-way elections provide a snapshot illustrating the progress of Taiwan's political reform. Given the presence of an opposition party, along with the newly liberalized election rules and democratic nominating procedures, standard political science hypotheses about democratizing states would predict significant changes in the conduct of the elections. And indeed, the 1989 elections were different in many ways from previous races. Nonetheless, the peculiarities of Taiwan's political system that we identified in Chapter 4 – personalistic voting, local factionalism, *tiau-a-ka* mobilization – continued to play a decisive role in 1989.

The 1989 elections and political reform

Some of the most powerful hypotheses about democratization come from modernization theory. According to this school of thought, social and economic trends associated with modernization (industrialization, improved communications, urbanization, rising standards of living, the development of a middle class) combine to create pressure for political change. As people move from a life of bare subsistence to one of middle-class comfort, their willingness to be ordered about by an authoritarian state declines. A modern economy diminishes citizens' dependence on the state, while improved access to education and information makes citizens aware of their relationship to the state and helps them imagine how it might be different. And it gives them confidence and resources to band together to change the situation.

In a general sense, modernization theory has much to offer students of Taiwan's reform process. Many leading democracy advocates fit the theory's description of well-educated, middle-class individuals frustrated with what they perceived as a backward, heavy-handed and unresponsive regime. But the 1989 elections showed that modernization theory was not a perfect match for Taiwan's experience.[26] The political changes underway in Taiwan had not changed the behavior of most Taiwanese. Party identification and issue-based voting were the exception, clientelism was the norm.

Historically, evidence for the modernization hypothesis has been weak in Taiwan. In a study of the 1980, 1983 and 1986 supplementary legislative elections, Ting T'ing-yu found significant correlations between the KMT's vote share and several variables related to modernization. But when he broke the data down more finely, Lin Chia-lung found no significant difference between KMT and Dangwai voters in terms of social class, whether measured by income or by subjective self-identification.[27] Lin did find significant differences among occupational groups.[28] These findings gain support from a study by Hu Fu and Chu Yun-han, who found that "KMT candidates drew relatively more votes from state employees, farmers, and housewives and retirees ... whereas DPP candidates gained *relatively* more support among the middle class, the business class and the working class."[29]

Ting, Lin, Hu and Chu agree that another variable, one which falls entirely outside the modernization model, was more important than socioeconomic factors in determining voting behavior: ethnicity. Not surprisingly, Ting found that predominantly Mainlander communities gave more of their votes to KMT candidates than Taiwanese communities. What was more striking was his finding that KMT vote shares in predominantly Mainlander areas increased with the level of socioeconomic development. That is, "Although by itself, high socio-economic development hurts the KMT, in neighborhoods and villages with high Mainlander population, it actually benefits the KMT."[30]

These studies describe a society in which support for the KMT "is not defined by capitalist production relations but by state power."[31] In other words, a social sector's loyalty to the ruling party reflects the degree to which that population is integrated into the KMT's party-state and its mobilizational networks. As we have seen, farmers are knitted into the mobilization system with several threads: the Farmers' Associations, the *tiau-a-ka* system and local factions. Public employees and soldiers are among the KMT's well-integrated "iron ballots" constituencies. Lin found that even workers were only weakly identified with the Dangwai, in part because their membership in state-sponsored corporatist labor unions kept most within the mobilization system's reach. Only independent entrepreneurs, of all of these groups, exist outside the KMT's mobilizational networks – and even they are not immune to the appeal of *tiau-a-ka*. This was true in 1989 as well as in earlier elections.

The absence of a socio-economic basis for the two parties' support is easier to understand when we recall that few Taiwanese select candidates for their party affiliation or issues stances. On the contrary, for most Taiwanese, the most important factor in choosing a candidate is the candidate's personal characteristics. Hsu Huo-yan analyzed data about voting choice in the 1989 legislative election, and found that, while voters were beginning to "develop images and preferences about them," the attachments voters had to parties were not strong enough to qualify as "party identification."[32] Indeed, voters' opinions of the parties were remarkably weak.[33] Most voters had no opinion about either of the major parties. When asked whether they liked or disliked the KMT, 55 percent answered "neither" or "don't know." For the DPP, the figure was 59 percent. Moreover, a significant number of respondents felt similarly toward both parties. Of the respondents who either liked or disliked at least one party, almost a fifth liked or disliked *both* parties.[34] In other words, they did not see the parties as occupying clear-cut, alternative positions. Finally, voters who did hold strong opinions about the parties did not necessarily vote according to their preferences. As Hsu put it,

> Voters who do not identify with or do not like the KMT do not necessarily vote for the DPP. However, loyal KMT *voters* are extremely likely to dislike the DPP. That is, the KMT has a base of iron votes, but the DPP's votes for the most part are floating or unaffiliated votes.[35]

Further evidence for the weakness of party identification as a factor in the 1989 elections comes from the widespread split-ticket voting that characterized the three-way competition. If voters were motivated by party loyalty, we would expect each party's vote share to be similar in each of the three simultaneous elections. For example, the DPP won 49 percent of the vote in the Taipei County executive race, but only 25 percent of the legislative vote. This kind of split-ticket voting was extremely widespread. The average difference between DPP's executive and legislative vote share in Taiwan's 21 municipalities was 17 percent; the discrepancy exceeded 10 percent in all but 6 municipalities. Nor did the gap between executive and legislative voting consistently fall on one side. In 13 municipalities, the DPP's executive vote share was larger than its legislative vote share, but in the other 8, the two were reversed. As Yang Tai-shuenn puts it, this ubiquitous and unpredictable ticket-splitting "clearly reflects a situation in which voters' orientation is toward 'choosing a person', not 'choosing a party.'"[36]

Mobilization in the 1989 elections

If candidate-oriented voting was the most widespread style of voting behavior in the 1989 elections, Taiwan's long-standing system of electoral clientelism played a major role in attracting those candidate-oriented votes. Candidates relied heavily on *tiau-a-ka* and local factions to bring out the votes they needed. In fact, because the elections were more competitive than usual, candidates invested even more heavily in their clientelistic networks. Two aspects of the 1989 elections demonstrate the importance of clientelistic mobilization especially well: the prevalence of vote buying, and the role of local factions.

Until the mid-1980s, KMT electoral strategy rested on the assumption that the pool of KMT votes was stable. As more and more opposition and maverick candidates defeated KMT nominees, this assumption lost its validity. Distrustful of a party strategy that could no longer guarantee their success, KMT candidates took to stealing votes from one another. It was no longer unheard of for voters to receive payments from several candidates for the same office. In 1989, most campaign activists and election observers agreed, a candidate could expect to receive only two votes for every ten "purchased." Obviously, buying votes is an expensive way to get a small number of votes. Why, then, would candidates risk prosecution by continuing? Vote buying gets a candidate's vote broker in the door, establishing the possibility of a vote. As Yang Tai-shuenn put it, "Candidates are not so naïve as to believe that votes are guaranteed as money changes hands. But vote-buying helps voters narrow their selection list. The money buys an opportunity of being compared with other candidates."[37]

Reports of vote buying were ubiquitous in 1989. The independent (but DPP-leaning) Clean Election Coalition collected these accusations in a report published by the Twenty-first Century Foundation. The report gave the prices of votes in various races, ranging from NT$200 for a legislative vote in Taoyuan County to NT$2,000 for a vote in the Taipei County executive race.[38] The report also described candidates' efforts to enlist *tiau-a-ka*:

> KMT county and city executives used clear methods to bribe neighborhood and ward heads under their jurisdictions in order to help candidates of their party. For example, Taipei County Executive Lin Feng-cheng told 109 ward heads in Sanchung City that according to the election results, those wards where [KMT candidate] Li Hsi-kun's vote share exceeded [DPP candidate] You Ch'ing's would receive an extra allowance of NT$100,000 from the county government. Another example was when the Keelung City government gave every

ward head a subsidy of NT$30,000 to go on an "inspection tour" in Southeast Asia. This was designed to raise morale for campaigning.[39]

In addition to drumming up *tiau-a-ka* and buying votes, candidates in 1989's three-way elections made use of yet another aspect of Taiwan's clientelistic mobilization system: local factions. For almost four decades, the KMT kept the upper hand in its relations with local factions in most municipalities. But as the Dangwai's influence increased, the balance of power between party and factions shifted subtly. First, the long-standing practice of trading political spoils for cooperation meant that the relationship between the KMT and local factions was based on interests, not loyalty. If the flow of benefits slackened, the ruling party could not count on the factions' continued cooperation. Second, the party center came to rely on local factions to mobilize votes, giving the factions leverage over the center. Third, the appearance of a serious opposition force gave credibility to factions' threats of desertion. Fourth, the opposition's growing electoral success convinced local factions that the KMT would not be able to maintain the flow of political and economic benefits forever. This weakened their resolve to cooperate with the party. This dynamic crystallized in 1989, when factions in several counties and cities concluded that their interests would best be served by rebelling against the party. At the same time, the party primary forced factional conflict into the open. As a result, the ruling party was left with two options: give in to local factions, or risk losing access to its mobilization network.

Factions played a key role in keeping the KMT in power in 1989. Faction-linked candidates won 44 percent of the Provincial Assembly votes cast; they won majorities in twelve municipal executive races. Factional participation in legislative races was actually greater in 1989 than in 1986 or 1983. Looking only at official KMT nominees, the proportion of faction-linked candidates is even higher. More than 65 percent of KMT-nominated Provincial Assembly members and 58 percent of legislators elected in 1989 were members of local factions.[40] But as Lui Fei-lung writes,

> while this strategy [nominating faction-linked candidates] has proven successful in winning elections, it has also fostered a tendency in the candidates and their local supporters toward self-reliance ... As a result, the losers in party nomination battle[s] would sometimes seek to sabotage the party's campaign.[41]

Had the 1989 elections included only the legislative and Provincial Assembly elections, the dissension among local factions might have been less damaging. In these races, the SVMM system damped the conflict, because it allowed for enough nominations in each district that each faction could obtain at least one. But the municipal executive races forced the KMT to choose between local factions, or to choose candidates with no factional affiliation at all. It is in the executive races that we can see most clearly the damage wrought by factional infighting. While every case was different, of course, the Taipei County executive contest illustrates the problem.

In Taipei County, the KMT faced a tight race between its "good government" nominee, National Taiwan University professor Li Hsi-k'un, and a well-known DPP legislator, You Ching. Given You's reputation as an intellectual, the KMT leadership was keen to select a candidate with similar qualifications. The problem was, the party leadership decided on Li before it announced its intention to hold a primary election. The "bosses" of local factions in several Taipei County towns decided to join the primary, not fully realizing that the party center had made its choice.[42] When Li won the primary, they accused the party of mobilizing military voters and other iron ballots in support of its "personnel selection plan."

Candidate Li described his opponents' reaction this way:

> Before they [the nominating committee] decided to use the primary method, they already had a consensus on me. They agreed on me as the most favorable and viable candidate. But I think the subsequent decision to use a primary was too late. Because the party's important elite definitely wanted to go for me. So when they suddenly announced, "Hey, we want to use a primary," this created problems. If you're going to have a primary, you cannot groom a candidate, right?

Putting himself in the place of his primary opponents, Li added,

> We Chinese value face. You could have told me a little sooner; given me a chance to stay out of the race. Then I'd be willing to support the banner of the party ... But once you tell me there is a free primary, and I join the competition, and suddenly I found [I didn't have a chance]. I can't blame them [for being angry].[43]

To make matters worse, each of the rejected factions clung to the hope of winning the nomination four years hence. If Li Hsi-kun were elected, however, the party almost certainly would nominate him for a second term. Thus, not only did the local factions have little incentive to support Li; what was worse, their interests actually lay in defeating him. Although the local factions dared not oppose Li outright, political activists and observers throughout Taipei County agree that they "pulled his back leg" (*che tade houtui*). The KMT's strategy included establishing a Li Hsi-k'un Support Organization (*houyuan hui*) in each of Taipei County's 29 towns and cities by the end of September. But disgruntled faction bosses stalled, and several of the county's largest towns did not have functioning organizations until very late. In the county seat, ward heads walked out of a meeting when the county KMT chair introduced Li Hsi-k'un.

The head of organization for Li Hsi-k'un's campaign calls the party's failure to unify the local factions a key reason for Li's defeat, and the election results support his conclusion. For example, in Panch'iao City, Li received 44 percent of the vote, compared to 57 percent for the KMT candidate in 1985. The DPP's You Ch'ing, who lost in 1985, saw his Panch'iao vote share increase from 38 percent to 54 percent. The pattern of vote-splitting in the county also was consistent with factional resistance. Two legislative candidates whose factions opposed Li Hsi-k'un received the lion's share of their votes in the towns in which You Ch'ing's vote share increased most from 1985 to 1989. Even if factional resistance did not affect a large number of voters, it still may have been decisive. You Ching's margin of victory was less than half a percentage point. As one of Li Hsi-kun's campaign aides pointed out, a 20-vote swing in each of Panch'iao City's 230 precincts would have reversed the outcome.

Learning from the 1989 elections

The 1989 three-way elections carried some important lessons. The biggest difference between the 1989 elections and previous races was the competitiveness created by the opposition party's presence. The increased competition sharpened existing contradictions within the KMT, because it gave disgruntled members a strategic outlet for their dissatisfaction. Also, with so much at stake in the elections, the KMT learned that it could not afford to strong-arm or ignore local factions. At the same time, however, many Taiwanese associated local factions with vote buying and corruption, which hurt the KMT among unaffiliated voters. In short, the ruling party found that in order to turn out its core constituencies, it must cede a large measure of control to local factions whose influence within the party offended many voters. The KMT has struggled with this dilemma ever since.

The 1989 elections also advanced the democratization process. First, as we have seen, the elections empowered grassroots political forces. While elevating the status and power of local factions may not seem like a positive step to most advocates of democratization, the challenges facing the

KMT in the 1989 elections showed that the society had become more autonomous from the state, and was forcing the regime to respond to the interests of social forces, as they themselves defined them. Voters who disapproved of factions' influence over the ruling party were free to punish the KMT in subsequent elections – and they did. Second, as Lamounier points out, the 1989 contests created numerous opportunities for Taiwanese to criticize the regime. Throughout the campaign, candidates and their supporters stood before large crowds and spoke forthrightly about what they perceived to be the regime's shortcomings. And when the votes were counted, the DPP had won a significant number of seats in the Legislative Yuan, Provincial Assembly, Taipei and Kaohsiung City councils and as municipal executives, each one of which became a pulpit from which to denounce the KMT.

Third, the 1989 elections showed that the opposition was becoming organized. Although the KMT's substantial seat bonuses indicate that it still was better able than the DPP to estimate and allocate its votes in SVMM races, the DPP's coalescence as a party with a unified strategy was an important first step toward full-fledged two-party competition. Finally, the 1989 elections demonstrated the voters' desire for reform, both in the DPP's expanding vote share and in responses to surveys. As Lamounier's theory predicts, KMT reformers gained an advantage over hard-liners because the citizens whose preferences determined the make-up of the legislature, Provincial Assembly and municipal governments desired democracy. This not only hobbled efforts to slow or roll back reform, but also motivated the reform faction to push forward.

7 The Lee Teng-hui years (1990–1996)

During Chiang Ching-kuo's presidency Taiwan experienced profound political, social and economic changes. The conflicts and controversies of the 1970s and 1980s solidified into a cleavage between the KMT, identified with both the economic successes and political shortcomings of the old regime, and the DPP, which represented change. The split between the KMT and the DPP was born out of the opposition's efforts to empower Taiwanese and hasten democratic reform. As a result, the opposition party crystallized along political and ethnic fault lines, not socioeconomic ones. It was a marriage of anti-KMT political forces with little in common beyond their shared desire to drive the Nationalists from power. In the short run, this identity won the DPP an important place in ROC politics. But would it be enough to make the DPP Taiwan's ruling party?

As institutional barriers to democracy fell, many of the opposition's most attractive platform planks became moot. In effect, winning the fight for political reform made it more difficult for the DPP to win political power. The party's pro-reform emphasis also collided with its broad-based anti-KMT structure. Some of the DPP's strongest vote-getters belonged to local factions; being affiliated with the opposition did not stop candidates from corralling *tiau-a-ka*, distributing patronage and buying votes. With Taiwanese occupying most high government posts and political reform a reality, protest politics and ethnic politics attracted few new supporters. In short, the DPP entered the 1990s facing new difficulties born of its past successes.

The KMT, for its part, also faced challenges in the 1990s. Its vote share was slipping steadily, especially in national elections. It was under tremendous pressure to expand national elections and increase the authority of elected officials, creating at least the theoretical possibility that the KMT might someday lose power. This possibility remained remote, however. The KMT continued to win elections at all levels by large margins. It had more than two million official members, and millions more Taiwanese were connected to the party through local factions and corporatist organizations. Many voters sincerely believed that the KMT's performance, ideology and promise were superior to those of the opposition.

Most political parties in democratic countries would consider the KMT's 60 percent vote share and 71 percent seat share in the 1989 supplementary legislative election a great victory. But for the KMT, its shrinking majority was a troubling trend, suggesting a crisis of legitimacy not only for the party but for the very state it had founded. And at the grassroots level, the cost of winning was increasing. To keep the mobilization system functioning in the highly competitive environment of the late 1980s, the KMT found itself caving in to demands from local factions. As Chen Ming-tong writes, "Local factions no longer could be held within existing boundaries. One result ... was to bring about the most direct strike yet on the central party apparatus: the demand that the center distribute its ruling power."[1]

Pacifying local factions meant turning a blind eye to vote buying and corruption. This, in turn, gave the opposition an issue to use against the ruling party. But when Kuan Chung's strategies for controlling factions failed in 1989, "the KMT's policy of replacing factions, which Chiang Ching-kuo had led since the end of the 1960s, came to an end."[2] Instead, the party reversed itself, and as Figure 7.1 shows, the number of faction-linked candidates rebounded.

This "tail wagging the dog" phenomenon allowed corrupt practices previously confined to local politics to infiltrate the national arena. Competition and reform stripped away the insulation between central decision-makers and societal pressures. The cost of campaigns skyrocketed, giving wealthy candidates ("golden oxen," or *jin niu*) and even gangsters an advantage. Even honest politicians were forced to raise huge sums while in office to pay off their campaign debts. Not surprisingly, cases of politicians profiting from the policies they made became more frequent. Even Taiwan's much-admired bureaucratic autonomy eroded as the ruling party traded policy favors for electoral support. Efforts to impose unpopular policies, from restricting investment on the mainland to building nuclear power plants to closing pirate radio stations, all were stymied by political pressure. In sum, by 1990, the unintended, unanticipated consequences of Taiwan's political reforms were piling up.

The 1990 presidential selection

Tattered campaign banners from the 1989 three-way elections were still fluttering along Taiwan's roads and bridges when a new political watershed

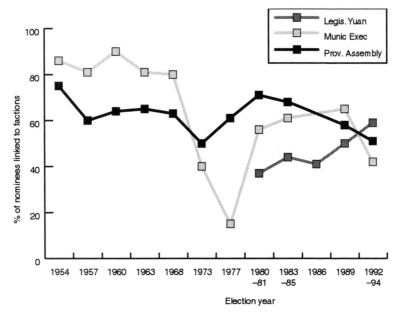

Figure 7.1   Factional nominations as a percentage of KMT nominees

Source: Chen Ming-tong, *Factional Politics and Taiwan's Political Evolution*, Taipei: Yuetan Publishing Company, Ltd, 1995.

arrived. In March of 1990, Lee Teng-hui would complete his term as Chiang Ching-kuo's replacement, and a new presidential election would be held. Choosing the president was the National Assembly's responsibility, and given the KMT's 86 percent majority in that body, there was no doubt that the ruling party's nominee would be selected. Thus, if there were to be resistance to another term for President Lee, it would have to come from within the ruling party. In fact, that is precisely what happened.

Controversy erupted in February. Lin Yang-kang, a senior party member and former vice premier, announced that he and Chiang Ching-kuo's half-brother, Chiang Wei-kuo, would challenge Lee Teng-hui and his running mate. Lin was a Taiwanese, but held conservative views. Lin and Chiang represented a tendency within the ruling party known as the Nonmainstream Faction. By early March, Lin and Chiang had assembled enough support to put them on the National Assembly presidential ballot, with or without the KMT's nomination. Lee Teng-hui and his faction negotiated with Lin, Chiang and other Nonmainstream leaders, hoping to persuade the alternative ticket to withdraw.

The Mainstream Faction, identified with President Lee and his close supporters, encompassed the KMT's reformist wing. Most Nonmainstream politicians were Mainlanders, and their votes largely came from Mainlanders in the electorate.[3] To the Nonmainstream politicians, Lee Teng-hui's concessions to the opposition amounted to abandoning the party's traditional commitment to political stability and Chinese nationalism. They believed Lee was too close to corrupt local politicians, and that he was moving Taiwan toward independence, which they opposed on both ideological and pragmatic grounds. They tried to derail reforms that appeared to put Taiwan ahead of a unified Republic of China; for example, the Nonmainstream opposed efforts to remove mainland-elected representatives from the national legislative bodies because, without them, who would represent the ROC's mainland provinces?[4]

While the KMT struggled to close the rift over the presidential nomination, the National Assembly session opened amid controversy. At the swearing-in ceremony, DPP members scandalized conservatives by addressing their oath to the people of Taiwan rather than to the Republic of China. And when a 94-year-old senior Assembly member was chosen to chair the meeting, DPP members violently disrupted the proceedings. Their goal was to undermine the National Assembly's legitimacy by portraying it as a chaotic, dictatorial anachronism. The strategy was effective; public opinion polls soon showed widespread popular dissatisfaction with the Assembly.[5]

Meanwhile, the KMT continued its efforts to rally the party around the Lee Teng-hui–Li Yuan-tsu presidential ticket. After weeks of negotiations and pressure from party elders, Lin and Chiang withdrew. The National Assembly re-elected President Lee with 641 of 688 votes. The challengers were not completely disappointed, however. They won a major concession for the Nonmainstream faction when President Lee appointed a Nonmainstream stalwart, General Hau Pei-tsun, to be his premier.

The National Affairs Conference

Lee Teng-hui responded to the upheaval in 1990 with a creative gesture of reconciliation directed at critics on both the left and right. He proposed a National Affairs Conference (*guoshihui*) at which representatives of various political tendencies would sit down together, along with scholars, business leaders and other luminaries, to seek a consensus on how Taiwan should proceed toward constitutional and political reform. The goal he set for the NAC was ambitious: to draw up a blueprint for the next stage of Taiwan's democratization, one that would be acceptable to all the major players in the political arena. The NAC was, in short, an extra-constitutional institution created to negotiate the conditions of a post-authoritarian state.

Preparations for the NAC began soon after the president's announcement. A broadly based preparatory committee including business people and academics as well as representatives of the two major parties met to plan the meeting. They identified four broad topics for discussion: the local government system, the central government system, constitutional revision and mainland China policy. The committee invited 150 of Taiwan's leading lights to attend the conference, scheduled to begin in late June. Before the NAC, the committee created opportunities for the general public to register its opinions.

Despite the organizers' efforts to present the NAC as an open forum for airing all sides of the issues, many Taiwanese (including many of the invitees) harbored suspicions about the event. Some scholars feared the conference would be a deal-making opportunity for the two main parties, leaving little room for viewpoints that contradicted the parties' own interests. Meanwhile, Lee's opponents in the KMT and the DPP worried that the president planned to use the conference to advance his own program of moderate, gradual reform. As a result of these concerns, some of those invited declined to attend, including several leading intellectuals who withdrew just before the conference began.

The DPP was divided over whether to accept the invitation. According to the New Tide faction, the NAC was a KMT ploy to strengthen ruling party control under the guise of bipartisan cooperation. But a majority of DPP standing committee members, believing that the DPP needed to stay on the playing field, even if the president had selected a new game, voted to attend the conference. Said Shih Ming-teh, "If the DPP did not participate ... what other way would be open for peaceful reform?"[6]

Despite the speed with which preparations for the conference proceeded, events overtook them, and some of the basic questions facing the NAC were mooted. In early April, DPP and KMT legislators introduced a resolution requesting the Council of Grand Justices to rule on whether or not the senior legislators could remain in office legally. On 21 June, a week before the conference opened, the justices ordered all life-tenure members of the Legislative Yuan, Control Yuan and National Assembly to step down by 31 December 1991. Meanwhile, on 22 May, President Lee announced his intention to abolish the Temporary Provisions, the source of his extra-constitutional powers, a year hence. Even so, there was plenty to discuss when the NAC opened on 28 June.

The NAC reached consensus on a number of important political issues, including direct election of the provincial governor and Taipei and Kaohsiung mayors and popular election of the president (although delegates debated the merits of an electoral college system versus direct election). Participants also agreed that the senior parliamentarians should retire, although some wanted them removed immediately, while others were willing to wait for the Grand Justices' deadline. The participants agreed to replace existing mainland and functional seats with at-large representatives chosen in proportion to each party's overall seat share and to increase local government autonomy. Finally, they recommended abolishing the Temporary Provisions and ending the Period of Mobilization for the Suppression of Communist Rebellion, and endorsed government-to-government talks with Beijing.

The National Affairs Conference did not put an end to the pressure for reform. Even with a consensus on major goals in place, working out the details of how to achieve those goals allowed plenty of room for controversy. The DPP continued to push the KMT to move more quickly and to enact farther-ranging objectives, including direct popular election of the president. The DPP also began promoting the idea that Taiwan should rejoin the United Nations. These positions enjoyed strong popular support. Eventually, the KMT was forced to adopt them in order to remain competitive. The early 1990s thus were a period of constant negotiation and renegotiation of basic political issues.

Mainland affairs and pragmatic diplomacy

One of the central challenges facing Taiwan in the 1990s was the two-headed problem of Taiwan's international status and cross-strait relations. Beginning in October 1987, Taiwan residents were allowed to travel to mainland China. At first, visits were restricted to Mainlanders visiting relatives, but the door soon opened to scholars, cultural groups and tourists. Taiwanese hoping to do business on the mainland quickly followed. Despite legal restrictions on cross-strait investment, the wealth of opportunities awaiting Taiwanese on the mainland proved irresistible, and money poured into Hong Kong, destined for reinvestment in the PRC. Most investors set up small, labor-intensive manufacturing facilities to take advantage of China's low wages while minimizing risk.

The results of the cross-strait traffic were ambiguous. On the one hand, it drew Taiwanese closer to the mainland, especially in economic terms. On the other hand, it gave Taiwan residents their first direct exposure to mainland China in forty years, and many were disappointed with what they found. The mainland was poor and backward; reunification, it seemed, could only hurt Taiwan.

Along with the increase in cross-strait interactions came a need for institutions to handle mainland affairs. These structures needed to operate within the framework of the ROC's policy of promoting reunification. In September 1990, the ROC government established a presidential advisory council on mainland affairs. The following March, the Executive Yuan approved the council's National Unification Guidelines. The guidelines established three preconditions for unification: democracy, freedom and equal prosperity on both sides of the Taiwan Strait. The guidelines established a three-stage process for unification including private exchanges; direct postal, transport and commercial links; and a period of consultation between the two sides to work out a mutually agreeable framework for unification.

In May of 1991, President Lee canceled the Period of Mobilization for the Suppression of Communist Rebellion, officially ending China's civil war. No longer would the ROC claim to be the rightful government of all of China. Instead, ROC leaders took the line that China was divided into two areas, under the jurisdiction of two states. ROC spokesman Jason Hu said in 1993,

> we recognized that the communist authorities were a political entity. We accepted the fact that the nation was divided, and that, prior to the unification of China, both the ROC and the Chinese communists exercise political authority in the areas under their de facto control. Each is entitled to represent the residents of the territory under its de facto control and to participate in the activities of the international community.[7]

In January 1991 the ROC government formed the Mainland Affairs Council (MAC), charged with planning, coordinating, evaluating and partially implementing the ROC's mainland policy. A month later, the Straits Exchange Foundation was formed. Technically, the SEF is not a government agency, but a private, non-profit organization. Because it is a private agency, the SEF skirts the ROC ban on government-to-government contacts with Beijing, although its actions are subject to MAC approval. The SEF handles technical and business matters and represents Taiwan in negotiations with its PRC counterpart, the Association for Relations Across the Taiwan Straits (ARATS).

At the same time as Taiwan was building an institutional framework for managing its relations with the PRC, a new approach to international relations was gaining strength in Taipei. This strategy, known as "pragmatic diplomacy" or "flexible diplomacy" was aimed at enhancing Taiwan's security.[8] Pragmatic diplomacy encompassed two broad strategies: forging official and unofficial relationships with other countries, and joining international organizations. Some small nations granted Taiwan full diplomatic ties, usually in exchange for development assistance (a practice critics called "checkbook diplomacy"). Most large nations maintained only unofficial ties with Taiwan, although the Ministry of Foreign Affairs worked hard throughout the 1990s to build popular support for Taiwan around the world. It undertook major public relations campaigns in the US and other countries, promoting Taiwan as a democratic, capitalist, peace-loving nation deserving of support, friendship and a voice in international bodies.

Foreign affairs experts in the ROC recognized that weaving Taiwan more tightly into the fabric of international interactions would raise the political cost to the PRC of strong-arming Taiwan into reunification on Beijing's terms. Taiwan belonged to some international non-governmental organizations already; throughout the 1990s, it worked to increase its representation in such groups. The ultimate prize was a return to the United Nations. Under the new "divided China" formula, Taipei no longer insisted that only one China could be represented in international organizations; instead, ROC leaders pointed to the examples of East and West Germany and North and South Korea to argue that dual recognition of divided states was acceptable both to Taiwan and to the world community. Beijing, for its part, rejected dual recognition and the "one-country, two-entities" formula, insisting that Taiwan was a province of the PRC. As for creating a second Chinese seat in the UN, Beijing condemned the idea.

The PRC suspected that pragmatic diplomacy, and especially the UN bid, would move Taiwan toward independence. Conservatives on Taiwan agreed. The KMT's Nonmainstream faction saw the policy shift as a retreat from the ROC's traditional pro-unificationist stance. The controversy put the Mainstream faction in a difficult position, because the UN bid was popular with the public. In late September 1991, a joint poll conducted by Taiwan Television and the *United Daily News* found that 60 percent of respondents favored a UN bid, while only 15 percent opposed the idea.[9] The DPP took advantage of the KMT's paralyzing Mainstream–Nonmainstream split to claim the UN issue as its own.

Adding to the pressure on the KMT, National Assembly elections were fast approaching. In response to the Grand Justices' ruling that the senior parliamentarians must step down, elections were scheduled for December 1991. The new body's most important responsibility would be to amend the constitution to allow popular presidential elections, either direct (as the DPP preferred) or through an electoral college (as the KMT advocated). Thus, the debates over pragmatic diplomacy, the United Nations bid, retiring the senior parliamentarians and reforming the presidential election system all were colored by the two parties' calculations of political advantage as they approached the December election. The election was important for both parties: removing the senior Assembly members eliminated the KMT's built-in advantage, leaving control of the Assembly in the hands of the voters for the first time.

The fact that the KMT was facing this challenge at all testifies to the extent to which its authoritarian control had deteriorated. Supplementary elections had been a low-risk way to fill empty seats in the parliamentary bodies while enhancing the regime's democratic image. Replacing the entire parliament in direct elections was a different matter. Although the KMT still enjoyed many advantages, so the likelihood of losing its majority was slim, total renovation of the parliamentary bodies eliminated the ruling party's built-in majority. For the first time, it would be forced to cope with the uncertainty that torments political parties in fully democratic polities. Why, then, did the Nationalist Party leadership push for legislation to remove the senior parliamentarians, then give the go-ahead for the Council of Grand Justices' decision in the case?

A key factor behind the Mainstream faction's willingness to give up its privileged position in the parliamentary bodies was electoral pressure. The DPP dogged the KMT for years with accusations that the "ten-thousand year legislature" constituted a one-party dictatorship. They attacked the seniors relentlessly, branding them "old bandits" and worse. These criticisms did not fall on deaf ears; the Taiwanese electorate agreed that retaining legislators chosen in the 1940s was irrational and undemocratic. In 1991, 30 percent of respondents in a national survey said they thought the pace of democratic reform was not fast enough; only 15 percent thought the reform process should slow down.[10] KMT politicians, especially those facing close races against DPP opponents, could not afford to uphold their party's unpopular policies. Jettisoning the senior legislators also became an issue in the Mainstream–Nonmainstream fight. Cultivating popularity with the voters was the Mainstream faction's most potent weapon; abandoning the "ten-thousand year legislature" could only increase its electoral advantage.

The 1991 National Assembly election

The DPP did not choose the UN bid to be the central issue in its 1991 electoral campaign. Instead, the party made a much bolder gamble: it revised its charter to call for a plebiscite in which the Taiwanese people would have the opportunity to vote for independence. According to Cheng Tun-jen and Hsu Yung-ming, the decision was a compromise between the moderate and radical factions within the DPP. The moderates (including most of the party's best-known politicians, but just under half of its top leaders) recognized that the party's growth depended upon keeping the radical New Tide faction in the opposition party. But the New Tide activists – for whom ideological purity was more important than electoral success – demanded a stronger party stance on the independence question. In order to pacify the radicals, the moderates agreed to change the party charter. In exchange, the New Tide faction supported moderate Hsu Hsin-liang's bid to become party chair. In addition, the moderates realized that giving the electorate an up-or-down vote on the independence issue would replace impassioned speculation with hard facts. If the voters rejected independence, DPP moderates would be able to put the debate within the party to rest.[11]

In addition to independence, the DPP platform called for direct presidential elections and pragmatic diplomacy, especially a UN bid, while the KMT campaigned under the slogan "reform, stability and prosperity." It claimed credit for Taiwan's past successes, both economic and political. On the constitutional questions facing the second National Assembly, the KMT's positions were ambiguous. The party rejected the DPP position that the constitution should be rewritten, as opposed to revised, but it could not reach a consensus as to what system the ROC should use for presidential elections. Above all, it attacked the DPP's independence plank as provocative, dangerous and indicative of the opposition's irresponsible outlook.

The ruling party's arguments proved persuasive with voters, who quickly revealed themselves more frightened of than inspired by the DPP's bold drive for independence. In a national survey taken in 1991, 71 percent of the respondents agreed with the statement, "Right now, it's most important to build a true democracy in Taiwan; we need not discuss the Independence–Unification issue now."[12] In fact, opinion was divided even on the question of whether or not people should be free to advocate Taiwan independence, with 37 percent for and 40 percent against.[13] It is not surprising, then, that well before the election most DPP candidates gave up their independence position in favor of a safer stance: opposing unification with the PRC.[14]

The 1991 election differed from previous elections in a number of ways. Most of Taiwan's most prominent politicians chose not to participate. The DPP in particular saved its biggest names for the more important legislative race planned for 1992. The campaign period was shorter than usual and spending rules were tighter but, for the first time, the rules allowed television commercials. Individual candidates still were forbidden to buy TV time, but the political parties received free TV access to publicize their messages. Television time was allocated according to the number of candidates each party nominated. The KMT thus received more than twice as many minutes as the DPP, and about five times as many as the Social Democratic Party and the Independent Alliance, a group of independent candidates who registered as a coalition in order to qualify for TV time. Most of the advertisements were high-concept infomercials. The KMT emphasized Taiwan's development from hard-luck case to Asian tiger, while the DPP's commercials used postmodern images to critique the conformism of education, politics and culture under the KMT. Only the Independent Alliance gave candidates a chance to speak for themselves, standing each one in front of a camera to briefly make his pitch to the voters. The Independent Alliance's quirky commercial was the most entertaining of the lot.

The number of seats up for grabs in 1991 was much higher than in any previous island-wide election. There were 225 seats in 58 geographical districts, as well as 80 at-large and 20 reserved for overseas Chinese. Seats in the latter two groups were assigned to the political parties which won more than 5 percent of the overall vote, in proportion to their vote share. The large number of districts meant that the size of each district was relatively small, facilitating the KMT's mobilizational tactics.[15]

The 1991 election was a clear victory for the ruling party – and for its mobilization system. It won 80 percent of the seats in geographical districts; including at-large and overseas seats, its share came to 78 percent. Moreover, the KMT's 71 percent vote share also constituted a landslide. By every measure – vote share, seat share, seat bonus – the KMT did astoundingly well.[16] Likewise, the DPP did poorly by every measure, especially in light of its strong showing in the 1986 and 1989 legislative contests. Its vote share fell from 30 percent in the Legislative Yuan election two years earlier to 24 percent. Its share of the district seats was 18 percent; with the at-large and overseas seats it claimed a meager 20 percent, well short of the one-fourth needed to veto constitutional amendments. The election was an especially big set-back for the New Tide faction and other independence stalwarts in the DPP. All but two of the strongly pro-independence candidates were defeated; nearly everyone interpreted the election as a repudiation of the DPP's independence stance.

A *New York Times* editorial attributed the KMT's strong performance to issue-oriented voting – mainly anti-independence voting. And indeed, issues did receive considerable attention during the National Assembly campaign. The two major parties offered a clear choice on several important ones, including independence and presidential elections. But voters attracted by the KMT platform still faced the question, "Which KMT candidate should I choose?" Issue voting cannot explain why KMT votes were allocated among ruling party candidates in a way that maximized the party's seat share. If candidate-oriented voting had predominated we would expect votes to be more – not less – concentrated. Candidates with high name recognition would have overshadowed political newcomers. In fact, however, as Figure 7.2 shows, few KMT candidates captured an excessively large share of the vote in their districts. The mobilization system, not issue or candidate voting, offers the best explanation for the distribution of KMT votes.

As we saw in Chapter 2, one criterion for judging a party's success in an SVMM election is how well it managed to control its members' entry into the competition. By this standard, the KMT performed well in 1991. Only 2.4 percent of all KMT members who registered as candidates did so without the party's authorization. The fact that these unauthorized (or "maverick") candidates took a mere 1 percent of their party's total votes indicates the KMT was able to prevent even those who *did* run from hurting its official nominees. Another criterion is the percentage of a party's nominees who are elected. If a party estimates its strength

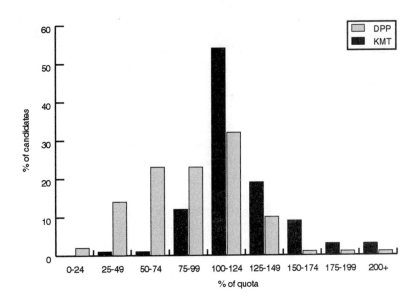

Figure 7.2   National Assembly, 1991

Source: Central Election Commission data

accurately, nominates the ideal number of candidates and allocates the votes available it to effectively, a high proportion of its nominees will win. In 1991, 86 percent of KMT nominees were elected, compared to 45 percent of DPP nominees and 2 percent of independents. A party's seat bonus is a third criterion, because the seat bonus measures a party's success in translating votes into seats. The KMT's large seat bonus in 1991 – it captured 78 percent of the contested seats with only 71 percent of the votes cast – indicates that the KMT distributed its votes more effectively than its opponents.

Finally, if we look at the frequency distribution from the 1991 elections, we can see that most KMT candidates finished with just a few more votes than they needed to be elected. Figure 7.2 shows the KMT's and DPP's vote distributions, respectively. The KMT's distribution is clearly much closer to the ideal (a single bar just above the quota) than is the DPP's. The opposition party's flatter distribution shows many votes wasted at both ends: some candidates received far more votes than the quota they needed to be elected; others received far fewer. As a result, the party failed to maximize the number of seats it won, given its share of the vote. Could the Kuomintang have achieved its result without using clientelistic tactics? According to KMT leaders, party-oriented voting explains their victory. In fact, a substantial majority of voters did indicate a preference for candidates running under the KMT label. But a strong preference for the KMT alone cannot explain the distribution of votes *among* KMT candidates. It was the mobilization system, not party-oriented voting, that allowed the KMT to achieve its nearly optimal distribution of votes, and the attendant large seat bonus.

The 1991 National Assembly election results reverberated through Taiwan's political arena. Moderates in both parties gained strength from the results, and their increased confidence set the stage for the next round of reforms – most notably the decision to allow direct presidential elections and the acceleration of pragmatic diplomacy. As for the DPP, its sagging popularity demonstrated the need to shed the image of an outsider party obsessed with Taiwan independence. It needed to propose realistic and responsible solutions to problems that mattered to ordinary Taiwanese. The party never again embraced the independence issue as it had in 1991; independence standpatters eventually quit the DPP in frustration, setting up the Taiwan Independence Party in 1997. In place of independence, the DPP emphasized the drive for a United Nations seat in its campaign for the 1992 legislative elections.

The National Assembly election results bolstered the KMT Mainstream. That the KMT could achieve a sweeping victory even with all the National Assembly seats up for grabs demonstrated Lee Teng-hui's ability to implement profound reforms without losing control. The KMT's strategist in 1991 was the party's secretary general, James Soong, another central figure in the Mainstream faction. The successful deployment of the mobilization system redounded to his credit. The election did not dislodge the Nonmainstream faction, however, and KMT leaders spent much of 1992 balancing pressures from the Nonmainstream against those coming from the Mainstream and the opposition on two crucial issues: constitutional revision and pragmatic diplomacy.

In March of 1992 the newly elected National Assembly met to amend the ROC constitution. Despite DPP disruptions, which helped to undermine popular respect for the body, the National Assembly managed to pass reforms that restructured the Control Yuan and subjected the posts of provincial governor, Taipei mayor and Kaohsiung mayor to direct election. The body did not act on the question of presidential elections because KMT leaders still had not reached a consensus on the issue. President Lee opened a debate on the matter at a KMT Central Committee meeting held during the National Assembly session. The president's own position leaned toward direct elections, but the matter proved too divisive to resolve. In April, three days of demonstrations in support of direct presidential elections intensified the pressure on President Lee.

A second issue pulling at the leadership was the question of how to balance cross-straits ties with pragmatic diplomacy. According to the Mainland Affairs Council's Su Chi, "the highly charged domestic political atmosphere in the early 1990s has given the government even more reason to synchronize these two policies and to prevent one from getting too far ahead of the other."[17] Under intense pressure from the Nonmainstream and from Beijing to advance cross-strait relations, the government moved forward on cross-strait negotiations while maintaining its rhetorical stance in favor of unification. Representatives of Taiwan's Straits Exchange Foundation met with their mainland counterparts from ARATS for the first time in March, and in May the ROC announced that it would set aside the question of sovereignty temporarily, in order to work on day-to-day problems. On the second track, Lee's government sought to advance its pragmatic diplomacy by, for example, actively pursuing membership in the Asia–Pacific Economic Cooperation forum (APEC) and the General Agreement on Tariffs and Trade (GATT, the precursor to the World Trade Organization).

Two foreign policy set-backs rejuvenated the campaign for pragmatic diplomacy in mid-1992. In August, one of Taipei's most valued diplomatic partners, South Korea, normalized relations with the PRC. Then the GATT decided to admit Taiwan as an observer, assigning it the status of Hong Kong and Macao – hardly the recognition Taipei desired. The DPP responded by stepping up its campaign for a UN bid. With the December legislative elections looming, many DPP candidates made the UN bid the centerpieces of their campaigns, a move that proved popular with voters. Indeed, by mid-1992, the KMT, too, was fully aboard the UN bandwagon; as James Robinson puts it, "the government declared a consensus of public opinion (without a referendum or even significant public opinion polls) in favor of joining the UN and announced a goal for implementation."[18]

The 1992 Legislative Yuan election

The momentum behind the UN and presidential elections issues made it increasingly difficult for the KMT leadership to hold together its deeply divided factions. Most elected officials were associated with the Mainstream faction, and as they approached the 1992 election, they faced intense pressure to embrace a more liberal position on international relations. Some KMT legislators supported the UN bid as early as 1991; more joined them as their re-election contests drew near. A few KMT candidates took foreign policy positions well beyond the UN proposal; legislative hopeful Chen Che-nan adopted the slogan "one China, one Taiwan."[19] Ultimately, grassroots demands for pragmatic diplomacy overwhelmed the KMT candidates, and they endorsed the UN bid and rejected unificationist rhetoric in droves. Given the fierce competition in their districts, they simply could not afford to mouth their party's one-China slogans.

The ruling party's in-fighting was not limited to foreign affairs. The run-up to the December legislative election was filled with controversy and dissension. Almost half the scheduled primary election races were canceled because party leaders feared they would cause more trouble than they were worth. Those that were held tended to over-nominate conservative, Mainland candidates whose popularity with KMT "iron ballot" constituencies contrasted sharply with the views of the general electorate. Next, KMT legislators opined that incumbents should receive automatic nominations; party strategists found this unacceptable. Meanwhile, many KMT candidates worried that if their party refused to support direct presidential elections, they would lose. Even the president agreed there was little grassroots support for the indirect method. President Lee insisted that party leaders discuss the matter at the plenary meeting in March, but they could not reach a consensus. Finally, the KMT announced that it would delay a decision on the matter until 1995.

In October, the KMT expelled four legislators from the party when they refused to support a cabinet proposal to tax stock transactions. The legislation was designed to rein in speculation, but it struck at the interests of wealthy investors. The legislators' unwillingness to support their party spotlighted two worrisome trends: the rise of "money politics" and the unraveling of KMT discipline in the legislature. As campaign costs spiraled upward, special interests and "golden oxen" – businessmen capable of financing their own campaigns – tightened their grip on politics.[20] Reformers decried this trend, especially because they believed much of the money went buy votes. But neither party had the resources to finance campaigns, so reversing the tide was nearly impossible. Meanwhile, KMT legislators facing tight re-election bids no longer followed the party line obediently; rather, they took note of a variety of opinions: their constituents', their supporters' and their financial contributors' – not necessarily in that order.

In the early 1990s, rampant real-estate speculation drove up land prices to the point that home ownership was out of reach for all but the very wealthy. In response, Finance Minister Wang Chien-hsuan proposed to tax excessive profits. The measure was intended as a populist gesture, but the speculators spun the proposal as an anti-Taiwanese move, since most undeveloped land belonged to Taiwanese. Anticipating a backlash from suburban and rural landowners and the DPP, President Lee refused to back Wang's proposal. Wang, who enjoyed considerable popularity among Taipei City's middle class for his refusal to capitulate to moneyed interests, resigned his post as finance minister and entered the legislative race. Because the KMT's list of nominees was already settled, Wang's entry threw the party's strategy into disarray. Shortly thereafter, another of the Nonmainstream faction's popular clean-government crusaders, Environmental Protection Agency head Jaw Shao-kong, followed Wang's example, quitting his cabinet post and joining the legislative contest.

On 19 December 1992, voters went to the polls in 27 districts to choose 161 representatives to the Legislative Yuan. Thirty at-large and 6 overseas Chinese representatives were chosen from party lists submitted before the election. The results gave the Kuomintang a solid majority in the legislature; nonetheless, both major parties interpreted the results as a set-back for the KMT. Ruling party nominees captured a bare majority of the vote (53 percent), while KMT members running without the party's nomination won another 8 percent. The DPP garnered 31 percent, up 7 percentage points from the 1991 National Assembly election and 6 points from its 1989 legislative performance. The KMT captured 96 seats, 60 percent of the total, while the DPP won 50 seats, or 31 percent.

Many political parties would be delighted to defeat their opponents so decisively. But, for the KMT, the 1992 legislative election brought disturbing tidings. Even though it had coopted the opposition's most popular issue – the UN bid – the ruling party's vote and seat share both fell. Above all, the election showed that the party leadership's ability to control the rank-and-file had deteriorated badly. As a result, the KMT label had lost its magic. Recall that in the 1950s and 1960s, KMT nominees for public office were all but guaranteed to win; their success rate consistently exceeded 75 percent. In 1992, the success rate for opposition party contestants (57 percent overall) exceeded that of KMT members (49 percent) for the first time. Even if we include only party nominees, the odds of winning were still better for a DPP contestant (65 percent) than for a ruling party representative (63 percent). The DPP also overcame its traditional problem of seat deficits, winning 31 percent of the seats with 31 percent of the vote.

DPP and independent candidates benefited from the KMT's reputation as a hotbed of money politics and corruption, but the ruling party's disappointing performance was due primarily to the collapse of party discipline and infighting among its own candidates. A quarter of the KMT members who took part in the elections ran without permission; an additional 13 percent received the party's endorsement, but not its nomination.[21] As Robinson and Baum point out, the ruling party could have nominated these mavericks, but chose not to for several reasons:

> Often these candidates opposed the major policies of President and Party Chairman Lee Teng-hui, or party officials believed that rewarding the dissidents would encourage others to ignore party discipline. When rebels won, they could not be disciplined and were often welcomed back into the ranks, thus undermining principles of discipline further.[22]

Left out of the distribution of turf, non-KMT candidates and mavericks had no reason to respect the boundaries of responsibility zones, and campaigned wherever they liked. This led to an explosion in the number of vote-buying complaints. The presence of so many competitors from outside the KMT also put pressure on the party's nominees, who overran the borders of their assigned turf in an effort to steal away enough votes from other candidates to make up for those they were losing to mavericks and non-KMT opponents.[23]

Figure 7.3 illustrates the KMT's discipline problem. If we compare Figure 7.3 with Figure 7.4 we can see that the KMT's votes were less well-distributed in 1992 than in the previous legislative election. Even more damaging to the ruling party was the shift of candidates from the category just above the quota (100–124 percent) to the bar just below the quota (75–99 percent). In a sense, the KMT's "problem" in 1989 was too many winners. The party's problem three years later was much worse: too many candidates competing for too few votes, with the result that a number of candidates lost. As Figures 7.3 and 7.4 show, the DPP consistently was less able than the KMT to distribute its votes evenly, although it improved somewhat from 1989 to 1992. But by controlling its nominations, the party avoided the problem of too many candidates chasing a limited pool of votes, and it managed to bring a larger fraction of its nominees in above the threshold for election.

Political scientist Chu Yun-han suggested that the tightening alliance between the KMT and local factions had squeezed out people with political ambitions but no factional connections, forcing them to run on their own.[24] Indeed, Soong Chu-yu's strategy of working with township-level factions did give faction-linked candidates a strong advantage. Fifty-nine percent of KMT nominees had connections to local factions, making the 1992 legislative race the first national contest in which a majority of KMT endorsements went to faction-linked candidates. Another third of the ruling party's candidates were sponsored by the military, leaving little room on the party's nominations list for candidates without organized support.

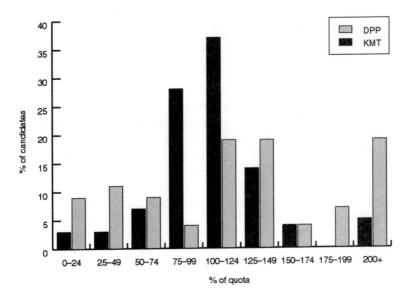

Figure 7.3   Legislative Yuan, 1992

Source: Central Election Commission data

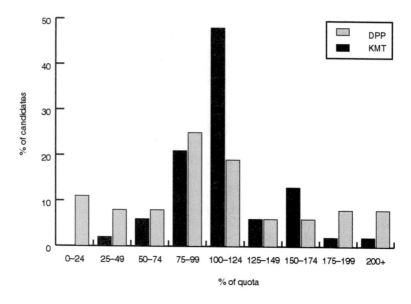

Figure 7.4   Legislative Yuan, 1989

Source: Central Election Commission data

Even the Mainstream–Nonmainstream conflict intruded into the election, causing headaches for the KMT. In past elections, party officials allocated the votes of military personnel and other strong KMT supporters – the so-called "iron ballots" – to those nominees most in need of them at the moment the election was held. But in 1992, the military hoarded its votes, heaping them on Nonmainstream candidates at the expense of Mainstream nominees. In a number of districts, military candidates were elected with enough extra votes to have elected additional KMT candidates, had the votes been distributed evenly. The two Nonmainstream former cabinet members who joined the race, Jaw Shao-kong and Wang Chien-hsuan, ignored the mobilization system. Both men finished first in their districts, drawing large numbers of votes away from other KMT nominees. Jaw captured 235,000 votes in a district in which the cut-off for election was only 36,000. If his votes had been distributed among the KMT nominees in his district, the party might have gained several more seats.

At first blush, the elections looked like a major victory for the Nonmainstream faction. Conservative candidates enjoyed a very high success rate: 11 of 12 New KMT Alliance candidates were elected. Meanwhile, the Wisdom Club, a Mainstream caucus, saw most of its leaders lose their seats in the legislature. However, the tide of battle between the two factions was turning against the Nonmainstream side. President Lee was under intense pressure to get rid of Premier Hau Pei-tsun, and the two men made less and less effort to conceal their differences of opinion on policy matters.[25] Street protests, media barrages and outbursts in the legislature – including some laced with vitriolic anti-Mainlander rhetoric – all contributed to a wave of opposition that crested in early 1993. In the end, the Mainstream leadership made common cause with the opposition party to force Hau out. The pretext for his removal was the election of the new Legislative Yuan. President Lee asked the cabinet to subject itself to the legislators' approval, and Hau and his cabinet resigned on 4 February. Lee chose a close Mainstream confederate, Lien Chan, to replace Hau.

The Kuomintang split

Hau Pei-tsun's sacking marked the triumph of Lee Teng-hui's predominantly Taiwanese Mainstream faction. It also sparked the break-up of the Nationalist Party. In May, legislators linked to the Nonmainstream faction and the New KMT Alliance announced their intention to form the Chinese New Party. They founded the party on 10 August, with a platform calling for direct presidential elections, human rights, greater economic integration with the PRC and fealty to Sun Yat-sen's ideology. The party down-played its position on unification, but its members were among Taiwan's strongest supporters of a unified China. The NP's founders were motivated by a number of factors, including dissatisfaction with Lee Teng-hui's Taiwan-first approach to cross-straits relations, what they perceived as his toleration of corruption, and his autocratic dealings with his opponents in the party. They also took inspiration from the success of Japan's New Party, which seemed poised to bring down the long-ruling Liberal Democrats.

The split damaged the KMT in several ways. It immediately reduced the KMT's legislative majority from 96 seats to 90. In addition, it complicated the KMT's electoral strategy, because the New Party's natural constituents were the KMT's iron ballots. It was impossible to predict how many of those voters would remain loyal to the party that had sustained and succored them for so many years, or transfer their support to the party that seemed most true to the KMT's founding ideology. Third, while some high officials associated with the Nonmainstream faction remained within the KMT, their political influence diminished greatly. Finally, the KMT's break-up marked a significant political and spiritual defeat for the party. Political observers had long predicted a split in the DPP. That the KMT fell victim to internal conflicts first was an especially sweet irony to its opponents.

The defection of many Nonmainstream figures to the New Party left Lee Teng-hui stronger than ever. Some of his critics even accused him of assembling dictatorial powers in the presidential office. Policy initiatives that had been stuck in the factional conflict bottleneck moved forward quickly after the Nonmainstream's eclipse. The KMT Central Committee recommended direct presidential elections to the National Assembly in April 1994, a year earlier than promised, and the Assembly approved the proposal in July. In August, Foreign Minister Chien Fu and Prime Minister Lien Chan both made speeches advocating Taiwan's return to the United Nations, signaling a major commitment to the UN bid. This acceleration of pragmatic diplomacy allowed diplomatic efforts to surge ahead of cross-straits relations.

Relations between Taipei and Beijing improved in the early 1990s. After 1987, millions of Taiwanese visited the mainland, and by 1993, estimates of Taiwan's business interests in the mainland ranged as high as US$15 billion.[26] Both governments had strong incentives to establish procedures and channels of communication for managing this traffic. On the ROC side, Taiwan's Mainland Affairs Council created regulations to manage Taiwan's burgeoning cross-straits investments, while Beijing founded ARATS, a nongovernmental counterpart to Taiwan's Straits Exchange Foundation, in 1991. The two agencies met in Beijing in March of 1992 to set up procedures for verifying documents. A year later, the two agencies' heads, the SEF's Koo Chen-fu and Wang Daohan of ARATS, met in Singapore. Koo and Wang signed agreements on document notarization, registered mail and future communications between the two sides. They also agreed on a schedule for tackling other problems, including fishing disputes, illegal immigration and protecting intellectual property rights. SEF and ARATS representatives continued to meet over the next several months.

Despite these improvements, however, the two sides still were far apart on fundamental issues. Beijing insisted on the following points: "one China" means the PRC; Taiwan is a province of the PRC; because the Taiwan authorities are local officials, government-to-government talks on an equal basis are impossible; reunification should occur under the one-country, two-systems model; Taiwan should not have international recognition, including a seat in the United Nations; and while the PRC would prefer peaceful reunification, it will not rule out the possibility of reunification by "non-peaceful means." The ROC, for its part, rejected each of these points, arguing that Taiwan and mainland China represented two equal parts of a divided nation. In Taipei's view, reunification would occur when the mainland and Taiwan reached the same level of political freedom and economic prosperity. Taiwan insisted that Beijing renounce the use of force against the island. It also argued that its quest for international recognition did not violate the one-China principle.

For a time, the two governments put aside their differences to discuss practical matters. But events soon derailed the negotiations. In March 1994, 24 Taiwanese tourists were murdered while boating on Qiandao Lake. Although PRC authorities quickly apprehended and executed three suspects, the victims' families believed the incident was mishandled. Some urged a boycott, but while many Taiwan residents distrusted the PRC authorities' ability and willingness to protect Taiwanese interests, Taiwanese businesses were too enmeshed in the PRC economy to abandon their mainland investments. In 1995, the Ministry of Economic Affairs estimated Taiwan's investment in the mainland at US$1.09 billion, while the number of visits to the mainland topped 1.27 million.[27]

If the Qiandao Lake Incident upset Taiwanese, Lee Teng-hui's comments to a Japanese magazine a month later infuriated Beijing.[28] The president compared himself to Moses leading Taiwan to freedom, and he bemoaned the fate of the Taiwanese, whom he said had fallen under the power of one foreign regime after another, including the Nationalists. In the economic realm, Lee began pushing hard for the "Go South" policy. This approach, which encouraged businesses to invest in Southeast Asia rather than mainland China, was designed to reduce Taiwan's economic dependence on the PRC. PRC leaders interpreted Lee's words and policies as proof that the Taiwanese president secretly supported Taiwan independence.

Despite these obstacles, 1995 began with conciliatory gestures from Beijing, and preparations for the next round of Koo-Wang talks resumed in May. But once again, outside events threw the negotiations off track. This time, the two halves of the ROC's foreign policy – improving cross-straits relations and promoting pragmatic diplomacy – collided with explosive force. A year earlier, the US government had denied Lee a visa to spend a night in Hawaii en route to Central America. The snub became a cause célèbre among Taiwan's friends and lobbyists in Washington. When President Lee's alma mater, Cornell University, invited him to the campus to speak, Taiwan's Congressional allies insisted that he be allowed to enter the US. PRC leaders responded with howls of outrage. They accused the US of interfering with China's internal affairs, canceled the Koo-Wang talks scheduled for June and launched military tests and maneuvers off the Taiwan coast. According to a poll commissioned by the MAC, the percentage of Taiwan residents who felt Beijing to be "hostile or unfriendly" to Taiwan reached 73 percent.[29]

Despite the ups and downs of cross-strait relations, Taiwan's domestic politics settled into a routine in the mid-1990s. The ruling party's decision to support direct presidential elections brought to fruition the last major item on the political reformers' agenda. With the Nonmainstream faction subdued, President Lee enjoyed enormous power. His close supporters Lien Chan and Soong Chu-yu held the offices of premier and provincial governor, respectively, so Lee could count on cooperation from the executive branch. The legislature, in contrast, had begun to show some independence.

In 1993, a coalition of DPP and KMT legislators passed a bill requiring public officials to disclose their financial assets, even though the party leadership did not support it. Late in the year, the DPP unveiled a plan for government-funded pensions for the elderly. The KMT initially opposed the idea on budgetary grounds, but political pressure soon forced it to present a plan of its own. In 1994, the ruling party rammed through funding for construction of a controversial nuclear power plant. Antinuclear activists collected enough signatures to require a recall vote on several pro-nuclear KMT legislators. Although the recall election results were overturned on technical grounds, the incident demonstrated the growing power of interest groups in ROC politics.

Electoral routine: 1993, 1994, and 1995

Local elections in the winter of 1993–1994 repeated the patterns established in previous election cycles. The municipal executive elections in December both rewarded and frustrated the DPP. On the one hand, the head-to-head competition in large districts encouraged voters to consider party affiliation and policy considerations instead of relying on candidates' name recognition and the advice of *tiau-a-ka*. This helped the opposition party raise its vote share to 41 percent. On the other hand, the built-in disproportionality of the single-member districts made it difficult to translate those votes into seats; the party won only six executive posts, the same number it had captured in 1989.[30]

In January, elections for municipal councils, township councils and township and village executives also followed a familiar pattern: the KMT won 67 percent of the council seats and 82 percent of the executive posts, while the DPP captured only 7 percent and 11 percent, respectively. In July, voters went to the polls to choose Taiwan's lowest-level elected officials: township representatives and village and neighborhood chiefs. Among these potential *tiau-a-ka* KMT members outnumbered DPP representatives fifty to one; out of more than three thousand basic-level officials, only two belonged to the New Party. This result both demonstrated and reinforced the dominance of the KMT and its mobilizational machine at the grassroots level.[31]

The KMT's success in these grassroots elections turned out to be a mixed blessing. Widespread allegations of vote buying by would-be municipal council speakers sparked a crackdown on corruption in which those many successful KMT candidates were the main target. One hundred and ninety KMT, 60 independent and 7 DPP councilors received prison sentences. The public viewed the incident as further proof of Taiwan's endemic political corruption. Meanwhile, many grassroots KMT officials felt betrayed: why suddenly begin prosecuting actions that for decades had constituted business as usual in local politics?

The elections at the end of 1994 included yet another "first": the first direct election of the provincial governor, which was the closest Taiwan had ever come to an island-wide election. The race was not quite island-wide, because the two special municipalities, Taipei City and Kaohsiung City, were not included. Their residents elected mayors at the same time, bringing back under popular control offices that had been made appointive decades earlier. These races set the KMT, DPP and NP in direct, head-to-head competition for meaningful stakes. And they offered voters their best opportunity ever to evaluate the three parties and express their preferences unambiguously.

The KMT was in a difficult position coming into the elections. Local factions expected nominations in the concurrent Provincial Assembly elections in exchange for mobilizing their supporters behind the KMT's gubernatorial candidate, Soong Chu-yu. But the vote-buying scandals in the county councils made cozying up to local factions unpalatable, especially for Soong, who wanted to rise above the unsavory world of local politics. The KMT as a whole was under heavy pressure from the opposition and the public to distance itself from local factions and money politics. To escape this dilemma, Soong devised a new approach: instead of negotiating the mobilization strategy with county-level faction heads, he would appeal directly to the township level bosses.[32] Soong later boasted that he had visited every one of Taiwan's more than three hundred urban and rural townships. During those visits he promised material and political assistance to township leaders.

To counter Soong's grassroots-oriented campaign, DPP and New Party candidates looked for issues with which to challenge him. Unfortunately, they found few policy matters that resonated with voters, and turned instead to the old stand-by, ethnicity. Because the provincial governor has no authority over national policy, the discussion degenerated into a debate over various candidates' ethnic background. DPP gubernatorial candidate Chen Ting-nan made much of the fact that Soong Chu-yu was a Mainlander, while the NP's candidate for Taipei mayor, Jaw Shao-kong, attacked his DPP opponent, Chen Shui-bian, for putting his Taiwanese identity ahead of the ROC's security.

In the end, the voters did not reward these tactics. Soong Chu-yu won a resounding victory, capturing 56 percent of the vote, to Chen Ting-nan's 39 percent. In Taipei City, Chen Shui-bian's mayoral bid nearly was torpedoed by Taiwan-first extremists in his own party before he noisily repudiated their position. Chen's rejection of radical Taiwan nationalism proved popular: he won the mayoral race with 44 percent of the vote. The NP's Jaw finished second with 30 percent, while the KMT's candidate, incumbent mayor Huang Ta-chou, trailed with 26 percent. In Kaohsiung City, the KMT defeated the DPP, 55 percent to 39 percent.

Legislative elections in December 1995 brought the KMT to the brink of losing its legislative majority. It lost 11 seats, ending up with only a 3-seat majority in the 164-member body.[33] The DPP picked up 4 seats, for a total of 54, while the NP garnered 21. To make matters worse, the KMT legislative delegation suffered from lax attendance and slack discipline. In one sense, the KMT's razor-thin majority looked more dangerous than it was, because a coalition between the two opposition parties – who are located on opposite sides of the ruling party ideologically – seemed unlikely. However, the opposition parties did work together on certain issues; for example, they joined forces to defeat a proposal for a fourth nuclear power plant.

The 1995 elections were not a fiasco for the ruling party by any means. The success rate of its district candidates was 64 percent, compared to 59 percent for the DPP and 46 percent for the New Party. And as Figure 7.5 illustrates, the KMT came closer than either of the opposition parties to achieving an ideal allocation of votes. The proportion of its candidates who obtained just enough votes to win not only was higher than that of its opponents, but also showed marked improvement over the previous legislative race. The sharp drop in its seat share is more a reflection of the New Party's defection and the KMT's reluctance to overnominate than a poor showing by the KMT. Although the DPP did not distribute its support as effectively as the KMT, it, too, did a better job in 1995 than in 1992. The DPP did not waste votes on superstars; the proportion of DPP candidates receiving at least twice as many votes as they needed fell from nearly 20 percent in 1992 to below 5 percent.

The New Party grabbed the headlines in 1995. Competing in its first legislative elections, the NP managed to win 13 percent of the seats with 13 percent of the vote. The news media focused especially on the NP's

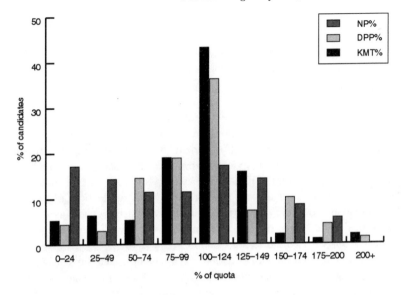

Figure 7.5 Legislative Yuan, 1995

Source: Central Election Commission data

performance in Taipei City. Because its Taipei-based supporters were highly motivated and relatively well educated, the NP avoided the learning curve for new parties in SVMM elections. The party achieved a nearly perfect allocation of its votes by assigning voters to candidates on the basis of their birth dates. Its success was due, in part, to the NP's conservative nominating strategy; in fact, New Party candidates won enough votes to have elected an additional candidate in each of Taipei's legislative districts.

The NP's success in the capital overshadowed serious difficulties in other districts. Even in Taipei County, which is part of the New Party's northern stronghold, it ran into difficulty. The party nominated 5 candidates, and its total vote share was sufficient to have elected all 5, but misallocation of votes cost the NP 2 seats. Together, Taipei City and Taipei County accounted for 9 of the NP's 16 successful district legislative candidates; the other 7 were scattered throughout the 24 remaining districts. Figure 7.5 shows that New Party candidates' vote shares varied widely, rather than clustering around the number they needed to be elected. Overall, the New Party elected a smaller percentage of its candidates in its first legislative race than the DPP had done in its first (legal) legislative trial in 1989. In short, the Taipei-based media's excitement over the New Party's strong performance in the metropolitan area obscured the party's weak showing in the rest of the island. This helps to explain the NP's disappointing performance in subsequent elections.

The 1996 presidential and National Assembly elections

The ink was not yet dry on the 1995 legislative ballots when campaigning began for the next round of balloting: Taiwan's first direct presidential election. From the beginning, incumbent president Lee Teng-hui was a sure winner. But while Lee's victory never was in doubt, the ruling party leadership worried that he might not capture a clear majority in the four-way race. Without at least half the votes, they feared, Lee not only would face stronger domestic opposition, but also would be viewed as a lame duck in Beijing. Thus, tension surrounded the election, even though the outcome was never in doubt.

Lee and his running mate, Lien Chan, campaigned on the KMT's record of prosperity, stability and political reform. Their campaign was confident, but took nothing for granted. The KMT mounted an impressive grassroots mobilization in support of Lee's re-election, blanketing the island with posters, flags and Lee–Lien baseball caps, and organizing thousands of campaign workers. Lee's competitors, too, campaigned aggressively. The DPP nominated Peng Ming-min and Hsieh Chang-ting as its presidential and vice-presidential candidates. Peng was a former National Taiwan University professor who escaped into exile to avoid a prison sentence for promoting Taiwan independence in the 1960s, and Hsieh was a well-known DPP legislator. The Peng–Hsieh campaign emphasized self-determination for Taiwan and attacked the KMT's record of authoritarianism and corruption. Peng's campaign logo was a purple and teal whale, designed to draw attention to Taiwan's independent, outward-looking, maritime heritage (which it implicitly contrasted with mainland China's inward focus and continentalism).

The remaining candidates were high KMT officials until shortly before the election. Lin Yang-kang was one of the most senior Taiwanese in the ROC government. He challenged Lee Teng-hui's first presidential bid in 1990, and when KMT conservatives urged him to join the 1996 race, he threw his hat into the ring once again. Expelled from the KMT for supporting New Party candidates in the 1995 legislative elections, Lin and his running mate, former premier Hau Pei-tsun, technically were independents. However, their organizational support and many of their votes came from the New Party. Lin and Hau fiercely criticized Lee Teng-hui's mainland China policy, which they said was leading away from unification and toward armed conflict. They also criticized the Mainstream faction's close ties with corrupt local factions, gangsters and "golden oxen."

The fourth presidential ticket consisted of Chen Li-an, who renounced his KMT membership and resigned from his post as Control Yuan president to run, and Wang Ching-feng, a Control Yuan member. Chen and Wang had two characteristics that set them apart from the other candidates: Wang was the only female member of any ticket, and theirs was the only campaign with a strong religious element. In the 1980s, Buddhist sects emphasizing discipline, charity and contemplation gained a wide following in Taiwan. These groups differed from conventional Taiwanese folk Buddhism in that they demanded more of their followers and tended to be highly centralized. One such group, the Tzu Chi movement, claimed to have more members than the KMT. The Chen-Wang campaign tapped this trend by criticizing the "dirtiness" of ROC politics and emphasizing clean government proposals. Chen and Wang also attacked Lee Teng-hui's Taiwan-first approach to cross-strait relations.

Although the first direct presidential election in Chinese history was itself a momentous event, a crisis erupted in February and March that nearly overshadowed it. The PRC government was still furious over Lee Teng-hui's trip to the US, and it bitterly opposed the idea of direct presidential elections in Taiwan. As long as the ROC president was chosen by the National Assembly, there was some pretext, at least, of participation by mainland representatives. But a direct election by the people of Taiwan alone would create a presidency whose legitimacy came entirely from the island of Taiwan, with no accountability, even in theory, to the mainland. This, to Beijing, was tantamount to independence. In addition, PRC leaders worried that a strong showing in the election would strengthen Lee Teng-hui, whom they accused of disingenuousness on the unification–independence issue. Finally, the election was a clear refutation of Beijing's argument that Chinese people were not suited for "Western-style" democracy.

Beijing issued numerous warnings in the months leading up to the election, urging the Taiwanese people to reject Lee Teng-hui and his "splittist" agenda. It reiterated its threat to use military force if Taiwan sought independence. When these measures did not diminish Lee Teng-hui's popularity, the PRC made its threats more explicit, conducting missile tests and military maneuvers in the area around Taiwan. There were few signs of panic on Taiwan itself, although the international press flocked to the island to cover the confrontation many foreigners expected. Beijing's fury reached fever pitch in mid-March, when the United States sent two aircraft carrier battle groups to the Taiwan Strait to calm the situation.

On 23 March, 74 percent of Taiwan's eligible voters defied Beijing's bluster and turned out to choose their president. Most observers agreed that the PRC's threats helped strengthen Lee Teng-hui, as Taiwanese voters demonstrated their defiance by supporting their much-maligned leader. Lee met his target, capturing a solid majority: 54 percent of the vote. Peng Ming-min finished second with 21 percent, while Lin Yang-kang received 15 percent and Chen Li-an 10 percent. As soon as the election was over, the cross-strait crisis dissipated. After insisting for months that Lee Teng-hui supported independence, Beijing totaled up the votes for Lee, Lin and Chen and declared that 79 percent of the Taiwanese people were pro-unification.

Some commentators called the election a set-back for the DPP, since its 21 percent share of the presidential vote was well below its usual performance, which had hovered around 30 percent in the last several elections. However, the results of the National Assembly elections held on the same day as the presidential race tell a different story. In the National Assembly polling, DPP candidates won 30 percent of the vote, and 30 percent of the seats. The New Party's National Assembly candidates underperformed the Lin-Hau ticket by 2 percentage points, while the KMT won exactly half the National Assembly votes, and 55 percent

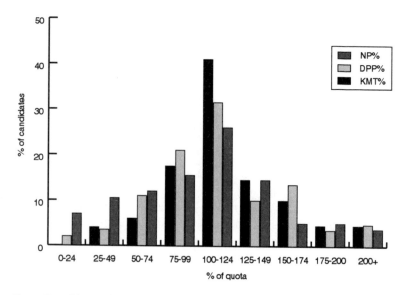

Figure 7.6   National Assembly, 1996

Source: Central Election Commission data

of the seats. The pattern of ticket splitting supports the view that Lee's victory was a personal triumph rather than an endorsement of his party. Meanwhile, the parties' distribution of votes echoed the pattern set in previous elections. (See Figure 7.6.)

The 1996 election was not only a triumph for President Lee. The presidential election overturned the last major institutional obstacle to democracy. From that point forward, all of Taiwan's top decision-making positions were filled in an electoral process that was reasonably fair and open. Of course, Taiwan's political system was far from perfect. Corruption and money politics, clientelism and local factionalism persisted. Citizens did not enjoy equal access to public offices and officials; nor were Taiwan's mass media flawlessly fair and accurate. Elections were not a perfect tool for citizens to supervise their government and communicate their preferences. But Taiwan is hardly alone in its imperfections. If we compare the Taiwan of 1996 to the Taiwan of 1966 or 1976, rather than to some ideal democracy that does not exist in any nation, we can recognize a political transformation to rival Taiwan's economic miracle.

8 Continuing challenges to Taiwan's democracy

As Huntington pointed out in *The Third Wave*, democracy is a set of procedures for selecting leaders and holding them accountable; it is not a guarantee of good government. Still, there are meaningful differences between life in a democracy and life under an authoritarian regime. At the most basic level, democracy gives public officials incentives to treat ordinary people well, since everyday citizens have the power to take away their authority.[1] In Taiwan, political reform did not create a perfect society, but it dissipated the cloud of fear and tension that hung over the island during the years of White Terror and political repression. Reform acted like an open window on a breezy day: it destabilized institutions, overturned established practices and let in many annoying things. But it also blew away years of stagnation and energized Taiwan's people.

If democracy matters, then it is worth asking how it comes about. Is it the inevitable product of socio-economic modernization? If it is, how much modernization and what kind is required to achieve it? Is it the creation of political leaders? If so, what made Chiang Ching-kuo decide to lead Taiwan toward democracy during a period of crisis, rather than attempting to shore up his regime through authoritarian retrenchment? Equally important, why, in the end, did the rest of the KMT follow him? And why did the political opposition – which all but disappeared after 1947 – re-emerge so strongly in 1977? It is my contention that in this case, Lamounier's theory of opening through elections provides the best chart for navigating through these questions.

Why respond to set-backs with reform, rather than retrenchment? Lamounier posits two central factors, each of which influences the decision in complex ways. First, even an authoritarian regime needs legitimacy, and the basis for that legitimacy must be consistent with the nation's historical and ideological heritage. Second, Lamounier argues that the electoral process produces its own momentum. Hu Fu alludes to this phenomenon when he writes of the "circumvolving" effect of elections on political reform. Both of these factors were at work in Taiwan's liberalization.

Legitimacy became a problem for the KMT regime shortly after retrocession. As Taiwanese became aware of their peripheral status in the ROC, their joy at returning to Chinese sovereignty turned into resentment. The February 28 Incident convinced many Taiwanese that the KMT was a conquering power, not a liberator. Thus, to build a safe harbor on Taiwan, the KMT regime needed to persuade the local people of its right to rule. The legitimacy formula it chose included two components: democracy and mainland recovery. Democracy was the ROC's fundamental promise, touted in every schoolbook, celebrated in every National Day parade, vaunted in every "Free China" boast. But the Nationalists asked Taiwanese to be patient in their democratic ambitions, because an even higher goal remained to be accomplished. Until the mainland was recovered, and all Chinese people were freed from behind the "bamboo curtain," Taiwan's democratic aspirations must be curtailed.

In the 1950s and 1960s, mainland recovery had a powerful claim on the hearts and minds of many Taiwanese. With the Cold War raging, the ROC leadership had reason to believe that the Western world supported its quest. But when international opinion shifted in favor of Beijing in the early 1970s, and the PRC consolidated its political and military control over the mainland, overthrowing the PRC was no longer a realistic goal. As more and more Taiwanese lost faith in mainland recovery, delaying democracy became increasingly difficult to justify. A growing number of Taiwanese began to suspect that the real reason for limiting democracy in the ROC was to keep the KMT in power. At the same time, human rights advocates overseas, no longer constrained by the fear of appearing soft on Chinese communism, began calling attention to the limitations of "Free China." Thus, with the party reform of 1972, the KMT began overhauling itself step by step, synchronizing its reality with its rhetoric. Reforms of state institutions followed, and the KMT touted them at home and abroad as evidence that it was living up to the name "Free China." At the same time, the ruling party offered elections as further justification for its "Free China" claim.

Even as the search for legitimacy drove the KMT to reform itself, elections were chipping away at the KMT's authoritarian base. The Nationalists established an electoral system on Taiwan for both practical and propaganda purposes. In propaganda terms, local elections helped the ruling party support its claim to democracy. In practical terms, elections identified authentic local leaders whom the Nationalists could recruit into the ruling party. They also provided an outlet for the Taiwanese people's political ambitions and competitive urges. And by rewarding local politicians and factions who joined the ruling party, elections helped Taiwanese overcome their distrust of the KMT and become active in politics through the ruling party.[2]

In its first two decades on Taiwan, the Nationalist Party managed to suppress the tendency of elections to act as a force for change, allowing it to enjoy their benefits at little or no cost. In 1960, the regime smashed the nascent Democratic Party and scattered its supporters. Certainly, Lei Chen and his collaborators' critical assessment of the regime in *Free China Fortnightly* provided the authorities with ample motivation for a crackdown. However, it is significant that the government tolerated Lei Chen's literary activities; it was only when he began working to coordinate his quest for democracy with Taiwanese politicians' electoral ambitions that he was arrested. Elections in the 1950s and 1960s reinforced the regime's legitimacy by regularly demonstrating its popularity. The KMT's record was extraordinarily strong, especially in small electoral districts and grassroots contests; its candidates routinely won between 70 and 80 percent of the vote in such races. As Lamounier predicts, this gave the regime confidence that it could control elections and elected bodies. Thus, opening supplementary seats in the Legislative Yuan and National Assembly to popular election looked like a low-risk way to simultaneously shore up the KMT's democratic claim and fill seats left empty by attrition.

Developments in the 1970s and early 1980s show that these carefully orchestrated elections were not without cost for the ruling party. In fact, they created regular opportunities for pro-reform activists to press their demands. The electoral calendar was extremely crowded, with major elections held almost every year. Each of these elections provided an occasion for island-wide political discussions in which dissident voices attracted the most attention. Because they were national (and therefore important) and yet only supplementary (and therefore not decisive), supplementary elections carried especially strong symbolic messages. This encouraged protest, or what Lamounier calls "plebiscitary," voting; that is, voting designed to send a message to the regime. Smaller-scale elections, such as those at the township, county and provincial levels, tended to be less symbolic, and of greater practical significance. Not surprisingly, the KMT maintained its overwhelming dominance in those races.

Grassroots elections also were a powerful force for political socialization in Taiwan. They taught Taiwanese to value elections – even if for selfish reasons – and to expect them. Canceling an election required a strong justification; some activists even opposed the postponement of the 1978 elections, which resulted from Taiwan's worst-ever foreign policy set-back. The strength of the electorate's attachment to elections was masked, however, by the KMT's monopoly at the local level. In the absence of inter-party competition, when more than 70 percent of the votes routinely were cast for KMT candidates, those elections seemed far more likely to reinforce the KMT's dominant position than to imperil it.

But when the Dangwai appeared in the mid-1970s, Taiwanese voters' comfort with electoral competition had unexpected ramifications. Although most voters remained loyal to the KMT, the number of Taiwanese who cast their ballots for opposition candidates increased steadily, as did the number who identified themselves as Dangwai and DPP supporters. The experience of voting in competitive local elections taught Taiwanese to express preferences; the presence of local factions taught them fierce loyalty to a political "side." These skills transferred to the opposition when it appeared. In short, as Lamounier observes, elections created and reinforced party identification, which made retreating from reform doubly difficult.

The results of these elections shaped both sides' responses. The KMT recognized that the Dangwai's small but significant base of support represented a latent threat, so it gave in to the opposition's demands selectively. On the one hand, it recognized the need to appear responsive to the popular will. Coopting popular reform proposals undercut the opposition at the same time that it enhanced the ruling party's popularity and allowed it to retain the initiative in the reform process. On the other hand, the KMT was careful to control the pace and direction of reform. This it was confident it could do, both because its mobilization system brought it large majorities in each election, and because Taiwan's institutional design insulated policy-making from elected officials. At the same time, the ruling party's smooth-running grassroots political machine brought it reassuring seat bonuses and commanding majorities. Thus, the KMT had little to lose and much to gain from reform.

At the same time, however, the authorities maintained enough of a repressive apparatus to keep dissidents nervous, even as they resorted to repression less frequently. The opposition, for its part, remained cautious (for example, eschewing contact with the overseas Taiwan Independence Movement), but at the same time constantly pushed the limits of the regime's tolerance. The Dangwai's steadily rising vote share in national elections encouraged it to continue working within the system. Dangwai candidates who took a radical line or participated in demonstrations were far more likely than their moderate colleagues to find themselves in trouble with the law; they also had less electoral success. For all but the most hard-bitten dissidents, this combination of carrots and sticks inspired moderation.

But if managing the opposition was the KMT leadership's main preoccupation, an equally serious threat lurked within the party itself. As we saw in Chapter 5, the turning point came in 1977, when the revolt of local factions revealed that the KMT could no longer control its electoral machine. Here, too, the underlying dynamic was rooted in the ballot box: as elections became more competitive, Taiwan's society became stronger, relative to the state. As long as electoral competition existed within the confines of a dominant party system, the state prevailed; its leaders defined the parameters in which political activity could occur. But once political actors outside the ruling party began to demonstrate an ability to deal significant set-backs to individual KMT candidates, the once-tame local factions found themselves facing new dangers, and holding new leverage. And because the relationship between the factions and the ruling party was based on utilitarian factors, not ideological commitment, as the factions adjusted to the new situation, they put their own interests ahead of the party to which they nominally belonged. The ruling party, for its part, was forced to choose between ceding more power to the society (i.e., democratizing) or seizing back its dominant position by force. And the KMT had learned in 1947 that force would not work.

After 1977, the reform process was irreversible. Efforts to suppress the opposition, including the 1979 crackdown on the *Formosa* group, had little long-term impact; new activists appeared to replace those arrested, and the public signaled its distaste for repression by voting for the defendants' surrogates. Opposition victories deepened the local factions' anxiety and further weakened their loyalty to the KMT. These trends accelerated throughout the 1980s. DPP legislators used their prominence (and the immunity of office) to attack KMT rule, while electoral pressures forced many KMT politicians to embrace pro-reform positions. The Mainstream–Nonmainstream competition created a bottleneck in the reform process, but after Premier Hau Pei-tsun resigned and the New Party broke away from the KMT, Lee Teng-hui and his "Taiwanese KMT" were free to take a final step toward procedural democracy: instituting direct presidential elections.

Challenges for the future

Transforming political attitudes and behavior

The macro-level reforms in Taiwan's political system have been accompanied by small, micro-level changes in individual attitudes and behavior. For example, party identification and party-oriented voting are on the rise. As we have seen, studies in the 1980s uncovered little evidence of party-based voting, but voting behavior studies in the 1990s found this trend weakening slightly. Political scientists Chen Yi-yan and Tsai

Meng-shi analyzed data on party and voting behavior from the 1996 presidential election.[3] Their findings paint a picture of limited change; almost half of young voters (48.4 percent) expressed neither like nor dislike for any political party, and more voters said they disliked all the parties (4.4 percent) than said they liked them all (3.0 percent). Voters also were unimpressed with the parties' performance. On a scale of 0 (dissatisfied) to 10 (very satisfied), the KMT's average score was 5.54. The DPP and NP both scored below the mid-point: 4.71 and 3.90, respectively.[4] In short, it is still the case that only a minority of Taiwanese identify with political parties, even among the "new generation" of voters. Moreover, Taiwanese have a remarkably low opinion of parties in general. Still, Chen and Tsai found that among those young voters who did have a party preference, that preference was a very strong predictor of their presidential votes, especially for KMT supporters.

Some political trends seem be taking Taiwan in a less democratic direction. For example, voter turn-out is falling.[5] As elections become routine, and traditional mobilizational devices are less effective, fewer Taiwanese are making the effort to vote. After the 1996 presidential election, the cachet of voting in a "first ever" election ceased to be a factor boosting voter participation. Primary elections, too, attract fewer and fewer voters. The KMT's first party-member poll in 1989 had an overall turn-out of 45 percent. The next two primaries' saw less than 30 percent participation, even though the party purged inactive members from the rolls after 1989.[6] Still, declining voter turn-out is a feature of many mature, consolidated democratic systems. Taiwan is unlikely to be an exception to this trend.

Balancing presidential and legislative power

In July 1997, the National Assembly passed a serious of amendments designed to streamline and strengthen the island's administrative apparatus. These reforms altered the balance of power between the president and the legislature and scaled back the provincial government. One of the most important gaps between the ROC constitution and the actual functioning of Taiwan's government is the concentration of power in the presidency. The ROC constitution established a parliamentary system with no reserved powers for the president at all. In reality, however, the ROC has functioned as a presidential system since its days in mainland China. Two factors played an especially important role in creating this state of affairs. First, emergency powers granted to the president under the Temporary Provisions effectively nullified the constitution's parliamentary emphasis. Second, the fact that nearly every ROC president served simultaneously as the Kuomintang party chair ensured that neither parliament nor prime minister could challenge presidential authority. The 1997 constitutional revisions will not alter this situation much. The revisions gave the president the power to appoint a premier without the consent of the legislature; however, the legislature can hold a vote of no confidence and force the premier out of office. Still, as long as the president is chair of the majority party, he or she still will may enjoy *de facto* powers beyond what the constitution states.

If changes in the presidency will have little effect, alterations to the Legislative Yuan are likely to be more significant. A major complaint of students of Taiwan politics has long been its weak legislative bodies. According to Hung-mao Tien, the Legislative Yuan lacks effective committee, party and leadership structures. In their absence, it tends to fall into "shouting matches and even physical confrontation." Moreover, the body requires "a substantial overhaul of existing practices to prevent an inefficient and sometimes chaotic legislature from becoming a serious impediment to democratic consolidation and national development."[7]

The 1997 constitutional amendments addressed these concerns by increasing the legislature's size and supervisory powers. They established procedures for breaking a deadlock between the executive and legislative branches. The Legislative Yuan now has the power to expel the premier with a vote of no confidence. The 1997 amendments also increased the size of the Legislative Yuan from 164 to 225 members in the hope of improving its functioning by distributing the workload more widely and facilitating an effective committee structure. Not all observers were convinced that these changes would have the desired effect. According to political scientist Lu Ya-li,

> The weaknesses of the Legislative Yuan may produce a serious situation: The sense of frustration and impotence felt by legislators may encourage them to engage in negative sorts of opposition and thus use their weapon of no confidence votes against the administration too freely, thereby creating instability.[8]

Nonetheless, the amendments show Taiwan's leaders' willingness to tackle institutional problems with constitutional reforms.

Despite its weaknesses, the second Legislative Yuan (elected in 1992) functioned less as a rubber stamp and more as an independent law-making body than did its predecessor, the "ten-thousand-year" legislature. One of its first independent actions was to pass the "Sunshine Bill" in 1993. This legislation, which requires high officials to disclose their personal wealth, was passed over the objections of the KMT leadership. Meanwhile, local governments also have begun wielding their authority more effectively. In early 1998, the newly elected DPP executive in Taichung County made national headlines when he blocked the planned construction of a German chemical factory. The project had the support of the provincial government, but the county's new leader insisted that the project be put before the voters for their approval. Political reforms empowered even ordinary citizens. In 1997, several ghastly crimes involving high-profile victims horrified Taiwanese. That summer, tens of thousands protested the government's failure to control violent crime, eventually forcing Premier Lien Chan to resign. In short, at each level of government, the public and its representatives are demanding accountability from Taiwan's once-dictatorial executive authorities.

Streamlining Taiwan's administration

The 1997 constitutional amendments also addressed a major anachronism of Taiwan's political system, the existence of provincial and central governments within the same territory. For years, the DPP advocated eliminating the provincial government, arguing that it duplicated the responsibilities of the central government and was a haven for corruption. Conservatives opposed the move on the grounds that doing away with the province would move Taiwan another step away from its identity as the Republic of China, and a step closer to independence. With the conservatives on the sidelines after 1993, Lee was free to adopt a reformist position on the issue. In December 1996, the National Development Conference (similar to the 1990 National Affairs Conference) recommended streamlining the provincial government; the National Assembly implemented the recommendation in 1997. It suspended elections for governor and Provincial Assembly at the end of their current terms (in December 1998), and made the provincial government an appointive body directly under the Executive Yuan.

In explaining its decision to downsize the provincial government, the National Assembly leadership emphasized the need for economy and efficiency. However, there was also a political dimension: the existence of two popularly elected executives (president and provincial governor) within the same territory could create serious conflicts. Provincial Governor Soong Chu-yu and the members of the Provincial Assembly fought fiercely to retain their status, but they failed to persuade the KMT leadership. Soong's willingness to stand up to President Lee gained him considerable popular acclaim. In early 1998, straw polls for the 2000 presidential election found Soong to be more popular than Lee's favorite, vice president Lien Chan.

Reducing clientelism and corruption

Despite its strong position on the issue of provincial government reform, the KMT leadership backed away from another set of reform proposals aimed at reducing electoral corruption. Political scientists are not alone in recognizing the links among local factionalism, grassroots electoral practices (including vote buying) and the SVMM system. Participants in the National Development Conference concluded that corruption, money politics and the pernicious influences of local factionalism would diminish if the bottom-most layers of the electoral system, where *tiau-a-ka* are recruited and rewarded, were eliminated. They recommended suspending elections for officials below the county level (that is, neighborhood and village heads, and town and township representatives and executives) and giving the power to appoint those officials to county executives. For similar reasons, the Legislative Yuan has considered proposals to replace the SVMM system with a combination of proportional representation and single-member districts (Japan implemented such a reform in 1994).

Both of these reform proposals were in limbo as of early 1999, thanks to opposition from incumbent officials. Not surprisingly, the targets of the reforms could not be persuaded to support them, and since the KMT still cannot afford to jettison the local factions' political assets, the proposals were stymied. Municipal elections in 1997 and 1998 undermined the KMT leadership's commitment to these reforms. The results of the November 1997 municipal executive races shocked the ruling party. For the first time ever, DPP nominees won a larger share of the vote (43 percent) than ruling party nominees (42 percent), despite the fact that the DPP had fewer candidates in the race. What is more, the DPP's support was widely distributed, allowing it to capture 12 executive positions to the KMT's 8 (independents won 3). The DPP's victories came in Taiwan's most populous and developed areas, so that the proportion of Taiwanese living under opposition executives exceeded 70 percent after these elections. According to KMT National Assembly member Chen Chih-nan, "the election results were 'irrefutable evidence' that the KMT's earlier agreement to cancel the local chief elections had shaken the roots of the party's power base to the very core."[9]

Once again, local factions were a major cause of the KMT's disastrous performance. Twelve KMT mavericks challenged their party's nominees in eight municipalities. The KMT expelled ten of the mavericks and suspended the other two, but they continued to campaign as independents. The dissenters, most of whom had local factions behind them, split the KMT vote in a number of counties. In desperation, the KMT pulled out all the stops. President Lee criss-crossed the island on behalf of the

KMT's nominees. In Taipei County he promised elderly residents a pension of US$160 monthly. In 1993, the DPP had proposed such a scheme, but the KMT blocked the measure. In late 1997, the Cabinet proposed expanding the offer to the entire nation. Opposition deputies tried to expose the KMT's true intentions by speeding the measure through the legislature. As they expected, the KMT ended up blocking the bill. As a result, whatever the merits of the KMT's responses, the appearance remained of a last-ditch campaign promise the party had little intention of fulfilling, a perception which underlined the KMT's desperation in the campaign.

In this climate, the proposal to put the power to select grassroots-level officials in the hands of county executives could hardly have had less appeal to the ruling party, both because it would increase the opposition's power and because it would further undermine local support for the KMT. Thus, in December, just after the election, the KMT announced that it was considering withdrawing its support for the reform proposal.

Its outstanding performance in the 1997 executive races energized the DPP, but the results of municipal council races held two months later were sobering: the opposition party won only 13 percent of council seats and 9 percent of city, township and village executiveships. (See Table 8.1.) These results reinforced the view that the KMT could use these grassroots officials to balance DPP executives. Also, the results were consistent with two long-standing electoral trends. First, they showed the shallowness of the DPP's grassroots penetration. The party's candidates actually performed well; however, there were very few of them. The DPP

Table 8.1 Basic-level election results, 1990–1998

| | Percentage of seats won | |
	KMT	DPP
1990		
Municipal council	77	6
Basic-level executive	92	2
1994		
Municipal council	59	11
Basic-level executive	82	7
1998		
Municipal council	60	13
Basic-level executive	73	9

Source: *Free China Journal*, 23 January 1998; James A. Robinson and Deborah A. Brown, "Local Elections Reveal the Problems and Promises of Taiwan's Emerging Democracy," published by Foreign Policy Research Institute, 17 March 1998, distributed electronically by FPRI@aol.com.

won 35 percent as many votes as the KMT, with only 25 percent as many candidates.[10] Second, the difference between November and January illustrates the fact that the DPP performs best in head-to-head competition; even after more than ten years in existence, the party still cannot equal the KMT in SVMM races. The KMT, for its part, did not have to face factional splits in the local races. In light of these trends, it is not surprising that proposals to scrap the SVMM formula have made little progress.

Strengthening political parties

Another of the challenges facing Taiwan is the need to strengthen political parties and party competition. Perhaps the DPP eventually will replace the KMT as the ruling party, either by gaining a majority in the Legislative Yuan or by winning the presidency. In either case, this almost certainly will come about as the culmination of incremental electoral gains, rather than a sudden overthrow of the ruling party. Or perhaps Taiwan will undergo party realignment, leading to an entirely new constellation of political forces. The political parties themselves may become more democratic, although progress toward that goal is halting. In describing the candidate selection process for the 1994 elections, Baum and Robinson wrote,

> [Two years ago], those who demanded greater democracy within parties seemed in ascendancy. And in a polity whose major symbols stress democracy, we projected that the trend toward frequent use of primaries and other intra-party democratic practices would be difficult to reverse. As it happened, however, each party's overriding interest to win elections demanded that leaders modify candidate selection processes in ways calculated to improve the party's chances in elections.[11]

To equal the KMT, the DPP must increase the size and depth of its grassroots membership and candidate pool. Executive elections and national races will continue to be the opposition's strong suit, but penetrating the grassroots must be a long-term goal if those DPP executives are to prove their mettle as policy-makers.[12] Becoming the ruling party also will require the DPP to overcome formidable impediments arising from its own history. As we have seen, the DPP began as a coalition of anti-KMT elements. Thus, while the party found its greatest support among the urban middle class, it also included traditional local factions in rural areas which, whether out of ideological conviction or concern for their vested interests, detached themselves from the ruling party and joined the DPP.

The opposition's basic agenda of democratization and Taiwanization held the movement together for a long time, for however fiercely those within it argued over how far and how fast its promised changes should proceed, they recognized that removing the KMT from power would require a unified opposition. But while the DPP's reformist agenda provided a unifying foundation for the opposition party, in the long run, it created complications. Maturing into a post-reform party has proven difficult, precisely because the party is a hodge-podge of anti-KMT forces. The DPP has had limited success in identifying new issues with which to re-energize its existing supporters and attract new ones. This is due both to the KMT's ability to coopt successful initiatives, and to contradictions among the DPP's major constituencies, which include both entrepreneurs and workers. Nor can the DPP attract a groundswell of new voters by continuing to flail away at the independence–unification issue. As Hu Fu and Chu Yun-han write,

> So far, emphasis on Taiwanese identity and self-determination has helped the DPP gain considerable electoral success and has given the DPP a clear political identity. But it is doubtful that this issue can help the DPP build up a winning electoral coalition in the future … Once the Taiwanese identity issue is disentangled from issues of democratic legitimacy and majority rule, its all-class appeal will attenuate.[13]

Despite the fanfare that greeted its creation, the New Party still is struggling to establish itself as a viable third force in Taiwan's politics. The party has done well in legislative elections, but its performance in local races is extremely poor. Internal disputes had grown so heated by 1997 that even in its Taipei County stronghold it managed to create a fiasco. A fight over the nomination caused one well-known NP legislator to quit the party, another to resign his seat in the party leadership and a third to declare his intention to support no one in the election. After the election, rumors flew that the KMT was seeking to lure New Party leaders back into the ruling party fold, not least in an effort to increase its legislative majority after the 1998 Legislative Yuan elections. New Party leaders rebuffed those advances, but a reconciliation of the two parties is not impossible, especially if the NP continues to struggle and the generation of leaders who sparked the KMT's break-up in 1993 fades from the scene.

The challenge of cross-strait relations

Managing its relationship with the People's Republic of China is by far the most daunting task facing Taiwan at the close of the twentieth century. Twenty years ago, mainland policy was made by a small group of party, government and military leaders. Today, it is shaped by a diverse array of institutions and driven by the imperatives of an electoral system in which the public perception of a political party's ability to manage cross-strait relations is a key determinant of its popularity.

After forty years in a state of war, relations between Taipei and Beijing began to thaw in the late 1980s. Since then they have been locked in a cycle of tension and relaxation. On the eve of Taiwan's 1996 presidential election, tensions were high enough to raise the possibility of war. Taiwan's stock market fell, and some residents bought foreign currency and prepared to flee. Yet as soon as the election was over, the threat receded. Beijing's leaders declared victory, and cross-strait economic relations resumed. In 1996 and 1997, relations between the two sides remained in a slump, but by early 1998 a new upswing was underway.

The two sides are held in this cycle by their disagreements on fundamental issues. These differences prevent a permanent resolution of the cross-strait dilemma, and complicate the process of negotiating about immediate concerns. So far, talks between Taipei and Beijing have concentrated on practical matters including economic ties, travel and communication, and dealing with crime and immigration. The two sides so far have not insisted on resolving the question of what kind of a relationship they ultimately will have. But how long will Beijing wait to accomplish its goal of unification? And how long will Taiwanese be willing to tolerate an unsettled status?

Conflict between Taipei and Beijing centers on two issues: unification and Taiwan's pragmatic diplomacy. Beijing is devoted to the idea of political unification as soon as possible. The PRC government would like to make Taiwan an entity within the People's Republic of China under the "one-country, two-systems" formula. This arrangement is unacceptable to most Taiwan residents, who believe this model would give the PRC government too much control over Taiwan's affairs. Despite Beijing's efforts to persuade the Taiwanese that the central government would allow them to manage themselves (the PRC even has offered to let Taiwan have its own military), most simply do not trust the PRC to keep its hands off.

The fact that most Taiwanese would not choose reunification on Beijing's terms does not mean that they support Taiwan independence, however. In fact, while the percentage of independence supporters has grown in recent years, a plurality of Taiwan's citizens still favors the status quo.[14] The status quo entails political autonomy for Taiwan, but eschews formal separation from China. In fact, most Taiwanese believe there is a meaningful historical and cultural bond between Taiwan and China. A 1998 study by Liu I-chou found that half of Taiwan residents believe "China" includes both Taiwan and the mainland, while 70 percent believe "the Chinese people" includes residents of Taiwan and the mainland.[15] When it comes to politics, however, Taiwanese are committed to self-determination: three-quarters of the respondents in Liu's study said Taiwan residents alone should have the right to decide the island's future, while only 11 percent said the opinions of mainland residents should be considered.[16] Based on these findings, we can conclude that Taiwan's populace would be most likely to accept unification in the form of a loose confederation based on historical and cultural ties, with full political autonomy for Taiwan. This is a far cry from what Taiwanese believe Beijing means by "one country, two systems."

In addition to their conflict over unification, Taipei and Beijing are at odds over Taiwan's campaign to raise its international profile. Domestic political considerations make it impossible for the ROC government to abandon pragmatic diplomacy; according to surveys taken in 1997, about 70 percent of Taiwanese want their government to pursue international relations even if doing so damages cross-straits ties.[17] Unfortunately, the PRC sees pragmatic diplomacy as a stealth campaign for Taiwan independence, while many Taiwanese view the PRC's campaign to keep Taiwan out of the international arena as evidence that Beijing's wishes to isolate Taiwan diplomatically so that it can more easily seize the island.

Cross-strait relations reached a low point in March 1996, and although the immediate crisis passed, the situation did not improve much until two years later. In February 1998, Beijing accepted Taipei's offer to hold talks on economic and business affairs, and agreed to a visit from Taiwan's Straits Exchange Foundation's chief negotiator. By March, the two sides had agreed to discuss both civil and political matters, and began planning a meeting of the SEF and ARATS heads, Koo Chen-fu and Wang Daohan. These advances were due, in part, to the efforts of the US government to push the two sides toward the negotiating room. In October 1997, US president Bill Clinton met with the PRC president Jiang Zemin. In subsequent weeks, a parade of highly placed former US officials trooped through Taipei. Each one urged Taiwan to resume negotiations with a realistic outlook. Although the visitors denied having any official role, many Taiwanese interpreted the visits as a message from Washington that it was time for Taiwan to give in to some of Beijing's demands. Taiwan's press was highly critical of what many characterized as pressure from Washington to sell out to the PRC. So were some foreign policy experts. Said Academia Sinica's Lin Cheng-yi, "So many China experts are impatient about the situation between Beijing and Taipei …: I'm concerned that there is a creeping US policy to endorse China's unification as the only option for the future of Taiwan."[18] Nonetheless, Taiwan can ill afford to antagonize the US, its most powerful backer.

The likelihood of reopening talks also benefited from a growing consensus among ROC political elites in favor of negotiations. In February, the DPP held a two-day symposium to hammer out guidelines for a new cross-strait policy, one that would be acceptable to all its major factions.[19] The discussions pointedly avoided the term "independence," emphasizing instead the notion of "sovereignty." (Sovereignty is considered less controversial, because all the parties agree that the ROC on Taiwan already possesses sovereignty; unlike independence, sovereignty need not be declared.) According to DPP official Julian Kuo, Taiwan needs to resume negotiations to avoid gaining a reputation internationally as a "troublemaker."[20]

Both DPP factions agreed that negotiations over economic and social issues should go forward, while political issues should remain off limits. However, they disagreed over exactly what Taiwan's goal should be. Some argued for a European Union-like arrangement, while others looked to the British Commonwealth as a model. Others rejected any such compromise. The DPP factions also differed over whether the party should encourage cross-strait economic activity. The Formosa faction argued that economic interdependence would reduce tensions and encourage moderation in Beijing, while the New Tide faction took the view that too much economic exchange would make Taiwan dependent upon, and therefore vulnerable to, the mainland. This debate reflects a deep-rooted conflict within Taiwan between those who wish to keep the mainland at a distance and those who believe good relations with the PRC offer Taiwan its best chance for continued economic success.

In sum, after a dry spell lasting nearly two years, cross-strait ties improved somewhat in 1998. In October, members of the Straits Exchange Foundation met with their ARATS counterparts and other PRC officials, including Chinese president Jiang Zemin. The two sides agreed to continue their exchange of visits, but the talks revealed profound differences between the two sides. Beijing rejected Taipei's fundamental condition for unification, the democratization of the PRC. Nor was Beijing willing to limit the talks to pragmatic issues, despite Taipei's strong desire to leave political discussions about the details of unification for later.

Taiwan, for its part, is determined to prolong the discussions and delay concrete action on unification. The danger is that Beijing may be unwilling to wait. The PRC is struggling to implement economic reforms, such as downsizing state-owned enterprises, that could spark civil unrest. And it faces these economic challenges just as the regional economy of East Asia is in its worst crisis in decades. Economic conditions could forestall precipitous action on the Taiwan issue, as Beijing may be reluctant to tackle the Taiwan issue at a time of uncertainty at home. However, the reverse also is possible. If economic conditions worsen and the leadership sees a need to enhance its popular legitimacy, a nationalistic campaign to recover Taiwan could ensue.

Working in favor of gradualism is Beijing's relatively stable political situation. When Jiang Zemin consolidated his hold on power, noisy protestations of patriotism (including promises to bring Taiwan back into the fold) gave way to more humdrum statements about economic and social policy. And having a strong leadership clarifies China's Taiwan policy. While the potential for a sudden hard-line shift is ever-present in Beijing, there is little sign of such a change on the horizon. As political scientist Chu Yun-han put it in March 1998, "The PRC's policy towards Taiwan has become more comprehensible and predictable."[21]

On 28 February 1997, Taiwan marked a poignant passage. The February 28 Incident altered forever the direction of the island's political evolution; on its fiftieth anniversary, the tragic date became a national holiday. Given those early days of bloodshed and heartbreak, it is remarkable how smooth and peaceful Taiwan's democratization has been over the past twenty years. As in any new democracy, short-comings and stumbling blocks remain. But unlike other young democracies, Taiwan can ill afford those mistakes, and it may well run out of time. Everything the Taiwanese people have accomplished since 1949 could be wiped out overnight if Beijing chooses to assert forcibly its claim to the island. Thus, the most important political issue facing the island will continue to be managing its relationship with its giant neighbor to the west. If Taiwan cannot maintain peaceful relations with the mainland, all of its political, social and economic triumphs could come to naught. Whether Taiwan's democratic political institutions will provide the tools necessary to accomplish this task remains to be seen. What is clear, however, is that the people of Taiwan chose the reforms that put these decisions in their own hands.

Notes

1 Voting for democracy

1 John Israel, "Politics on Formosa," in Mark Mancall, ed., *Formosa Today*, New York, Praeger, 1963, p. 60.
2 Despite Taiwan's high level of development and population density, its central mountains are so impassable that some areas remain unexplored. In 1998, scientists discovered a 900 hectare forest of rare beech trees in the high mountains of Ilan County.
3 Very few Chinese moved to Taiwan during the Japanese colonial period, so most "Taiwanese" families had been on the island for at least two generations at the time of retrocession.
4 This book refers to the Taiwanese and Mainlanders as "ethnic groups." This is a controversial point. Some people prefer to call this a "sub-ethnic" division, arguing that all Han Chinese belong to the same ethnic group. Ethnicity theory does not give a clear answer to the question. But the two communities behave very much like ethnic groups when it comes to politics: they tend to live near others in the same group (although this trend is diminishing), they tend to vote for members of their own group and their political views tend to be closer to one another than to members of the other group. For this reason, I have chosen to refer to the two groups as "ethnic." This does not mean, however, that they do not share a Han Chinese identity.
5 Liu I-chou, "The Taiwanese People's National Identity – A New Survey Method" (*Taiwan minzhong de guojia rentong – yi ge xin de celiang fangshi*), paper presented to the 1998 Annual Conference of the ROC Political Science Association, Taipei, 1998.
6 See, for example, Thomas B. Gold, *State and Society in the Taiwan Miracle*, Armonk, M.E. Sharpe, 1986; Hung-mao Tien, *The Great Transition: Political and Social Change in the Republic of China*, Stanford, Hoover Institution Press, 1989; Daniel Metraux, *Taiwan's Political and Economic Growth in the Late Twentieth-Century*, Lewiston/Queenston/Lampeter, Edwin Mellen Press, 1991; Peter R. Moody, *Political Change on Taiwan: A Study of Ruling Party Adaptability*, New York, Praeger, 1992; Jauhsieh Joseph Wu, *Taiwan's Democratization: Forces Behind the New Momentum*, Hong Kong, Oxford University Press, 1995; Linda Chao and Ramon H. Myers, *The First Chinese Democracy: Political Life in the Republic of China on Taiwan*, Baltimore, Johns Hopkins University Press, 1998; Hung-mao Tien, ed., *Taiwan's Electoral*

Politics and Democratic Transition: Riding the Third Wave, Armonk, M.E. Sharpe, 1996.

7 Juan Linz has even argued that leadership can be a necessary and sufficient condition for democratization in some cases. See Linz and Alfred Stepan, eds, *The Breakdown of Democratic Regimes: Crisis, Breakdown and Reequilibration*, Baltimore, Johns Hopkins University Press, 1978, p. 5.

8 Adam Przeworski, "Democracy as a Contingent Outcome of Conflicts," in Jon Elster and Rune Slagstad, eds, *Constitutionalism and Democracy*. Cambridge, Cambridge University Press, 1988, pp. 59–81.

9 See Fu Hu, "The Electoral Mechanism and Political Change in Taiwan," in Steve Tsang, ed., *In the Shadow of China: Political Developments in Taiwan since 1949*, Honolulu, University of Hawaii Press, 1993, pp. 134–168; Fu Hu and Yun-han Chu, "Electoral Competition and Political Democratization," in Tun-jen Cheng and Stephan Haggard, eds, *Political Change in Taiwan*, Boulder, Lynne Rienner Publishers, 1992, pp. 177–203; Yun-han Chu, *Crafting Democracy in Taiwan*, Taipei, Institute for National Policy Research, 1992; Lin Chia-lung "Local Elections and Marketization of the KMT Regime: From Authoritarian Consolidation to Democratic Transition (1946–1994)" (*Taiwan difang xuanju yu Guomindang zhengquan de shichanghua: cong weiquan gonggu dao minzhu zhuanxing*) in Chen Ming-tong and Cheng Yungnian, eds, *Basic-level Elections and Socio-political Change on Both Sides of the Strait* (*Liang an jiceng xuanju yu zhengzhi shehui bianqian*), Taipei, Yuedan Publishing Company Ltd, 1998, pp. 169–260.

10 Fu Hu and Yun-han Chu, "Electoral Competition and Political Democratization," op. cit., p. 197.

11 Samuel Huntington, *The Third Wave*, Norman, University of Oklahoma Press, 1991, p.7.

12 Of course, voters always operate under constraints. They may be afraid of how voting for a party or candidate will affect the economy or social welfare programs on which they depend. Or they may consider the international ramifications of electing a particular candidate. For example, Taiwanese voters cannot help but consider how the PRC might react to results of elections on the island. Many voters choose the KMT because they believe hostilities between Taiwan and the PRC are less likely under a KMT government. However, this does not mean that Taiwan's electoral process is not democratic. During the Cold War, many US voters chose presidential candidates at least in part on the basis of how well they thought they would manage relations with the Soviet Union, yet few would argue that this made US elections undemocratic.

13 The concept of democracy is hotly contested , and some would argue with my definition of democracy and my characterization of Taiwan as democratic. For example, in his 1996 National Day address, President Lee Teng-hui applied a substantive definition of democracy and found Taiwan lacking. He said, "We must understand that democracy is more than just a political system, it is a way of life. Only when the ideals of democracy are deeply inculcated in the mind can they continually grow." (Quoted in James A. Robinson, "Western Theories of Democratization and Taiwan Politics: Is Taiwan Democratic?" in Winston L. Yang and Deborah A. Brown, eds, *The Republic of China on Taiwan in the 1990s*, Center of Asian Studies, St Johns University, 1997, pp. 76–77.) Even if we choose a procedural definition of democracy, as I have done, it is

possible to argue that Taiwan falls short, because of the limitations of its electronic media. In particular, the fact that three of the island's four broadcast television stations are linked to state agencies is an important shortcoming. However, I would argue that the existence of a fourth broadcast station since mid-1997 and the widespread availability of independent information through cable television, radio and print sources makes this a much less significant drawback than it was even as recently as 1995.

14 Bolivar Lamounier, "Authoritarian Brazil Revisited: The Impact of Elections on the Abertura," in Alfred Stepan, ed., *Democratizing Brazil: Problems of Transition and Consolidation*, New York, Oxford University Press, 1989, p. 69.

15 Ibid., p. 56.

16 Ibid., p. 52.

17 Ibid.

18 Ibid., p. 70.

19 Ibid., p. 62.

20 This is not to say that either the process or the outcome is inevitable. Authoritarian regimes do have other options than to allow electoral momentum to drive them toward reform. They may abort the process by canceling elections or imposing military coups. However, where there is a history and ideology supporting elections, these solutions will be unstable. For example, governments in South Korea, Thailand, Mexico, Chile and other countries have been dragged back to the ballot box after numerous authoritarian interludes.

21 Chen Ming-tong, *Factional Politics and Political Change in Taiwan* (*Paixi zhengzhi yu Taiwan zhengzhi bianqian*), Taipei, Yuedan Publishing Company Ltd, 1995, p. 267.

22 Taiwan's Western allies, especially the US, were not blind to "Free China's" limitations. They were willing to accept an authoritarian ally in order to reduce the PRC's influence. However, the ROC's democratic veneer facilitated friendly relations between these nations. Western politicians and scholars pointed to the existence of elections and Taiwan's tiny "opposition" parties as evidence that the ROC was worthy of their nations' support.

23 It is interesting to note how radically the ROC's claim to international legitimacy has changed. Until the 1990s, the Taiwanese government insisted that the ROC was the sole legitimate government of all of China. But in 1991, President Lee Teng-hui acknowledged the existence of the Beijing government, and based his foreign policy on the idea that the people of Taiwan deserve international recognition – even if they must share it with the PRC. This approach urges foreign governments to recognize Taiwan for both moral and practical reasons, because it is a democratic state, an economic powerhouse and a cooperative international player.

24 Wu, op. cit., pp. 12–13.

25 See, for example, the quotations from Chiang Ching-kuo in Chao and Myers, op. cit., pp. 112–113.

26 Teh-fu Huang, "Elections and the Evolution of the Kuomintang," in Hung-mao Tien , ed., *Taiwan's Electoral Politics and Democratic Transition: Riding the Third Wave*, Armonk, M.E. Sharpe, 1996, p. 121.

27 In an island-wide survey conducted in July 1996, a quarter of the respondents (25.5 percent) replied that Taiwan should not unify with the PRC, even if the mainland achieved a level of economic, social and political development

comparable to Taiwan. See Naiteh Wu, "National-Identity Conflict and Democratic Consolidation in Taiwan," working paper published by the Conference Group on Taiwan Studies of the American Political Science Association, 1996.

28 See, for example, Joseph Bosco, "Taiwan Factions: Guanxi, Patronage, and the State in Local Politics," *Ethnology*, 31:2 (1992), pp. 157–183; Chao Yung-mao, *A Survey of Taiwan's Local Politics and Local Construction (Taiwan difang paixi yu difang jianshe zhi zhanwang)*, Taipei, Te-hsin-shih Publishers, 1978; Bruce J. Jacobs, "Preliminary Model of Particularistic Ties in Chinese Political Alliances: *kan-ch'ing* and *kuan-hsi* in a rural Taiwanese Township," *China Quarterly*. 78 (1979), pp. 237–273; Shelley Rigger, "Machine Politics in the New Taiwan," unpublished PhD thesis, Harvard University, 1994.

29 Wu, op. cit., p. 44.

30 Lamounier, op. cit., p. 57.

31 Hu and Chu, op. cit., p. 184.

32 Linda Chao and Ramon Myers, *The First Chinese Democracy: Political Life in the Republic of China on Taiwan*, Baltimore, Johns Hopkins University Press, 1998, *passim*, especially footnote 87, p. 326.

33 Ibid., p. 124.

34 Bruce Dickson, "The Kuomintang before Democratization: Organizational Change and the Role of Elections," in Hung-mao Tien, ed., *Taiwan's Electoral Politics and Democratic Transition: Riding the Third Wave*, Armonk, M.E. Sharpe, p. 49.

35 Ibid., p. 58.

36 Hu, op. cit., p. 149.

37 Chao and Myers, p. 108.

38 Wu, op. cit., p. 164. Wu's book was published before Taiwan's first popular presidential election.

39 Lamounier, op. cit., p. 62.

40 Yang Kuo-shu and Chu Hai-yuan, eds, *Social Change in Taiwan, Basic Survey Plan (Taiwan shehui bianqian jiben diaocha jihua)* Academia Sinica, Institute of Social Science, 1993; Chu Hai-yuan, ed., *Social Change in Taiwan, Basic Survey Plan (Taiwan shehui bianqian jiben diaocha jihua)* Academic Sinica, Institute of Social Science, 1991; and Chu Hai-yuan, ed., *Social Change in Taiwan, Basic Survey Plan (Taiwan shehui bianqian jiben diaocha jihua)* Academia Sinica, Institute of Social Science, 1996.

41 Wu, op. cit., p. 163.

42 Chu, op. cit., 1991.

43 Huang, op. cit., p. 111.

44 Chu, op. cit., p. 55.

45 William L. Parish and Charles Chi-hsiang Chang, "Political Values in Taiwan: Sources of Change and Constancy," in Hung-mao Tien, ed., *Taiwan's Electoral Politics and Democratic Transition: Riding the Third Wave*, Armonk, M.E. Sharpe, 1996, pp. 27–41.

46 I-chou Liu, "The Behavior of Taiwanese Voters in 1992: Consolidation of Partisan Ties," in Hung-mao Tien, ed., *Taiwan's Electoral Politics and Democratic Transition: Riding the Third Wave*, Armonk, M.E. Sharpe, 1996, p. 226.

47 Ibid., p. 229.

48 Hu and Chu, op. cit., pp. 184–185.

49   Hu, op. cit., p. 153.
50   Dickson, op. cit., p. 49.
51   Ibid., p. 62.
52   Tun-jen Cheng and Yung-ming Hsu, "Issue Structure, the DPP's Factionalism, and Party Realignment," in Hung-mao Tien, ed., *Taiwan's Electoral Politics and Democratic Transition: Riding the Third Wave*, Armonk, M.E. Sharpe, 1996, p. 152.
53   According to Lin Chia-lung's calculations, between 1950 and 1993, non-nominated local factions challenged KMT candidates in 24 municipal executive races, supported opposition candidates 32 times and passively boycotted KMT nominees 50 times. Opposition candidates won about 40 percent of these races, compared to only 3.5 percent of races in which factions either supported KMT candidates or had no reaction (Lin Chia-lung, op. cit., p. 56). See also Shelley Rigger, "The Risk of Reform: Factional Conflict in Taiwan's 1989 Municipal Elections," *American Journal of Chinese Studies*, 2:2 (October 1993), pp. 201–232.
54   Ming-tong Chen, "Local Factions and Elections in Taiwan's Democratization," in Hung-mao Tien, ed., *Taiwan's Electoral Politics and Democratic Transition: Riding the Third Wave*, Armonk, M.E. Sharpe, 1996, p. 181.
55   Huang, op. cit., pp. 133–134.
56   Chen, op. cit., p. 185.

2   Learning to vote: the origins of Taiwan's electoral system

1   Lai Tse-han, Ramon Myers and Wei Wou, *A Tragic Beginning: The Taiwan Uprising of February 28, 1947*, Stanford, Stanford University Press, 1991, p. 25.
2   Taiwan was divided into eight prefectures.
3   George H. Kerr, *Formosa: Licensed Revolution and the Home Rule Movement, 1895–1945*, Honolulu, University Press of Hawaii, 1974, p. 169.
4   Chen Ming-tong and Lin Jih-wen, "The Origins of Taiwan's Local Elections and the Changing Relations between State and Society" (*Taiwan difang xuanju de qiyuan yu guojia shehui guanxi zhuanbian*) in Chen Ming-tong and Zheng Yungnian, eds, *Basic Level Elections and Socio-Political Change on Both Sides of the Strait*(*Liang an jiceng xuanju yu zhengzhi shehui bianqian*) Taipei, Yuedan Publishing Company, 1998, p. 30.
5   Chen Ming-tong and Lin Jih-wen point out that the property qualification in these early elections limited the franchise to Taiwan's wealthy class. In their view, these early elections established the pattern of local factionalism that endures today, prompting them to speculate that had the Japanese not imposed these restrictions, Taiwan's political landscape might have developed class-based political cleavages rather than the vertical patron–client linkages that characterize its faction-based politics (Chen and Lin, op. cit., 34n.).
6   Chen and Lin, op. cit., pp. 32–33.
7   This description of the League's activities in the 1935 elections is drawn from Chen and Lin, op. cit., pp. 37–38.
8   Ibid., p. 37.
9   Ibid., p. 38.
10   Ibid., p. 39.

11 Kerr, op. cit., p. 171.
12 Lai *et al.*, op. cit., p. 44.
13 Ibid., p. 68.
14 Ibid., p. 69.
15 Chen and Lin, op. cit., p. 42.
16 Ibid., p. 44.
17 In 1995, Taipei City and Kaohsiung City each were divided into two legislative districts. Of the remaining 23 districts, 21 consisted of the individual counties and cities of Taiwan province. The other two were the islands of Mazu and Jinmen, which are municipalities under Fujian province. In the supplementary legislative elections held prior to 1992, some districts encompassed more than one municipality.
18 There is one exception to this rule. Taiwan's election law establishes a quota for women. If not enough women are elected from a particular district, the top-finishing woman replaces the male candidate who finished at the bottom of the winning group. This makes for interesting strategies, as parties use female candidates to pick up "free" seats. Paradoxically, it has meant that many female candidates receive little campaign help from their parties, because they are considered to be outside the normal competition. This makes it difficult for more than the minimum quota of women to be elected.
19 In Taiwan, certain groups (including veterans who belong to the KMT's Huang Fu-hsing Special Party Branch, the Railway Workers Union, the Postal Workers Association, police, and teachers) are reliable enough to be assigned in this fashion. See I-Chou Liu, "The Electoral Effect of Social Context Control on Voters: The Case of Taipei, Taiwan," unpublished PhD dissertation, University of Michigan, 1990, p. 61.
20 For a very thorough explanation of this process see Liu, ibid., pp. 57–86. The DPP and NP have attempted to use similar strategies. However, achieving an effective division of the vote is extremely difficult for small parties, especially in the competitive environment created by political liberalization.
21 The KMT employed three patterns of nomination. Where there were no more factions than available seats and the party was strong, it usually nominated a candidates for every contested seat (full nomination). If all the factions could be accommodated, but party organization was weak, the party nominated fewer candidates than seats, to avoid the possibility of non-KMT candidates defeating KMT nominees. Where the party felt little risk from independents, but factional competition was fierce and the number of seats was not sufficient to reward all the factions, the KMT sometimes chose not to nominate anyone, so that the inter-factional competition could squeeze out opposition competitors without the party appearing to "play favorites." Lin Chia-lung studied these strategies and found that, statistically, the net result was to give the KMT more seats than it otherwise would have won (Lin Chia-lung, "Local Elections and Marketization of the KMT Regime: From Authoritarian Consolidation to Democratic Transition, 1946–1994" (*Difang xuanju yu Guomindang zhengquan de shichanghua*) in Chen Ming-tong and Cheng Yungnian, eds, *Local Elections and Socio-Political Change on Both Sides of the Taiwan Strait* (*Liang an jiceng xuanju yu zhengzhi shehui bianqian*) Taipei, Yuedan Publishing Company Ltd, 1998, pp. 200–201.
22 The information in this paragraph is drawn from Liu I-chou, op. cit., pp. 60–61.

23 There is a Mandarin translation of this expression, *zhuangjiao*, but because *tiau-a-ka* are a grassroots phenomenon, and grassroots politics in Taiwan is conducted overwhelmingly in Taiwanese, not Mandarin, the phrase *tiau-a-ka* is more familiar and widely recognized.

24 Liu, op. cit., p. 71.

25 Lin Chia-lung, op. cit., p. 205.

26 Thomas R. Rochon, "Electoral Systems and the Basis of the Vote," in John C. Campbell, ed., *Parties, Candidates, and Voters in Japan: Six Quantitative Studies*, Ann Arbor, University of Michigan, 1981, pp. 6–7.

27 Ibid., *passim*.

28 Yang Tai-shuenn, "*Woguo xuanju zhidu de tese*" ("The Peculiarities of our Electoral System"), *Zhongguo Xianzheng*, 24:12 (1989), p. 12.

29 Survey respondents were asked to choose as many of the following factors as applied: personal relations (71.7 percent), social relations (9.0 percent), political organizations (26.4 percent), candidates' political views (30.4 percent), candidates' qualifications (71.7 percent), personal factors (11.5 percent), other (3.4 percent) (*The Voting Behavior of the Electorate* [*Xuanmin de toupiao xingwei*] Taipei, *Zhongyang xuanju weiyuanhui* [Central Election Commission], 1987, p. 156.)

30 Liu, op. cit., p. 132.

31 Fu Hu and Yun-han Chu, "Electoral Competition and Political Democratization," in Tun-jen Cheng and Stephan Haggard, eds, *Political Change in Taiwan*, Boulder, Lynne Rienner Publishers, 1992, p.196.

32 See Lin Chia-lung, op. cit., p. 205.

33 Jih-wen Lin, "Consequences of the Single Nontransferable Voting Rule: Comparing the Japan and Taiwan Experiences," unpublished PhD dissertation, University of California Los Angeles, 1996, *passim*.

34 This, in turn, contributes to the tendency of Taiwan's political parties to be ideologically heterogeneous and not very cohesive. Because most members of the majority party in an SVMM system are concerned primarily with providing benefits to their own supporters, Lin calls these parties "distributive coalitions" (Ibid., p. 65).

35 Based on surveys conducted after the 1989 elections, I-chou Liu estimated the percentage of Taipei City voters who are influenced by the responsibility-zone system at roughly 35 percent (Liu, op. cit., p. 122). Because Taipei has the largest percentage of middle-class and well-educated voters, the percentage of voters who respond to the mobilization system is probably lower there than in most areas of Taiwan.

36 Ibid., p. 155.

37 Yang Tai-shuenn, *Elections* (*Xuanju*), Taipei, Yungran Cultural Publishers Ltd, 1991, p. 219.

38 In a study of preference voting (an electoral formula under which voters cast one vote for a party and another for a candidate), Richard Katz noted a similar phenomenon. The larger the district magnitude, the more likely a candidate was to lose to a member of his or her own party. So to survive intraparty competition – in which programmatic and party label distinctions were of little use – candidates relied on personal organizations and connections. (See Richard Katz, "Preference voting in Italy: votes of opinion, belonging, or exchange," *Comparative Political Studies* 18 (1985) pp. 229–249.)

39 Fei-lung Lui, "The Electoral System and Electoral Behavior," in Tun-jen Cheng and Stephan Haggard, eds, *Political Change in Taiwan*, Boulder, Lynne Rienner, 1992, p. 152.

40 See Yung-mao Chao, "Local Politics on Taiwan: Continuity and Change," conference paper delivered at the International Symposium, Tufts University, December 1989, pp. 10–11; and Huang Teh-fu, "Elections, Local Factions and Political Transition: Reflections on the 1989 Elections" (*Xuanju, difang paixi yu zhengzhi zhuanxing: qishiba nien sanxiang gongzhirenyuan xuanju zhi xingsi*) *The Journal of Sunology: A Social Science Quarterly*. 5:1 (1990), p. 93.

41 Hu Fu, "The Function of Elections in an Evolving Society," (*Xuanju zai bianqian shehui de zuoyong*), *Zhongguo Luntan*, 240 (1989), p. 67.

42 Until the 1992 election "renovated" the legislature, only 18 of its approximately 300 members represented the opposition party.

43 During the 1991 legislative session the DPP captured a majority of seats in the Judiciary Committee. The speaker, Liang Su-yung, berated his KMT comrades, whom he said had become so preoccupied with "economic meddling" (*gao jingji*) that they had let the DPP take over the committee.

44 Fu Hu, "Elections under the Emergency Rule: The Case of Taiwan," paper presented to the Conference on Power and Social Responsibility: Elections in Asia and the Pacific, University of the Philippines, Quezon City, February 1986, p. 6.

45 In 1997, the opposition Democratic Progressive Party introduced legislation to make the top bureaucratic posts in municipal governments subject to political appointment rather than civil service promotion. Otherwise, DPP legislators argued, non-KMT executives find it impossible to implement their policy initiatives. The legislation was defeated in December 1997.

46 Hung-mao Tien, *The Great Transition: Political and Social Change in the Republic of China*, Stanford, Hoover Institution Press, 1989, p. 124.

47 In general, public spending is uneven in Taiwan. For example, average per capita spending on economic and communications construction in Taipei City was NT$1,903, three times the amount spent in second-place Taichung City (NT$638). In Yunlin County, spending was less than 5 percent of the Taipei City rate (NT$90). Chao Yung-mao, *A Survey of Taiwan's Local Politics and Local Construction*, (*Taiwan difang zhengzhi yu difang jianshe zhi zhanwang*), Taipei, Te-hsin-shih Publishers, 1978, p. 108.

48 Tien, op. cit., p. 132.

49 Edwin A. Winckler, "Roles Linking State and Society," in Hill Gates and Emily Martin Ahern, eds, *The Anthropology of Taiwanese Society*, Stanford, Stanford University Press, 1981, p. 68.

50 Gerald L. Curtis, *Election Campaigning Japanese Style*, New York, Columbia University Press, 1971, p. 254.

51 Julian Baum and James A. Robinson, "Party Primaries in Taiwan: Reappraisal," *Asian Affairs: An American Review* 22:2 (1995), p. 93.

52 Liu, op. cit., p. 51.

53 Many observers have noted the legal restrictions on mass media coverage of political campaigns in Taiwan. However, practical problems are equally overwhelming. Until 1997, Taiwan had three broadcast television stations, all of which covered the entire island. As a result, the only local TV news coverage and advertising was on cable networks, which themselves were illegal until the mid-1990s. Even without legal restrictions, coordinating TV access for the

hundreds of candidates competing in local elections each year would be nearly impossible. Without broadcasts targeted at local markets, only a tiny fraction of potential viewers would be in each candidate's own district, making TV an expensive and inefficient way to campaign. Daily newspapers are better able to accommodate the large number of candidates, because they publish zoned local editions. Still, most media election coverage focuses on parties, not candidates, even though party identification plays only a small role in the voting decision.

54 From time to time a party may sacrifice this objective to achieve an even more valued result. In the 1991 National Assembly election, the KMT over-assigned votes to one of its nominees in Hsinchu City, because party leaders decided it was more important to have a KMT candidate finish first in the high-profile contest than to distribute its votes evenly.

55 Deborah A. Brown, Eric P. Moon and James A. Robinson, "Taiwan's 1998 Local Elections: Appraising Steps in Democratization," unpublished paper, 1998, pp. 14–15.

56 A party's seat bonus is defined as the difference between the percentage of seats it wins in an election and the percentage of votes it wins. A positive seat bonus indicates that the party was more successful than its opponents in maximizing the effectiveness of the votes it received.

57 Liu, op. cit., p. 107. (The differences are statistically significant at the 0.001 level.)

58 Liu, op. cit., p. 104.

59 The fact that the second-largest group of candidates fell just *below* the quota illustrates the problem of overnomination – too many KMT candidates competing for the same votes.

60 Chen and Lin, op. cit., p. 27.

3 Party-state authoritarianism in the pre-reform era (1945–1972)

1 Li Hsiao-feng, *Forty Years of Taiwan's Democracy Movement* (*Taiwan minzhu yundong sishi nian*), Taipei, Independence Evening Post, 1987, p. 27.

2 George Kerr, *Formosa Betrayed*, Boston, Houghton Mifflin Company, 1965, pp. 73–74.

3 Li, op. cit., p. 30.

4 Lai Tse-han, Ramon H. Myers, and Wei Wou, *A Tragic Beginning: The Taiwan Uprising of February 28, 1947*, Stanford, Stanford University Press, 1991, p. 66.

5 Li, op. cit., p. 29.

6 Quoted in Li, op. cit., p. 32.

7 Quoted in Li, op. cit., p. 43.

8 Lai *et al.*, p. 120.

9 The ROC's Judicial Yuan admits to more than 29,000 cases of political imprisonment between 1950 and the early 1990s. (Fran Buntman and Tong-yi Huang, "The Role of Political Imprisonment in Developing Democratic Elites: A Comparative Study of South Africa and Taiwan," paper presented to the American Political Science Association, 1997, p. 4.)

10 Discrimination on the basis of provincial origin was not accidental. The 1947 constitution limited the number of civil service employees that could be recruited from each province, presumably to distribute opportunities more

widely. On Taiwan, however, this provision was used as a legal justification for limiting the number of Taiwanese in public service. When the National Assembly amended the constitution in 1994, it set aside this provision. I am indebted to James A. Robinson for bringing this item to my attention.

11 The central government later created two provincial-level special municipalities, Taipei City and Kaohsiung City, which reduced the overlap between the central and provincial governments. Also, the ROC controls two small islands on the mainland coast; these are recorded as "Fukien Province" in official documents.

12 Edwin Winckler, "The Politics of Regional Development in Northern Taiwan: case studies and organizational analysis," unpublished PhD dissertation, Harvard University, 1974, p. 79.

13 Ping-lung Jiang and Wen-cheng Wu, "The Changing Role of the KMT in Taiwan's Political System," in Tun-jen Cheng and Stephan Haggard, eds, *Political Change In Taiwan*, Boulder, Lynne Rienner, 1992, p. 91.

14 Two legal "opposition" parties, the Young China Party and the Democratic Socialist Party, have no base or appeal in Taiwan, and so are effectively moribund. A few representatives of these parties came with the KMT from the mainland in 1949. The Kuomintang propped them up politically and economically in order to preserve the fiction of multi-party politics in the ROC. However, neither party made a significant contribution to politics on Taiwan.

15 Hung-mao Tien, *The Great Transition: Political and Social Change in the Republic of China*, Stanford, Hoover Institution Press, 1989, p. 71.

16 Yangsun Chou and Andrew Nathan, "Democratizing Transition in Taiwan," *Asian Survey*, 27:3 (1987), p. 278.

17 J. Bruce Jacobs, *Local Politics in a Rural Chinese Cultural Setting: a field study of Mazu Township, Taiwan*, Canberra, Contemporary China Centre, Research School of Pacific Studies, Australian National University, 1980, p. 25.

18 Lin Chia-lung, "Local Elections and Marketization of the KMT Regime: From Authoritarian Consolidation to Democratic Transition (1946–1994)", (*Difang xuanju yu Guomindang zhengquan de shichanghua: cong wequan gonggu dao minzhu zhuanxing*) in Chen Ming-tong and Cheng Yungnien, eds, *Basic Level Elections and Socio-Political Change on Both Sides of the Strait*(*Liang an jiceng xuanju yu zhengzhi shehui bianqian*), Taipei, Yuedan Publishing Company, 1998, p. 177.

19 Yung-mao Chao, "Local Politics on Taiwan: Continuity and Change," in Denis Fred Simon and Michael Y.M. Kao, eds, *Taiwan: Beyond the Economic Miracle*, Armonk, M.E. Sharpe, 1992, p. 51.

20 Jacobs, op. cit., p. 30.

21 Tien, op. cit., p. 86.

22 Statistics drawn from Monthly Bulletin of Statistics of the Republic of China and Statistical Summary published by the Bureau of Statistics, Directorate-General of Budget, Accounting and Statistics, Executive Yuan, 1997.

23 Lai *et al.*, op. cit., p. 35.

24 Ibid., p. 39.

25 Thomas B. Gold, *State and Society in the Taiwan Miracle*, Armonk, M.E. Sharpe, 1986, p. 66.

26 Gold, op. cit., p. 184.

27 Tun-jen Cheng and Stephan Haggard, "Regime Transformation in Taiwan: Theoretical and Comparative Perspectives," in Cheng and Haggard, eds, *Political Change in Taiwan*, Boulder, Lynne Rienner Publishers, 1992, p. 9.

28 The GINI Index averaged 0.298 during these years. Tun-jen Cheng and Yung-ming Hsu, "Issue Structure, the DPP's Factionalism, and Party Realignment," in Hung-mao Tien, ed., *Taiwan's Electoral Politics and Democratic Transition: Riding the Third Wave*, Armonk, M.E. Sharpe, 1991, p. 154.

29 Tien, op. cit., p. 111.

30 For a detailed discussion of the regime's efforts to promote an ROC identity – and the reactions of Taiwanese to that effort – see Alan Wachman, *Taiwan: National Identity and Democratization*, Armonk, M.E. Sharpe, 1994. See especially the sections on education (pp. 82–84), language (pp. 107–110) and the status of Taiwan (pp. 110–112).

31 Chen Ming-tong, *Factional Politics and Taiwan's Political Evolution* (*Paixi zhengzhi yu Taiwan zhengzhi bianqian*), Taipei, Yuedan Publishing Company, 1995, p. 114.

32 Chin-chuan Lee, "Sparking a Fire: The Press and the Ferment of Democratic Change in Taiwan," in Lee, ed., *China's Media, Media's China*, Boulder, Westview Press, 1994, p. 166.

33 Emma Wu, "The View from Down South," *Free China Review* June 1993, p. 19.

34 Tien, op. cit., p. 197.

35 Ruth Berins Collier and David Collier, "Inducements versus constraints: disaggregating 'corporatism'," *American Political Science Review* 73 (1979), p. 968 (emphasis in original).

36 See, for example, Chiang quoted in Chi-yun Chang, *The Rebirth of the Kuomintang, the Seventh National Congress* translated Yuan-ching Nee, Taipei, China Cultural Service, approx. 1955, p. 34.

37 *The Kuomintang Manifesto and Platform Adopted by the Seventh National Convention, October 1952*. Taipei, China Cultural Service, 1954, p. 33.

38 Arthur Lerman, *Taiwan's Politics: The Provincial Assemblyman's World*, Washington DC, University Press of America, 1979, p. 212.

39 Chen, op. cit., p. 111.

40 Tien, op. cit., p. 50.

41 Benedict Stavis, *Rural Local Governance and Agricultural Development in Taiwan*, Ithaca NY, Cornell University Center for International Studies, 1974, p. 104.

42 Huang Teh-fu and Liu Hua-tsung, "Farmers Associations and Local Politics: The Cases of Taichung County and Kaohsiung County," (*Nonghui yu difang zhengzhi: yi Taizhong Xian yu Gaoxiung Xian wei lie*) *Journal of Election Studies* (*Xuanju Yanjiu*) 2:2 (November 1995), *passim*.

43 Stavis, op. cit., p. 99.

44 The source for this section is an article titled "There's a General Chiang K'ai-shek [bank note] Hiding in the Straw Hat," *The Journalist* (*Xin Xinwen Zazhi*), 16 December 1991, pp. 12–27. The content of the article is consistent with information from other sources.

45 Stavis, op. cit., p. 81.

46 In March 1993, a DPP activist in Chiayi County was murdered after he began investigating a scheme in which the Chiayi District Fishermen's Association was collecting substantial fees from fishermen seeking to purchase

government-subsidized fuel to which they are legally entitled. According to the Chiayi's DPP legislator Tsai Shih-yuan, the association was collecting as much as NT$5–10 million (US$200,000–$400,000) annually. According to Tsai, "the income is one way of funding support for the faction which controls the fishermen's group and other rural councils as well as most other major posts in the county government" (*Far Eastern Economic Review* , 6 May 1993, p. 17).

47 Tien, op. cit., p. 47.
48 Stavis, op. cit., p. 99.
49 Quoted in Aksel DeLasson, *The Farmers' Association Approach to Rural Development – the Taiwan Case*, Goettingen, Germany, Institute for Rural Development, University of Goettingen, 1976, p. 181.
50 Jacobs, op. cit., pp. 23–24.

4 Electoral mobilization in the pre-reform era (1945–1972)

1 Success rates calculated from election results reported in Chen Ming-tong, *Factional Politics and Taiwan's Political Evolution* (*Paixi zhengzhi yu Taiwan zhengzhi bianqian*), Taipei, Yuedan Publishing Company, 1995, pp. 224–227.
2 Lin Chia-lung, "Local Elections and Marketization of the KMT Regime: From Authoritarian Consolidation to Democratic Transition, 1946–1994" ("*Difang xuanju yu Guomindang zhengquan de shichanghua*") in Chen Ming-tong and Zheng Yungnian, eds, *Basic-level Elections and Socio-Political Change on Both Sides of the Strait* (*Liang an Jiceng Xuanju yu Zhengzhi Shehui Bianqian*), Taipei, Yuedan Publishing Company Ltd, pp. 180–181.
3 Jih-wen Lin, "Consequences of the Single Nontransferable Voting Rule: Comparing the Japan and Taiwan Experiences," unpublished PhD dissertation, University of California Los Angeles, 1996, p. 24.
4 John Duncan Powell, "Peasant Society and Clientelist Politics," *American Political Science Review*, 64:2 (1970), p. 416.
5 Immediately after retrocession, island-wide political factions did exist, but the KMT leadership believed they were implicated in the February 28 Incident, and it soon eliminated them. For a detailed discussion of this period, see Chen Ming-tong, op. cit., pp. 132–137.
6 Chen, op. cit., p. 150.
7 Chen, op. cit., p. 153.
8 Yang Yung-i, "The New Face of Factional Politics," (*Paxi zhengzhi de xin mianmao*), *The Intellectual* (*Daxue*), 188 (1985), p. 9.
9 Chen, op. cit., p. 177.
10 Lin Chia-lung, op. cit., p. 195.
11 Arthur Lerman, *Taiwan's Politics: The Provincial Assemblyman's World*, Washington DC, University Press of America, 1978, p. 51.
12 Bernard Gallin, *Hsin Hsing, Taiwan: A Chinese Village in Change*, Berkeley, University of California Press, 1966, p. 22.
13 Interviews with the author, June and October 1991.
14 Chao Yung-mao, "The Relationship Between Local Factions and Elections – An Attitude Structure Analysis" (*Difang paixi yu xuanju zhi guanxi – I ge gainian jiagou de fenxi*) *Zongshan Shehui Kexue Jikan* 4:3 (1989), p. 61.
15 Quoted in Chen, op. cit., p. 108.
16 Chen, op. cit., p. 110.
17 Interview with the author, April 1991.

18 Details of the *tiau-a-ka* system vary from county to county, and even within counties. For example, the best-developed *tiau-a-ka* network can be found in some rural townships. There, the identities of *tiau-a-ka* responsible for particular types of projects and problems are common knowledge among villagers. Relationships between politicians and *tiau-a-ka*, *tiau-a-ka* and voters, are stable and enduring. In other areas, *tiau-a-ka* have lost much of their political influence and social status; their activities have become largely routine and their relationships with politicians and voters are distant and unpredictable. This account will emphasize the general characteristics of the *tiau-a-ka* system, recognizing the wide variation that exists within this pattern.

19 Gallin, op. cit., p. 116. None of the authors discussed in this section cites the 28 February 1947 massacre of Taiwanese elites as a cause of the landlords' declining influence. Jacobs mentions that the township he studied differed from its neighbors in that the February 28 Incident had no repercussions there (see Jacobs, 1980, p. 116). Contemporary Taiwanese writers place much more importance on the February 28 Incident, which they say so terrorized the landholding rural elite that many of those who were not killed withdrew from public life. Nai-teh Wu takes up this issue in his dissertation, arguing that the largest turnover of local leadership occurred in the 1950 and 1951 elections, the first elections held after the February 28 Incident, before the land reform was implemented (see Wu Nai-teh, *The Politics of a Regime Patronage System: Mobilization and Control Within an Authoritarian Regime*, unpublished PhD dissertation, University of Chicago, 1987, pp. 212–220.). The notion that land reform transformed rural society by liberating farmers from the landlords' control is an important KMT dogma; it appears in all the ROC literature on land reform published before about 1985. This could be the reason why these authors did not look to the February 28 Incident to explain the landlords' fall from power. Another likely reason is the extreme reluctance of rural people to talk about the Incident. Even in 1991, after it had become a topic of open public debate, some elderly farmers who suffered its effects refused to discuss it. The barriers to those seeking information about it in the 1970s must have been all but insurmountable. Finally, it may be that in the cases these scholars studied, the February 28 Incident simply was not a significant factor in the transformation of rural elites in the 1940s and 1950s.

20 Ibid.

21 The existence of many different institutions of mobilization does not imply KMT failure or lack of control. The ruling party founded many of these organizations; most of the rest are affiliated with it. The party benefits from their diversity in that they allow for multiple routes of access to voters; for example, a voter who disapproves of the KMT as a party and his village head as an individual may be willing to cooperate with a Farmers' Association loan officer.

22 I-chou Liu, *The Electoral Effect of Social Context Control on Voters: The Case of Taipei, Taiwan*, unpublished PhD dissertation, University of Michigan, 1990, p. 67.

23 Interview with the author, May 1991.

24 Interview with the author, November 1991.

25 "*Tong xing, tong xue, tong xiang*" often are reeled off in a single breath, in response to questions about how people make their voting decisions. Many Taiwanese treat them as components of a single phenomenon; in effect, they

are a cliché representing the constellation of relationships Taiwanese people understand to be relevant in political decision-making.

26 The Farmers' Association case study in Chapter 3 describes in detail how associational *tiau-a-ka* in one organization are mobilized.

27 Interview with the author, April 1991.

28 According to a survey of Legislative Yuan members, more than half reported attending more than thirty weddings and funerals each month. On average, legislators said they received 3.5 service requests from constituents each day (Hung-mao Tien, *The Great Transition*, Stanford, Hoover Institution Press, 1989, p.143).

29 The Yu family's behavior is consistent with Powell's description of the clientele system, in which he said,

[i]mpersonal communications between persons low and high in the system hierarchy are as ineffective as they are rare. A low-status participant may, on occasion, personally approach a high-status participant in the same clientele system, but normally he depends on a series of linkages with intermediate brokers.

(Powell, op. cit., p. 423)

30 Yang Kuo-shu and Chu Hai-yuan, eds, *Social Change in Taiwan, Basic Survey Plan* (*Taiwan shehui bianqian jiben diaocha jihua*) Academia Sinica, Institute of Social Science, 1993.

31 See Wu, op. cit., pp. 46–54, *passim*.

32 Quoted in Wu, ibid., p. 52.

33 Quoted in ibid., p. 51.

34 The first character in the Taiwanese expression *tiau-a-ka* is "pillar" (*zhuang*); the third is "foot" (*jiao*).

35 Liu, op. cit., p. 82.

36 Brian Woodall, *Japan under construction: corruption, politics, and public works*, Berkeley, University of California Press, 1996, *passim*.

37 A 1994 study found that the voters who are most likely to be mobilized by *tiau-a-ka*, those who support local factions, are less ideological, less well informed, less likely to identify with a party and more apathetic than other Taiwanese voters (Chen Ming-tong, "Xunzhao Paixi Xuanmin," cited in Lin Jih-wen, op. cit., p. 125).

38 Wu, op. cit., pp. 264–265.

39 If a particular neighborhood post is contested especially fiercely, the ward or village head may hold an election, but most neighborhood heads are appointed.

40 I am indebted to Hwang Jau-Yuan for pointing out the political implications of local officials' private philanthropy.

41 Yung-mao Chao, "Local Politics on Taiwan: Continuity and Change," in Denis Fred Simon and Michael Y.M. Kao, *Taiwan: Beyond the Economic Miracle*, Armonk, M.E. Sharpe, 1992, p. 49.

42 *Free China Journal*, 15 December 1992.

43 Quoted in Lerman, op. cit., p. 112.

44 Quoted in ibid., p. 111.

45 Ibid., p. 127.

46 Ma Ch'i-hua, *Research on Contemporary Political Problems* (*Dangqian zhengzhi wenti yanjiu*) Taipei, Li-ming Cultural Publishing Company, 1991, p. 161.
47 *Free China Journal*, 25 September 1992.
48 *World Journal* (*Shijie Ribao*) , 17 December 1992.
49 *World Journal* (*Shijie Ribao*), 17 July 1992.
50 This trick is not new; it is mentioned in the Lerman and Jacobs books.
51 *Independence Evening Post* (*Zuli Wanbao*), translated in JPRS-CAR-93–0006, 2 February 1993.
52 In 1989, the Clean Election Commission, a private organization committed to stamping out electoral corruption, distributed stickers showing an NT$1,000 bill under a red circle and slash with the words "My family does not sell votes." The idea was that voters would put these on their houses to send a message to *tiau-a-ka*. The wife of a reporter I interviewed in a small town in southern Taiwan said the stickers showed how out of touch the anti-bribery crusaders were with the culture of ordinary Taiwanese. While her family never receives bribes (the *tiau-a-ka* are afraid of journalists), she said she could never put such a sticker on her house because it would insult her neighbors. "Everyone would say we think we're better than they are," she explained.
53 I once asked the teenage daughter of a DPP activist if she knew of anyone who bought votes in her village. "Of course," she laughed. "Our next-door neighbor, the ward head, buys votes. But not ours, because everybody knows we're for the DPP." The teenage daughter of a National Taiwan University professor living in Taipei City, however, has no first-hand experience of vote buying. As her father explained, candidates do not believe vote buying will help them in the family's urban, middle-class neighborhood.
54 Yang Tai-shuenn, *Elections* (*Xuanju*), Taipei, Yung-jan Cultural Publishing Ltd, 1991, p. 273.
55 Chen, op. cit., pp. 238–241.
56 Chen, op. cit., p. 254.

5 Political reform under Chiang Ching-kuo (1972–1988)

1 Li Hsiao-feng, *Forty Years of Taiwan's Democracy Movement* (*Taiwan minzhu yundong 40 nian*), Taipei, Independence Evening Post Publishing Company, 1987, p. 71. The Taiwanese opposition was still complaining about these very abuses thirty years later.
2 For example, Chiang Ching-kuo preferred the quiet Lee Teng-hui to other, more prominent, Taiwanese politicians (such as Lin Yang-kang) precisely because he had no connections to local forces. According to his advisor, Chen Li-fu, Chiang once told him, "Lin Yang-kang has a clique (*xiaozu*), but Lee Teng-hui has none, so he is better; indeed, he is quite capable." Quoted in Chen Ming-tong, *Factional Politics and Taiwan's Political Evolution* (*Paixi zhengzhi yu Taiwan zhengzhi bianqian*), Taipei, Yuedan Publishing Company, 1995, p. 169.
3 Li, op. cit., p. 78.
4 Sixteen years later, Fei became the founding chair of Taiwan's first opposition party, the Democratic Progressive Party.
5 Li, op. cit., p. 81.
6 To prevent a third embarrassment, the central government gave Taipei "special municipality" status in 1967, suspending mayoral elections until 1994.

Cleverly, however, the center chose the incumbent Kao to be the first appointed mayor; a few years later, Kao was brought into the cabinet, effectively neutralizing him as an electoral threat.

7 This was not impossible, however. One of the most prominent Taiwan Independence activists of the 1950s, Liao Wen-yi, repudiated the movement and returned to Taiwan in 1965.

8 Incredibly, one of the would-be assassins, Cheng Tzu-tsai, returned to Taiwan in 1991 to campaign for his wife's National Assembly bid. He made several public speeches in which he described the planning and execution of the assassination plot.

9 Ralph Clough, *Island China*, Cambridge MA, Harvard University Press, 1978, p. 41.

10 The Tiaoyutai conflict reignited in the 1990s when right-wing Japanese erected a light and flag on one of the islands. One Hong Kong Chinese was killed when he attempted to swim to the Tiaoyutai in rough seas to plant a PRC flag; patriotic demonstrations in Beijing eventually were suppressed, as they threatened the PRC government's good relations with Japan. In Taiwan, radical Chinese nationalists also protested the ROC's weak response to the Japanese "insult."

11 Peter Moody, *Political Change on Taiwan: A Study of Ruling Party Adaptability*, New York, Praeger Publishers, 1992, p. 77.

12 The *Ta Hsueh* group strongly advocated expanding the national bodies; however, it did not reach out to local politicians, as the *Free China Fortnightly* activists had done.

13 Quoted in Linda Chao and Ramon Myers, *The First Chinese Democracy: Political Life in the Republic of China on Taiwan*, Baltimore, Johns Hopkins University Press, 1998, p. 112.

14 Teh-fu Huang, "Elections and the Evolution of the Kuomintang" in Hung-mao Tien, ed., *Taiwan's Electoral Politics and Democratic Transition*, Armonk, M.E. Sharpe, 1996, p. 115.

15 Clough, op. cit., p. 63.

16 Bruce Dickson, "The Kuomintang before Democratization: Organizational Change and the Role of Elections," in Hung-mao Tien, ed., *Taiwan's Electoral Politics and Democratic Transition*, Armonk, M.E. Sharpe, 1996, p. 52.

17 Dickson, op. cit., p. 50.

18 Dickson, op. cit., p. 58.

19 Edwin Winckler, "Institutionalization and Participation on Taiwan: From Hard to Soft Authoritarianism?" *China Quarterly*, 99 (1984), *passim*.

20 Later, in the 1990s, the opposition's demands became more radical. The demand to implement the ROC constitution gave way to the demand for a new constitution, and Taiwan independence replaced Taiwanization of the ROC in the opposition's platform. But in the 1970s and 1980s, these positions had little currency, except among the most radical dissidents, most of whom were in exile.

21 Moody, op. cit., p. 78.

22 Chen, op. cit., p. 190.

23 The KMT admitted as much in internal party documents. See Chen, op. cit., p. 269.

24 Li., op. cit., p. 125.

25 *Forever our Old County Executive, Yu Teng-fa (Yongyuan de lao xianzhang, Yu Dengfa)*, Yu Cheng-hsian/Yu Ling-ya Joint Service Center, 1989, p. 38.

26 John F. Copper, *The Taiwan Political Miracle: Essays on Political Development, Elections and Foreign Relations*, Lanham MD, University Press of America, 1997, pp. 190–191.

27 Ibid., p. 138.

28 The difference between the KMT's vote share and that of the Dangwai is the vote share of independent candidates not affiliated with the Dangwai group. Some of these candidates belonged to the traditional small parties. Others were sympathetic to the Dangwai, but it is a difficult and subjective project to try to separate the various tendencies among the independents. Thus, the most reliable way to measure support for the Dangwai is to count only the candidates formally affiliated with it.

29 Shih Ming-teh's attorney You Ching was elected to the Control Yuan by the members of the provincial assembly and the Taipei and Kaohsiung City councils. After 1980, the government substituted at-large seats for geographical constituencies in Control Yuan elections. The stated reason for the switch was to eliminate vote buying, but it also had the effect of making it nearly impossible for Dangwai candidates to win election to the Control Yuan.

30 Copper, op. cit., p. 210.

31 For the views of presidential adviser Tao Pai-chuan, see Chao and Myers, op. cit., p. 123.

32 According to Peter Moody, the KMT's problems in this period resulted in part from Chiang Ching-kuo's worsening health. Without President Chiang firmly in control, the KMT tended to drift, and problems got out of control. Moody, op. cit., p. 90.

33 Human rights pressures were not entirely ineffectual. In 1984, Chiang Ching-kuo released a number of political prisoners from the White Terror period, and he commuted the sentences of two Kaohsiung defendants, Lin Yi-hsiung and Reverend Kao Chun-ming.

34 Moody, op. cit., p. 89.

35 The DPP's position on Taiwan's identity called for "self-determination," not independence.

36 Copper, op. cit., pp. 68–69.

37 The national security law that replaced martial law allowed some forms of censorship. In particular, advocacy of Taiwan independence was defined as subversive and banned. Thus, in 1991, five young activists were tried on subversion charges related to Taiwan independence activism. Even the modified restrictions on free speech proved unenforceable in the 1990s. The "Taiwan Independence Five" were released with a warning after an enormous public outcry. The case marked the death knell for speech restrictions.

38 Janis Connolly, "Mass Media Explodes: Taiwan's Media Market is Practically Bursting at the Seams," *Topics: Issues on International Business in Taiwan*, 1996 (August), p. 18.

39 Ibid.

40 *The Republic of China Yearbook, 1997*, Taipei, Government Information Office, p. 116.

6 The watershed elections of 1989

1 John F. Copper, *The Taiwan Political Miracle: Essays on Political Development, Elections and Foreign Relations*, Lanham MD, University Press of America, 1997, p. 145.

2 *Independence Evening Post* survey, quoted in Jauhsieh Joseph Wu, *Taiwan's Democratization: Forces Behind the New Momentum*, Hong Kong, Oxford University Press, 1995, p. 121.

3 Linda Chao and Ramon H. Myers, *The First Chinese Democracy: Political Life in the Republic of China on Taiwan*, Baltimore, Johns Hopkins University Press, 1998, p. 172.

4 Shao Tzung-hai, "A Discussion of the Development of Party-Oriented Voting From the Perspective of the 1989 Election Results" ("*Cong chishiba nian gongzhi renyuan xuanju jieguo lun zhengdang quxiang toupiao xingwei de fazhan*"), *Theory and Policy* (*Lilun yu zhengce*), 4:2 (1990), p. 41.

5 Eligibility to vote in Taiwan's party primaries is limited to registered party members, who constitute a small minority of ROC voters. They are a strictly private affair, with no mass participation or government involvement.

6 Organization Department document, quoted in Yang Tai-shuenn, *Elections* (*Xuanju*), Taipei, Yungran Cultural Publishing Company, 1991, p. 255.

7 *Ibid.*, p. 267.

8 Ming-tong Chen, "Local Factions and Elections in Taiwan's Democratization," in Hung-mao Tien, ed., *Taiwan's Electoral Politics and Democratic Transition*, Armonk: M.E. Sharpe, 1996, p. 187.

9 Lin Chia-lung, "Local Elections and Marketization of the KMT Regime: From Authoritarian Consolidation to Democratic Transition (1946–1994)" (*Difang xuanju yu Guomindang zhengquan de shichanghua*), in Chen Ming-tong and Zheng Yungnian, eds, *Basic Level Elections and Socio-Political Change on Both Sides of the Taiwan Strait*, (*Liang an jiceng xuanju yu zhengzhi shehui bianqian*), Taipei, Yuedan Publishing Company, 1998, p. 226.

10 Chen, op. cit., p. 181.

11 Yang, op. cit. p. 257.

12 *Ibid.*, p. 260.

13 This assertion is supported by Yang Tai-shuenn's study of the gap between first- and last-finishing KMT candidates. Ideally, in SVMM elections, all candidates of a single party should receive about the same number of votes. That way, no votes are wasted, and the party maximizes its share of seats. To measure the KMT's success in achieving this standard, Yang looked at the ratio of the vote shares of the KMT's first- and last-finishing candidates in each district. In the 1986 legislative elections, the top KMT finishers in all districts averaged 1.52 times the vote share of the bottom KMT finishers, proving, as Yang says, the "efficiency of the party's vote allocation arrangement." In 1989, however, the party's vote allocation strategy was less effective, with the average top-finisher winning 1.66 times more votes than his last-finishing KMT comrade. In some districts the gap was very wide indeed; one candidate received 4.7 times as many votes as his most laggardly KMT colleague. *Ibid.*, p. 271.

14 Quoted in *ibid.*, p. 269.

15 The average turn-out of military voters was 55 percent, compared to 42 percent for other party organizations. I-Chou Liu, "The Electoral Effect of

Social Context Control on Voters: The Case of Taipei, Taiwan," unpublished PhD dissertation, University of Michigan, 1990, p. 43.

16 Ibid.

17 Shao, op. cit., p. 43.

18 The two parties' issue positions are summarized in Martin Lasater, *A Step Toward Democracy: The December 1989 Elections in Taiwan, Republic of China*, Washington DC, AEI Press, 1990, pp. 36–41.

19 Copper, op. cit., p. 255.

20 Shao, op. cit., p. 43.

21 Ibid.

22 I-Chou Liu, op. cit., p. 132.

23 For example, Taipei County Executive You Ching mounted a long-standing battle with the central government to prevent the construction of a second nuclear power plant in the county, while Kaohsiung County Executive Yu Chen Yueh-ying helped compel the government to provide health insurance coverage to farmers when she extended the benefit to farmers in her county.

24 Hsu Huo-yan, "Party Identification and Voting Choice" ("*Zhengdang rentong yu toupiao jueze*"), *Journal of Humanities and Social Sciences* (*Renwen ji shehui kexue jikan*), 4:1 (1991), p. 18.

25 Ibid., p. 17.

26 For example, modernization theory predicts that opposition voting will be strongest in those districts in which modernization is most advanced – the urban, industrialized areas. In fact, however, Taiwan's voting patterns were considerably more complicated than this. The KMT's overall vote share in legislative races was 60 percent. And, as modernization theory predicts, the ruling party exceeded this performance in several rural counties (Nantou, 63 percent; Taitung, 64 percent; Hualien 87 percent). However, the KMT also did better than average in Taiwan's largest city, Taipei (64 percent) and some other urban areas (Keelung, 74 percent; Taichung, 66 percent). In other cities, the KMT's vote share in the legislative races fell well below its overall performance (Hsinchu, 47 percent; Chiayi, 32 percent; Kaohsiung, 42 percent), and it also did poorly in some of Taiwan's most rural counties (Ilan, 32 percent; Pingtung, 47 percent).

27 Lin Chia-lung, "Who Supports the KMT? Who Supports the DPP?" (*Shei zhichi Guomindang? Shei zhichi Minjindang?*), *Zhongguo Luntan*, 33 (1989), p. 10.

28 Lin emphasized that the Dangwai did not enjoy majority support among *any* social group. Perhaps, writes Lin, the best way to describe the KMT is as a catch-all party, while the DPP is a party for Taiwanese. Indeed, his strongest statistical finding was that 96.5 percent of DPP supporters in 1986 were Taiwanese (Lin, ibid.).

29 Fu Hu and Yun-han Chu, "Electoral Competition and Political Democratization," in Tun-jen Cheng and Stephan Haggard, eds, *Political Change in Taiwan*, Boulder, Lynne Rienner, 1992, p. 192.

30 Ting T'ing-yu, *Socio-Economic Development and Voting Behavior: An analysis of Kuomintang vote share at the village and neighborhood level in the 1980, 1983 and 1986 supplementary Legislative Yuan elections* (*Shehui Jingji Fazhan yu Toupiao Xingwei: Minguo 69, 72, 75 nian qucheng zenger liwei xuanju guomindang depiaolu cunli jueding insu zhi fenxi*), Taipei, Kuei-kuan Book Company, 1992, p. 73.

31 Ibid., p. 193.

32 Hsu Huo-yan, op. cit., p. 39.
33 Although the data on which this study is based were collected under the most rigorous of standards and practices, it is possible that a lingering atmosphere of political repression may have caused some respondents to answer less than candidly.
34 Hsu, op. cit., p. 20.
35 Ibid., p. 41. Emphasis in original.
36 Yang, op. cit., p. 276.
37 Yang Tai-shuenn, *Free China Journal*, 8 December 1992.
38 Cited in Lasater, op. cit., p. 46.
39 Kau Ying-mao, *Selected Papers from the Conference on Election Reform* (*Xuanju gaige yantaohui lunwenji*), Taipei: 21st Century Foundation, 1991, p. 4.
40 Huang Teh-fu, "Elections, Local Factions and Political Transition: Reflections on the 1989 Elections" (*Xuanju, di fang paixi yu zhengzhi zhuanxing:qishiba nian sanxiang gongzhi renyuan xuanju zhi xingsi*), *The Journal of Sunology: A Social Science Quarterly*, 5:1 (1990), pp. 90–92.
41 Fei-lung Lui, "The Electoral System and Voting Behavior in the Republic of China on Taiwan," paper submitted to the Conference on Democratization in the Republic of China, Taipei, January 1989, p. 19.
42 Taipei County, unlike Taiwan's other municipalities, does not have county-wide factions. Its factions are specific to each of its cities.
43 Interview with the author, Taipei, October 1991.

7 The Lee Teng-hui years (1990–1996)

1 Ming-tong Chen, "Local Factions and Elections in Taiwan's Democratization," in Hung-mao Tien, ed., *Taiwan's Electoral Politics and Democratic Transition: Riding the Third Wave*, Armonk, M.E. Sharpe, 1996, p. 188.
2 Ibid., p. 189.
3 Although the Mainstream faction was predominantly Taiwanese and the Nonmainstream faction predominantly Mainlander, the division between the factions was more political than ethnic. There are many exceptions to the ethnic generalizations; for example, one of the Mainstream leaders, Soong Chu-yu, is a Mainlander, while a leading Nonmainstream figure, Lin Yang-kang, is Taiwanese.
4 According to Chen Ming-tong, the Mainstream and Nonmainstream factions both sought allies among the local factions during the presidential election struggle. As a result, Mainstream leaders found themselves expending more resources than ever, cultivating local factions in order to keep them out of the Nonmainstream camp. This further increased the local factions' political influence. Chen Ming-tong, *Factional Politics and Taiwan's Political Evolution* (*Paixi zhengzhi yu Taiwan zhengzhi bianqian*), Taipei, Yuedan Publishing Company Ltd, 1995, pp. 233–235, *passim*.
5 Linda Chao and Ramon H. Myers, *The First Chinese Democracy: Political Life in the Republic of China on Taiwan*, Baltimore, Johns Hopkins University Press, 1998, p. 193.
6 Quoted in Ts'ai Ling and Ramon H. Myers, "Manichaean Suspicions and the Spirit of Reconciliation: Currents of Public Opinion in Taiwan on the Eve of

the 1990 Conference on the Republic of China's Destiny," *American-Asian Review* (Summer 1991), p. 21.

7 Jason Hu, speech dated 23 September 1993, Government Information Office, p. 5.

8 Chi Su, "International Relations of the Republic of China During the 1990s," *Issues and Studies*, 29:9 (1993), p. 8.

9 FBIS-CHI-91-184, 23 September 1991, pp. 69–70.

10 Ch'u Hai-yuan, ed., *Social Change in Taiwan, Basic Survey Plan* (*Taiwan shehui bianqian jiben diaocha jihua*) Nankang, Academia Sinica, Institute of Social Science, 1991.

11 Tun-jen Cheng and Yung-ming Hsu, "Issue Structure, the DPP's Factionalism, and Party Realignment," in Hung-mao Tien, ed., *Taiwan's Electoral Politics and Democratic Transition: Riding the Third Wave*, Armonk, M.E. Sharpe, 1996, p. 14.

12 Ch'u, op. cit.

13 Ibid.

14 John F. Copper, *The Taiwan Political Miracle: Essays on Political Development, Elections and Foreign Relations*, Washington DC, University Press of America, 1997, p. 278.

15 For an explanation of why this is so, see Yang Tai-shuenn, *Elections* (*Xuanju*), Yungran Cultural Publishing Company Ltd, 1991, p. 213.

16 Neither the Social Democratic Party nor the Independent Alliance had much success in the election. Together, the two main parties captured 95 percent of the vote. The Social Democrats did not win any seats; independents won just 5 seats, or 2 percent.

17 Su, op. cit., p. 9.

18 Robinson, op. cit., p. 42.

19 When members of the Nonmainstream faction sought to have Chen expelled from the party for this heresy President Lee tried to quiet the conflict. But when Chen attacked his critics, calling them "traitors to Taiwan," even the president could not protect him. He lost his party membership despite holding the KMT's nomination for Legislative Yuan.

20 A Changhua County legislative candidate (KMT) boasted to reporters that he planned to spend NT$600 million on his campaign. According to the *Far Eastern Economic Review*, the average KMT candidate spent around NT$150 million. Most DPP candidates' expenditures were below NT$100 million. (Julian Baum, "Tactical Alliance," *Far Eastern Economic Review*, 17 December 1992, p. 15.)

21 One-tenth of the DPP-affiliated candidates ran without the party's nomination.

22 Julian Baum and James A. Robinson, "Party Primaries in Taiwan: Reappraisal," *Asian Affairs: An American Review*, 20:2 (1993), p. 92.

23 According to an *Independence Evening Post* report, some *tiau-a-ka* accepted money from several different candidates. In an effort to be fair, these vote brokers "allocated them [votes] according to the amount of cash they have received. As a result, the chairman of the KMT is unable to allocate the votes. On the contrary, a delicate situation arises with the vote bosses [*tiau-a-ka*] in control." (Translated in JPRS CAR-93-015, 3 May 1993, p. 43.)

24 Julian Baum, "Tactical Alliance," *Far Eastern Economic Review*, 17 December 1992, p. 15.

25 For examples of the disputes between Hau and Lee, see Chao and Myers, op. cit., pp. 270–271.
26 Chi Huang and S. G. Wu, "Inherited Rivalry, A Chronology," in Tun-jen Cheng, Chi Huang, Samuel S. G. Wu, eds, *Inherited Rivalry: Conflict Across the Taiwan Straits*, Boulder, Lynne Rienner, 1995, p. 258.
27 *The Republic of China Yearbook, 1997*, Taipei, Government Information Office, 1997, p. 116.
28 For excerpts see Chao and Myers, op. cit., p. 292. For the original article, see Shima Ryotaro, "*Basho no kurishimi: Taiwanjin ni umareta hiai*" ("A place of agony: The tragedy of having been born a Taiwanese"), *Shukan asahi* (*Asahi Weekly*), 6–13 May 1994, p. 44.
29 The percentage was 58 percent in February 1995 (*Republic of China Yearbook, 1997*, op. cit., p. 115).
30 The New Party won only 3.1 percent of the vote overall, but its large vote share in Taipei County split the conservative vote, thus contributing to the DPP's success.
31 The author shadowed a DPP candidate for township representative in Kaohsiung County during this election. Despite an energetic campaign, the candidate lost in every polling district in the township, even in his home neighborhood. The reasons for his defeat included his refusal to buy votes (most candidates had campaign workers openly handing out cigarettes at polling stations). Also, this candidate was not a member of the Black Faction, which held executive power in both the township and the county. Thus he would have been unable to obtain material assistance or constituent services for his supporters. In short, without access to the mobilization system, he was not a viable candidate.
32 This description of the KMT's strategy in 1994 is drawn from Chen, *Factional Politics*, op. cit., pp. 254–255.
33 The party subsequently lost a seat when it expelled one legislator.

8 Continuing challenges to Taiwan's democracy

1 Michael Coppedge has written a fascinating article in which he argues that the existence of electoral competition made Venezuelans less vulnerable to violence and exploitation than Mexicans. See Michael Coppedge, "Parties and Society in Mexico and Venezuela," *Comparative Politics*, 23:2 (April 1993), pp. 253–271.
2 In 1983, I had the privilege of living with a Taiwanese family in Hualien, a small city on Taiwan's remote east coast. One night, after his children were in bed, the father of the family confessed his hatred for Mainlanders. He said, "They are not only not of the same country (*guojia*) as us, they are not the same nationality (*minzu*)." However, this man (a physician) actively supported the local KMT branch and had excellent relations in the Hualien County government. He saw no contradiction between despising Mainlanders and the central government they dominated, and participating in local politics. In his mind, the local KMT apparatus was part of the local scene, entirely distinct from national politics. Thus, he was a KMT activist in spite of his distrust of the national leadership.
3 Chen Yi-yan and Tsai Meng-shi, "Party Orientation and Voting Choice of the New Generation of Voters: An Analysis Based on the 1996 President

Election," (*Xinshidai xuanmin de zhendang quxian yu toupiao juece – Shouju minxuan zongtong de fenxi*), *Chinese Political Science Review* Vol. 29 (December 1997), pp. 63–91. Data drawn from the National Chengchi University Election Research Center survey of voters.

4 The score for the NP had a very large standard deviation, suggesting that opinion was polarized.

5 Eric Moon and James Robinson, "Grassroots races vital for democratic process," *Free China Journal*, 23 January 1998, p. 7.

6 James A. Robinson and Julian Baum, "Party Primaries in Taiwan: Footnote or Text in Democratization?" *Asian Affairs: An American Review* 20:2 (1993), p. 93.

7 Hung-mao Tien, "Elections and Taiwan's Democratic Development," in Hung-mao Tien, ed., *Taiwan's Electoral Politics and Democratic Transition: Riding the Third Wave*, Armonk, M.E. Sharpe, 1996, p. 21.

8 Quoted in *Free China Review*, October 1997, p. 45.

9 *Free China Journal*, 12 December 1997.

10 Deborah A. Brown, Eric P. Moon and James A. Robinson, "Taiwan's 1998 Local Elections: Appraising Steps in Democratization," unpublished paper, 1998, p. 15.

11 Julian Baum and James A. Robinson, "Party Primaries in Taiwan: Reappraisal," *Asian Affairs: An American Review* 22:2 (1995), p. 95.

12 Frustration with its inability to win grassroots offices and the advantage this gives the KMT in mobilizing votes in higher-level elections makes the DPP the strongest advocate of eliminating elections below the municipal level. There is some irony in the fact that a political party born out of the desire for democratic reform is now fighting to reduce local autonomy and democratic control.

13 Fu Hu and Yun-han Chu, "Electoral Competition and Political Democratization," in Tun-jen Cheng and Stephan Haggard, eds, *Political Change in Taiwan*, Boulder, Lynne Rienner Publishers, 1992, p. 198.

14 According to Liu I-chou's research, 49.9 percent support the status quo, compared to 18.3 percent for independence, either immediate or gradual, and 20.5 percent for unification, either immediate or gradual. Liu I-chou, "The Taiwanese People's National Identity – A New Survey Method," (*Taiwan minzhong de guojia rentong – yi ge xin de celiang fangshi*), paper presented to the 1998 Annual Conference of the ROC Political Science Association, 1998, p. 14.

15 Ibid., pp. 8–9.

16 Ibid., p. 10.

17 Ho Szu-yin, "Taking the Middle Road," paper presented to the Workshop on Cross-Strait Relations, University of British Columbia, 21–22 August 1998, p. 6.

18 Quoted in Julian Baum, "Strait Talking", *Far Eastern Economic Review*, 26 March 1998, p. 29.

19 The New Party was grappling with these issues, too. In February, ten elected officials from the NP drew fire from party leaders when they endorsed a one China, two Chinese states formula.

20 Quoted in *Free China Journal*, 20 February 1998.

21 Quoted in Baum, "Strait Talking," op. cit., p. 29.

Suggestions for further reading

Taiwan's democratization

Chao, Linda and Myers, Ramon H., *The First Chinese Democracy: Political Life in the Republic of China on Taiwan*, Baltimore, Johns Hopkins University Press, 1998.

Cheng, Tun-jen and Haggard, Stephan, eds, *Political Change in Taiwan*, Boulder, Lynne Rienner Publishers, 1992.

Chu, Yun-han, *Crafting Democracy in Taiwan*, Taipei, Institute for National Policy Research, 1992.

Copper, John F., *The Taiwan Political Miracle: Essays on Political Development, Elections and Foreign Relations*, Lanham MD, University Press of America, 1997.

Dickson, Bruce, *Democratization in China and Taiwan: The Adaptability of Leninist Parties*, Oxford, Clarendon Press, 1998.

Gold, Thomas B., *State and Society in the Taiwan Miracle*, Armonk, M.E. Sharpe, 1986.

Leng, Shao-chuan, ed., *Chiang Ching-kuo's Leadership in the Development of the Republic of China on Taiwan*, Lanham MD: University Press of America, 1993.

Metraux, Daniel, *Taiwan's Political and Economic Growth in the Late Twentieth-Century*, Lewiston/Queenston/Lampeter, The Edwin Mellen Press, 1991.

Moody, Peter R., *Political Change on Taiwan: A Study of Ruling Party Adaptability*, New York, Praeger, 1992.

Tien, Hung-mao, *The Great Transition: Political and Social Change in the Republic of China*, Stanford, Hoover Institution Press, 1989.

Tien, Hung-mao, ed., *Taiwan's Electoral Politics and Democratic Transition: Riding the Third Wave*, Armonk, M.E. Sharpe, 1996.

Tsang, Steve, ed., *In the Shadow of China: Political Developments in Taiwan since 1949*, Honolulu, University of Hawaii Press, 1993.

Winckler, Edwin A., and Greenhalgh, Susan, *Contending Approaches to the Political Economy of Taiwan*, Armonk, M.E. Sharpe, 1988.

Wu, Jauhsieh Joseph, *Taiwan's Democratization: Forces Behind the New Momentum*, Hong Kong, Oxford University Press, 1995.

Yang, Winston L., and Brown, Deborah A., eds, *The Republic of China on Taiwan in the 1990s*, Center of Asian Studies, St Johns University, 1997.

Pre-reform Taiwan

Clough, Ralph, *Island China*, Cambridge, Harvard University Press, 1978.

DeLasson, Aksel, *The Farmers' Association Approach to Rural Development – the Taiwan Case*, Goettingen, Germany, Institute for Rural Development, University of Goettingen, 1976.

Finkelstein, David Michael, *Washington's Taiwan Dilemma, 1949–1950: from abandonment to salvation*, Fairfax VA, George Mason University Press, 1993.

Garver, John W., *The Sino-American Alliance: Nationalist China and American Cold War Strategy in Asia*, Armonk, M.E. Sharpe, 1997.

Jacobs, J. Bruce, *Local Politics in a Rural Chinese Cultural Setting: a field study of Mazu Township, Taiwan*, Canberra, Contemporary China Centre, Research School of Pacific Studies, Australian National University, 1980.

Jacoby, Neil H., *U.S. Aid to Taiwan*, New York, Praeger, 1966.

Kerr, George H., *Formosa: Licensed Revolution and the Home Rule Movement, 1895–1945*, Honolulu, University Press of Hawaii, 1974.

Lai Tse-han, Myers, Ramon, and Wou, Wei, *A Tragic Beginning: The Taiwan Uprising of February 28, 1947*, Stanford, Stanford University Press, 1991.

Lerman, Arthur, *Taiwan's Politics: The Provincial Assemblyman's World*, Washington DC, University Press of America, 1979.

Stavis, Benedict, *Rural Local Governance and Agricultural Development in Taiwan*, Ithaca NY, Cornell University Center for International Studies, 1974.

Wolf, Margery, *The House of Lim: A Study of a Chinese Farm Family*, ?Appleton-Century-Crofts, 1968.

Social issues

Berman, Daniel K., *Words Like Colored Glass: The Role of the Press in Taiwan's Democratization Process*, Boulder, Westview Press, 1992.

DeGlopper, Donald R., *Lukang: Commerce and Community in a Chinese City*, Albany, State University of New York Press, 1995.

Gates, Hill, *Chinese Working-Class Lives: Getting By in Taiwan*, Ithaca, Cornell University Press, 1987.

Gates, Hill, and Ahern, Emily Martin, eds, *The Anthropology of Taiwanese Society*, Stanford, Stanford University Press, 1981.

Lee, Chin-chuan, ed., *China's Media, Media's China*, Boulder, Westview Press, 1994.

Rubinstein, Murray, ed., *The Other Taiwan: 1945 to the Present*, Armonk, M.E. Sharpe, 1994.

Simon, Denis Fred, and Kao, Michael Y.M., eds, *Taiwan: Beyond the Economic Miracle*, Armonk, M.E. Sharpe, 1992.

Wachman, Alan, *Taiwan: National Identity and Democratization*, Armonk, M.E. Sharpe, 1994.

Wolf, Margery, *Women and the Family in Rural Taiwan*, Stanford, Stanford University Press, 1972.

Clientelism and local politics

Bosco, Joseph, "Taiwan Factions: Guanxi, Patronage, and the State in Local Politics," *Ethnology*, 31:2 (1992), pp. 157–183.

Jacobs, J. Bruce, "Preliminary Model of Particularistic Ties in Chinese Political Alliances: *kan-ch'ing* and *kuan-hsi* in a rural Taiwanese Township," *China Quarterly*, 78 (1979), pp. 237–273.

Rigger, Shelley, "Machine Politics in the New Taiwan," unpublished PhD thesis, Harvard University, 1994.

Rigger, Shelley, "The Risk of Reform: Factional Conflict in Taiwan's 1989 Municipal Elections," *American Journal of Chinese Studies*, 2:2 (October 1993), pp. 201–232.

Cross-strait relations

Cheng, Tun-jen, Huang, Chi, and Wu, Samuel S. G., eds, *Inherited Rivalry: Conflict Across the Taiwan Straits*, Boulder, Lynne Rienner, 1995.

Copper, John F., *Words Across the Taiwan Strait*, Lanham MD, University Press of America, 1995.

Garver, John W., *Face off: China, the United States, and Taiwan's Democratization*, Seattle, University of Washington Press, 1997.

Leng, Tse-kang, *The Taiwan-China Connection: Democracy and Development Across the Taiwan Straits*, Boulder, Westview, 1996.

Wu, Hsin-hsing, *Reaching Across the Strait: Taiwan, China and the Prospects for Unification*, Hong Kong, Oxford University Press, 1994.

Chronology

1895	China cedes Taiwan to Japan in the Treaty of Shimonoseki .
1921	Taiwanese living in Japan form the Taiwan Culture Society to advocate home rule for Taiwan.
1935	Japanese colonial government orders the election of local assemblies on Taiwan.
25 Oct 1945	Japan relinquishes Taiwan to China.
1946	Elections held for district, city and township consultative councils.
28 Feb 1947	Clashes between Taiwanese and Mainlanders lead to an island-wide uprising that is violently suppressed.
May 1948	Temporary Provisions Effective During the Period of Mobilization for the Suppression of Communist Rebellion are promulgated.
May 1949	Martial law imposed.
Dec 1949	ROC government moves to Taipei.
June 1950	United States Seventh Fleet sails to the Taiwan Strait.
1950	Municipal elections.
1953	Land to the Tiller Act promulgated.
1954	First direct election of Provincial Assembly, municipal elections.
1957	Provincial assembly and municipal elections.
1960	*Free China Fortnightly* publisher Lei Chen is arrested and jailed. Provincial and municipal elections.
1963	Provincial elections.
1964	Municipal elections.
1965	National Taiwan University professor Peng Ming-min is arrested, goes into exile.
1967	ROC declares Taipei City a "special municipality," abrogating mayoral elections.

1968	Provincial and municipal elections.
1969	First supplementary elections held for seats in the National Assembly, Legislative Yuan and Control Yuan.
1971	ROC loses its United Nations seat to the People's Republic of China.
Dec 1972	Elections for supplementary members of National Assembly and Legislative Yuan, and for Provincial Assembly members and municipal executives.
April 1975	Chiang Kai-shek dies, replaced by vice president Yen Chia-kan.
1975	Supplementary elections for the Legislative Yuan.
Nov 1977	Dangwai participates in Provincial Assembly elections and municipal executive elections; violence breaks out at the Chungli vote-counting station in Taoyuan County.
1978	Chiang Ching-kuo elected president of the ROC by the National Assembly.
Dec 1978	National supplementary elections canceled due to the announcement of normalized relations between the United States and PRC.
10 Dec 1979	Kaohsiung Incident: violent encounter between police and demonstrators at a rally in Kaohsiung City sponsored by *Formosa* magazine leads to the arrest of more than forty dissidents; eight are court-martialed.
28 Feb 1980	Kaohsiung Incident defendant Lin Yi-hsiung's family is murdered while their home is under police surveillance.
Dec 1980	Supplementary elections for National Assembly and Legislative Yuan.
1981	Provincial and municipal elections.
1983	Supplementary elections for Legislative Yuan.
March 1984	Taiwan Provincial Governor Lee Teng-hui named ROC vice president; provincial and municipal elections.
1985	Provincial and municipal elections.
Sept 1986	Democratic Progressive Party founded in Taipei.
Oct 1986	President Chiang Ching-kuo tells *Washington Post* interviewer that he intends to lift martial law.
Dec 1986	Supplementary elections to Legislative Yuan and National Assembly.
June 1987	Legislative Yuan passes National Security Law to replace martial law.
15 July 1987	Martial law is lifted.

Oct 1987	Taiwan residents are permitted to travel to mainland China for family visits.
Jan 1988	Chiang Ching-kuo dies, replaced by vice president Lee Teng-hui.
July 1988	Lee Teng-hui elected chairman of Kuomintang at 13th Party Congress.
July 1989	First primary elections held by KMT to select candidates for December elections.
Dec 1989	Newly legalized opposition parties compete with KMT in elections for supplementary Legislative Yuan seats, Provincial Assembly, municipal executives and municipal councils. DPP wins 35 per cent of the vote.
1990	Mainland Affairs Council created.
March 1990	Lee Teng-hui elected president of the ROC by National Assembly.
April 1990	Central Standing Committee of the KMT passes plan for the voluntary retirement of senior parliamentarians.
May 1990	Hau Pei-tsun appointed premier.
June 1990	National Affairs Conference; Council of Grand Justices rules that senior parliamentarians must step down by 31 December 1991.
Oct 1990	National Unification Council established .
Nov 1990	Straits Exchange Foundation founded.
May 1991	President Lee declares the termination of the Period of Mobilization for the Suppression of Communist Rebellion.
Dec 1991	Elections for the Second National Assembly held (the first non-supplementary national elections); senior parliamentarians step down.
Nov 1992	Peng Ming-min returns to Taiwan.
Dec 1992	Elections for Legislative Yuan (non-supplementary).
Feb 1993	Premier Hau Pei-tsun resigns.
Aug 1993	Chinese New Party founded.
1993	Municipal elections.
March 1994	Qiandao Lake Incident.
1994	Soong Chu-yu elected Provincial Governor in first direct gubernatorial election; direct mayoral elections restored in Taipei City and Kaohsiung City.
June 1995	Lee Teng-hui visits Cornell University.
1995	Elections for Legislative Yuan.

July 1997	National Assembly passes constitutional amendments aimed at streamlining administration.
1997	Municipal elections.
23 March 1996	Lee Teng-hui elected president in first direct, popular presidential election; National Assembly elections held concurrently.

Index